The Possible Dream

How the 2004 Red Sox Reversed History

Vin Femia

To alex and Kevin,

Hope that we all can enjoy more World Series wins to come.

Vin Femia

ISBN 1-886284-76-8

Library of Congress Catalog Card Number 2004117989

First Edition
ABCDEFGHIJK

Cover Design by Tamas Jakab

Published by

Chandler House Press, Inc.
335 Chandler Street
Worcester, MA 01602 USA

Chandler House Press books are available at special discounts for bulk
purchases. For information contact Sales Department Chandler House Press –
508-756-7644 – 335 Chandler Street, Worcester, MA 01602, USA or
info@tatnuck.com

Table of Contents

Preface

Like most New Englanders and many other baseball fans who grew up in the 1960s, I was a die-hard Red Sox fan. I would listen to games on the radio every night and watch them on TV whenever they were on. There was, in fact, no more glorious or happy year in all of my years of watching sports than 1967 with the miracle Red Sox coming from a ninth place finish the preceding year to winning an absolutely thrilling pennant race in 1967. That was the Impossible Dream Year, a magical year that will probably never be duplicated by any team, in any sport, in my lifetime.

The love of the Red Sox and the glow from 1967 carried over into the mid-1970s. The Red Sox were a good team, and surely, we all thought, they will win a championship one of these years. Unfortunately, the years went by and, through 2003, still there was no championship. Dreams and hope ultimately turned into tragedy and despair. The incredible collapse of 1978, when the Red Sox had a 14 game lead over the dreaded Yankees in July and wound up losing the lead, a playoff game with the Yankees, and the American League East pennant race, turned these feelings further into cynicism and doubt that the Red Sox would ever win that elusive championship. Over a quarter-century later, after the 2003 season, fans were still waiting. Meanwhile, since 1967, the Yankees had won 6 more World Series Championships, giving them 26 championships since the Red Sox won their last in 1918.

All of that changed in 2004. The Red Sox forged a season that will go down in history. They won the World Series, and the championship, but they also won it in historic fashion. They became the first team to come back from an 0-3 deficit to win a playoff series, and in the process, beat the vaunted New York Yankees. They then beat a St. Louis Cardinals team that had won 105 games and was viewed as one of the strongest (non-Yankee) teams in many years. They won more consecutive post-season games than any other team had done in winning its championship. They made believers out of everyone.

This book examines the historical reasons that the Red Sox had not won until this time, and what changed to have the team bring home the championship in 2004. It describes how the problems of the past, from ownership, through general managers, managers, and players, turned into renewed optimism with the ownership of John Henry, Tom Werner, and Larry Lucchino, and with the work of the new general manager, Theo Epstein. It describes how that optimism was rewarded with a comeback for the ages and with an amazing world championship run.   The new owners and GM were determined to do everything that they could to build a championship team, and they did so. Their positive moves and the great season of the team's players finally completed the job of building a championship team.

The book then is divided into three sections. The first section describes the reasons why the team continued to fail in its championship quest, with chapters describing in detail how such factors as ownership, playing style, bad trades, and even Major League Baseball itself, contributed to the Red Sox' championship drought. The second section chronicles the 2003-2004 off-season and the 2004 season month-by-month to show the ups and downs of the championship season from a fan's perspective. The third section describes what the world is like for Red Sox followers now that the championship quest has finally been satisfied.

Almost everything in this book is straight from the heart and memory. That is the way that it should be for a real fan. The triumphs and tragedies that come from following a team are emblazoned in the minds of the fans of any team, but particularly one that had come so close so often but failed to reach its ultimate goal. Following a team like the Yankees that wins regularly is easy and many of the steps toward winning are easily forgotten in the glow of victory. Following a team that has provided as tantalizing a history as have the Red Sox is difficult, and every near-miss is remembered in great detail, as is every key step that was made to finally winning that championship.

While most of what is written in this book is from memory, I do want to acknowledge the help of my son, Michael, who provided some details such as scores of recent playoff games and information about the team in the 1980s and 1990s when I had lost a good deal of interest in the team for reasons that will be all too clear from reading the first section that follows. Some information from years prior to 1961 has been culled from reading many books about Red Sox history, and facts about scores from the early part of the twentieth century (before my time) were found and checked in multiple sources. There is also some information quoted from some of the best sportscasters and sportswriters the media has offered over this time, people like Bob Costas, Jackie MacMullan, Al Hirschberg, and Ken Coleman. I have enjoyed reading their opinions and listening to them and some of their colleagues over the years, and I thank them for hours of pleasure that they have provided.

In mentioning my son, I also am reminded of what could have been one of our failings as parents. Although we had started our kids out as Red Sox fans (and had Michael cheer the Red Sox and boo the Reds as a 18-month old during the 1975 World Series), I had hoped after 1978 that we could convince all of our children not to become die-hard Red Sox fans so that they could spare themselves the agony that we knew could come from such efforts. Unfortunately, 2 of our 3 children have become Red Sox fans, and so had suffered along with us over the years (the third was a fan of the St. Louis Cardinals for a while, but then lost interest in baseball). Though that has helped provide some of the information in this book, I often was sorry for not protecting them from this history. However, they were then all happy to share the exhilaration that came from winning the title in 2004, so I can only hope that some of it was worth it for them.

In any case, I hope that the information provided here can give them and all readers the background as to why the team had not won a World Series for so many years and what was done to have the team finally win that championship for their fans and themselves.

Hope that you enjoy reading what's here, and here's hoping that we can all enjoy more of this same ride for many seasons to come!

Somewhere in this favored land, the sun is shining bright.
The band is playing somewhere, and somewhere hearts are light
Somewhere men are laughing, and somewhere children shout
But there was no joy in Fenway …
(with apologies to Ernest Lawrence Thayer and his poem "Casey at the Bat")

The above words were valid … but only until October 2004.

The Possible Dream

This book is dedicated to my mother, Anna (Glorioso) Femia, who died on November 17, 2004. She was a lifelong Red Sox fan, who was born on February 14, 1916, and was an infant when the Red Sox won championships in 1916 and 1918.

Every April for the last few decades she would say about the Red Sox "I think they're going to do it this year". Well, they finally did do it, and I'm glad that she was able to enjoy that they did -- although much too briefly before she died.

It's too bad that she won't be around for next season. She would have loved seeing them come onto the field as champions.

SECTION 1 – HISTORICAL PERSPECTIVE: WHY THE SOX NEVER WON

Chapter 1 – Introduction

The date was October 16, 2003 – and it happened …. AGAIN!

The Boston Red Sox once again in 2003 brought their long-loyal, and long-disappointed fans to the brink of what would have been a tremendous triumph, only to turn a near-sure victory into a crushing defeat. It was now 85 years – and counting -- without a World Championship for the Red Sox. The loss in 2003, however, may have been the most excruciating of all. It is one which left the worst taste of defeat in the mouths of many Red Sox fans for months, as it came at the hands of the team that has been absolutely dominant over them for most of those 85 years, the dreaded, hated, New York Yankees. Winning and going to the World Series would have been great. Winning and going to the World Series by beating the Yankees to do so – finally beating the Yankees in a game for the pennant – would have been fantastic. Unfortunately, it was not the way that things turned out in 2003.

What can be done to change this, fans wondered? What can be done to have the team finally, at long last, even just once, beat the Yankees with the pennant on the line, or go on to the World Series, or, ideally, both?

In *The Life of Reason, Volume 1, 1905* George Santayana states that "Those who cannot remember the past are condemned to repeat it." So, in order to understand what needed to be done for the Red Sox to finally win, it would be necessary to understand why they have always lost. Why was it, for example, that …

> For every Aaron Boone, who had done nothing for the Yankees since being acquired in mid-season of 2003, there is a Bucky Dent.

> For every Carl Yastrzemski, who had a home run and another key hit in the 1978 playoff but will be remembered more for popping up to Nettles to end the game, there is a Tim Wakefield, who was the hero for Boston after 6 games in 2003 but wound up on the mound when the pennant-winning home run was hit.

> For every John McNamara, who left Bill Buckner at first base in game six of the 1986 World Series, even though he had substituted for him defensively all season long, there is a Grady

Little, leaving Pedro in in the 8th inning of Game 7, though he had always taken him out late in games all season.

For every Don Zimmer, who let Bill Lee and Bernie Carbo rot on the bench in 1978 and pitched Bobby Sprowl in a key game against the Yankees in September, there was a Grady Little pinch-running for Jason Varitek, who had been one of his best -- and only -- hitters in the playoffs, in the 9th inning of a tied 7th game.

For every Joe Torre who moved a slumping Jason Giambi from 3rd to 7th in the batting order and helped his team win a game, there is a Grady Little (note a pattern here?) who did not do the same with a slumping Nomar Garciaparra, and thus had Nomar leaving a lot of runners on base during the ALCS.

For every Bill Buckner there is a Kevin Millar, falling down and not making what should have been an out at first.

For every Reggie Jackson getting his revenge against Bob Welch in the 1978 Word Series, there is Jorge Posada getting the game tying hit off Pedro after the two had words and kept pointing at their heads in Game 4.

For every Derek Jeter making a great play and toss to throw out Jeremy Giambi at home in game 3 of the 2001 ALDS, there is no one covering 2nd base for Boston in the 8th inning of game 7 of the 2003 ALCS, allowing Jorge Posada to get to 2nd on his bloop game-tying hit.

For every Don Zimmer, who managed the Red Sox to a colossal collapse in 1978 and the Cubs to a loss in the 1989 playoffs, there is a Don Zimmer, whose most significant baseball accomplishment was becoming friends with Joe Torre and who gets yet another ring primarily because he has Joe Torre for a friend.

For every 3-0 Red Sox lead over the Reds in game 7 of the 1975 World Series, there is a 3-0 Red Sox lead over the Mets in game 7 of the 1986 World Series, and there is a 4-0 Red Sox lead over the Yankees in game 7 of the 2003 ALCS, and there is a 14 game lead over the Yankees in July of 1978. No lead is ever big enough for this team.

The Yankees always seemed to find a way to win. The Red Sox always seemed to find a way to lose. The feeling was that if these two teams played 100 times with the pennant on the line, such that the winning team moved on and the losing time went home for the winter, the Yankees would win 100 times. Something had to be done to

The Possible Dream

change that inglorious history. In many ways, the 2003 season provided a microcosm of what had happened with and to the Red Sox for at least 40+ years of their almost 90 year drought – bad managing, questionable personnel decisions (though that now seems to be a bright spot for the future), player mistakes, and so on.

In order to determine what had to be done (and what was ultimately done) to break this 85-year history of futility, we will start examining in detail the reasons why the Boston Red Sox had, before 2004, consistently been one of the most disappointing franchises in North American professional sports history. As mentioned above, it is only by understanding the dismal past that we can also understand what needed to be done for the future. So, after examining the reasons for this continued streak of championship-less seasons, this book will provide a summary of what did change in 2004, and how the magical 2004 season progressed, building on the moves that were made in 2003 that brought them oh so close to actually beating the Yankees when it counted, and moving on to the World Series.

Chapter 2 – Misses, Near-Misses, and Total Collapses: Red Sox History 1961-2003

Route 128 encircles Boston. Thousands of cars travel that highway every day. A number of technology firms have established themselves along 128, causing the road to be referred to as "America's Technology Highway". 128 was also a significant number in recent Red Sox history, since, as the Red Sox started the 2004 season, their legacy was that they had appeared in exactly *1* World Series in the preceding *28* years. That record of futility is almost incomprehensible for a team that has had such good players and good teams. The Minnesota Twins have not been a good franchise and were almost eliminated when baseball considered contracting in 2001, and yet they had appeared in more World Series during this 28 year period than have the Red Sox. The Kansas City Royals, San Diego Padres, and Toronto Blue Jays, who just came into existence in 1969, 1969, and 1977 respectively, had also made more World Series appearances in this time than Boston. The Philadelphia Phillies, who have appeared in only four World Series in their entire history, have had two of those appearances during the last 28 years. More to the point, the Twins, Blue Jays, Royals, and Phillies have all won a championship during this time. The Red Sox had not. Why is that?

Before we begin examining the reasons, let's review the chances that the Red Sox have had and what has happened to trip them up along the way. In order to limit the focus of this analysis, we will concentrate on the time since baseball first expanded in 1961. This is also the time that I first became interested in baseball and began adding my name to the list of long-suffering Red Sox fans, so it is also a time over which I can provide first-hand knowledge of Red Sox futility.

The Red Sox were a miserable team during the first 6 years of this era, 1961-1966. They finished 6th, 8th, 7th, 8th, 9th, and 9th again in a 10-team league during those years, never winning more than 76 games in a 162 game season. There were plenty of stars, such as Carl Yastrzemski, Dick Radatz, and Tony Conigliaro, but no cohesive team. However, fans who were paying attention in late 1966 saw the beginnings of a team that was starting to come together. The team had one of the best records in the league over the second half of the season. It allowed them only to rise out of last place into ninth place by season's end, but there were some positive signs to carry over into 1967. Jim Lonborg began establishing himself as a good pitcher, moving from a 9-17 record in his rookie season of 1965 to 10-10 in 1966. Carl Yastrzemski continued to show himself to be one of the best hitters in the American League, and Tony Conigliaro one of the best young sluggers. Other players, such as George Scott and Rico Petrocelli, were also playing well. The pieces were in place for the team to be much better in 1967.

Not only did 1967 turn out to be a better year for the Red Sox than its predecessors, it was, quite simply, the best year in Red Sox history. The team played well, played hard, and played excellent fundamental baseball all year. In one of the most dramatic pennant races in baseball history, the Red Sox were locked in a year-long struggle with the Detroit Tigers, Minnesota Twins, and Chicago White Sox for the American league pennant. On one day in September, there was a three-way tie for first place, with the fourth place team only a half game behind and only percentage points away from the lead. The race was that close. This type of drama is no longer possible in baseball with 6 divisions and wild card entries in the playoffs, but this 1967 pennant race had gripped the nation.

The White Sox were in the driver's seat going into the last week of the season, but lost games to the lowly Kansas City A's and Washington Senators and dropped out of the race. Going into the final weekend of the season, though, it was still a 3-team race. The standings on Saturday morning, September 30 showed how close the race was:

	W	L	Games Behind
Minnesota	91	69	--
Boston	90	70	1
Detroit	89	69	1

To add to the drama, Minnesota was in Boston for the final two games of the season. The Tigers were playing double-headers with the California Angels both on Saturday and Sunday to end the season.

Boston won the first game against Minnesota to pull into a first place tie with the Twins. Jose Santiago pitched for Boston and Jim Kaat pitched for Minnesota. Kaat had pitched well for the Twins all year and was particularly tough on the Red Sox, but had to leave the game early after hurting his elbow. A big home run by George Scott gave the

The Possible Dream

Red Sox a 3-2 lead in the game, and then a monster three-run shot by Carl Yastrzemski, the 44th home run of what had become a dream season for Yaz, gave them a 6-2 lead. With a runner on in the Twins ninth, Dick Williams ordered his pitcher, Gary Bell, not to work around Twins' slugger Harmon Killebrew. Williams did not want Killebrew to walk and have the Twins rally and win the game. Killebrew promptly hit one into the screen to cut the lead to 6-4 but the rally was over. The 6-4 lead held up, pulling the Red Sox into a tie for first place with the Twins with one game left in the season. Meanwhile, in Detroit, the Tigers and Angels split a double-header. Thus, going into the last day of the season, the standings were now:

	W	L	Games Behind
Minnesota	91	70	--
Boston	91	70	--
Detroit	90	70	1/2

Sunday dawned bright and was a day full of anticipation for Red Sox fans. Undoubtedly thousands of prayers were said on behalf of the team as Red Sox fans attended Sunday Mass and church services throughout New England. The Red Sox and Twins were about to play the most important game of their seasons. The loser would be out. The winner would either finish in a tie with Detroit for the pennant and be forced to play a 1-game playoff for the pennant, or would win the pennant outright if the Tigers lost 1 of the 2 games of their double-header. Not only was the game a decisive game, but it matched two of the three best pitchers in the American League. Dean Chance, with a 20-13 record, was Minnesota's starter. Jim Lonborg, with a 21-9 record, started for Boston. Chance and Lonborg would be facing each other with the AL Cy Young award on the line – not to mention the American League pennant.

The game did not start well for Boston. The Twins took a 2-0 lead thanks in part to misplays in the field by left-fielder Carl Yastrzemski and first baseman George Scott, two of the Red Sox best fielders during the season. When Jim Lonborg came to bat to lead off the bottom of the sixth inning, the Red Sox fans gave him polite applause, but it seemed that the season was over. Lonborg, a Stanford graduate and very smart player, noticed that the Twins third baseman was playing deep and so dropped a bunt down the third base line to lead off the inning with a hit. Jerry Adair and Dalton Jones followed with singles, so the bases were loaded with Carl Yastrzemski coming to the plate. Fenway Park was in pandemonium. Who could ask for anything more? Yaz, the star of the season, was at the plate with the bases loaded in a game for the pennant. Yaz promptly lined a single to center to knock in two runs and tie the score. Jones went to third on the hit and scored the go-ahead run on a fielder's choice by Ken Harrelson, which moved Yaz on to second base. Yastrzemski then went from second to third and then third to home on two wild pitches by Twins pitcher Al Worthington. The Twins continued to unravel during that inning, as an error by Harmon Killebrew on a grounder to first allowed the fifth run of the inning to score. With their rally in the sixth the Red Sox had taken a 5-2 lead, capitalizing on their own timely hitting (the four straight hits to start the inning, capped by the big clutch hit by Yastrzemski), as well as these miscues by the Twins.

There was one more heroic effort before the game was over. With Tony Oliva and Harmon Killebrew on base with two out in the Twins eighth, slugger Bob Allison hit a shot into the left-field corner. It looked like a sure double and at least one run in, with the tying runs in scoring position. However, that was not to be. Yastrzemski raced over and got Allison's hit and threw a perfect strike to second base to get the sliding Allison. One run scored, but the inning and rally were over. An inning later, Lonborg got Rich Rollins to pop up to Rico Petrocelli for the final out in a 5-3 Red Sox win. Fans raced onto the field and lifted Lonborg onto their shoulders in celebration.

The Red Sox then gathered into the clubhouse to listen to the second game of the Tigers-Angels double-header. The Tigers had won the opener and could force a playoff with a win in the nightcap. However, the Angels rallied, took an 8-5 lead into the ninth inning, and won the game as Detroit's Dick McAuliffe grounded into a season-ending double play (the first and only double play that McAuliffe hit into all year – proving once again that sometimes you also have to have luck on your side to win). The final standings were:

	W	L	Games Behind
Boston	92	70	--
Minnesota	91	71	1
Detroit	91	71	1
Chicago	89	73	3

The Red Sox had won the pennant! No Red Sox fan who was alive and following the team will ever forget that season.

What turned the Red Sox from also-rans into winners? The team really played as a team all year. They played excellent fundamental baseball all year, for the first time in years. There were plenty of heroes. Jerry Adair went from being a utility infielder with Baltimore and Chicago to being a vital cog for Boston, including capping a Red Sox comeback in August against the Angels from being down 8-0 to winning 9-8 behind an Adair home run. Gary Bell came over from Cleveland and won 12 games. Tony Conigliaro was one of the top sluggers in the league with 20 homers and 67 RBI before his season ended on August 18 when Tony was hit in the head by a pitch from Jack Hamilton and was badly hurt.

Jose Tartabull was one of the players who replaced TonyC in right down the stretch and he helped the Red Sox win a key game in Chicago late in the season by throwing out speedy Ken Berry at the plate as Berry tried to score the tying run in the ninth inning. At the other end of that play was Elston Howard, a late-season acquisition who leaped to catch Tartabull's throw and came down blocking the plate and tagging out Berry to end the game.

George Scott, Reggie Smith, Rico Petrocelli, Dalton Jones, Jose Santiago, and others also made key contributions. One unsung hero was pitcher Billy Rohr, who pitched a near-no-hitter against the Yankees in the third game of the season, on April 14 in Yankee Stadium. Rohr held the Yankees hitless until there were two out in the ninth inning when Elston Howard (who, ironically, later that season was to join the Red Sox) hit a line single to right. Earlier that inning, the no-hitter was preserved on a great catch by Carl Yastrzemski in left field off a long drive by Tom Tresh. Those of us who were listening to the game can still recall the words used by radio announcer Ken Coleman in calling the play:

> Rohr winds ... here it comes ... fly ball to deep left ... Yastrzemski is going back ... way back ... and he dives and makes a TREMENDOUS catch ... one of the greatest catches that I have ever seen, by Yastrzemski in left field ... Everybody in Yankee Stadium on their feet roaring, as Yastrzemski went back and came down with that baseball.

Rohr won that game and then beat the Yankees again a week later at Fenway Park. Unfortunately, he really did not do much for the Red Sox after that, as those were his only 2 wins, but many believe that this near no-hitter really helped to bring the Red Sox together as a team, and really helped to establish the character and identity of the 1967 Red Sox.

However, despite the heroics of these players and the great team play of the Red Sox that season, three men stand out as the stars of the 1967 season. Dick Williams was added as manager before the season began and, when asked for a prediction said "We'll win more than we'll lose." Since he was taking over a team that had finished in ninth place in a ten-team league the season before, with a record of 72-90, this was a bold prediction. Yet Williams had the Red Sox working hard from the start of spring training and led the team to the pennant with the best managing job ever seen at Fenway Park.

Carl Yastrzemski had been a good hitter for 6 years, but during the off-season had worked harder than ever to build himself up. The results were fantastic. Yastrzemski won the American League triple crown with a .326 batting average, 44 home runs (finishing tied with Harmon Killebrew) and 121 RBI. Yaz not only had the statistics but was the heart and soul of the team and had one of the greatest seasons hitting in the clutch that baseball has ever seen. Yaz tied a key game in Detroit with a 9th inning home run, threw out Allison to kill a Minnesota rally on the final day of the season, and, in one of the best examples of clutch hitting baseball fans had ever seen, had 7 hits in 8 at bats in the final two games of the season with the pennant on the line, clinching the Saturday game with a big three-run homer and tying the Sunday game with a bases loaded single. Yaz was the league's MVP and baseball's last triple crown winner. There have been very few seasons anywhere, anytime, to match Yaz' 1967 season.

Jim Lonborg began pitching inside and became a 22-game winner and AL Cy Young Award winner. He was the best pitcher in all of baseball that year. Not only did he win the pennant-clincher on the last day of the season, but he then went on to pitch one of the best games in World Series history. In game 2 of the World Series against the Saint Louis Cardinals, Lonborg had a perfect game before walking Curt Flood in the seventh inning and a no-hitter until giving up a double to Julian Javier in the top of the eighth. Lonborg finished with a one-hit shutout. He then came back to win the fifth game 3-1, taking a two-hitter into the ninth inning and allowing the Cardinals just three hits for the game. Lonborg tried to come back on just two days rest in game 7, but was too tired, and wound up the loser to Bob Gibson 7-2. I am one of many fans who believe that if it had only rained and the seventh game pushed out a day or two, that Lonborg would have done it again and won the World Series for Boston. Unfortunately, rain came in two other Red Sox World Series appearances since 1961 (in 1975 and 1986) but not in 1967, so the Red Sox miraculous season fell one game short.

The baseball world felt that the Red Sox were a coming dynasty. They had Yastrzemski, Lonborg, and Conigliaro as the nucleus, young stars in Scott, Smith, Andrews, Petrocelli, and others, and up-and-coming prospects such as pitcher Ken Brett, who had become the youngest man ever to pitch in the World Series when he faced the Cardinals as a 19 year old. With Yastrzemski at 28 the oldest player among the core, things certainly seemed promising. However, that did not come to be.

Let's look at the seasons since 1967 to see what happened to derail the burgeoning dynasty of 1967 and then what happened since that kept the Red Sox from winning that elusive championship through 2003. We will only look at years in which they had a real chance or came close, so we will not discuss years like 1971 or the early 1980's, where the team was not really a contender. Nevertheless, as you will see, there were plenty of opportunities for the Red Sox to have won, and plenty of missed chances. We'll also see some of the reasons that they have continually lost these opportunities, which will be described in more detail in subsequent chapters.

1967 As we have just described, this was the Red Sox' best year, period. They won the pennant and took the powerful St. Louis Cardinals to a seventh game in the World Series. It took three strong pitching performances by Bob Gibson to beat the Red Sox. The Sox still might have won if they had been able to pitch Jim Lonborg on his usual rest instead of having to bring him back to pitch game seven on two days rest after he had already pitched three very tough games (all complete game victories) in the preceding eleven days: the pennant clincher on the final day of the season, and brilliant victories over the Cardinals in games two and five of the World Series. Still, this is the season that will always shine brightly in the memories of Red Sox fans everywhere.

1968 The Red Sox were defending AL champions but were bested by injures. Tony Conigliaro's vision after being beaned in 1967 was not good; he missed the entire season. Jim Lonborg had broken his leg skiing in the off-season and was not the same pitcher when he returned. He went from a 22-9 record in 1967 to 6-10 in 1968. Jose Santiago was off to a very good start with a 9-4 record when he injured his elbow and was lost for the season. Also, George Scott, one of the key performers in 1967, had a horrendous season in 1968, dropping in batting average from .303 to .171. Despite these problems, Dick Williams led the team to an 86-76 record and a fourth-place finish behind Detroit.

1969 The American League split into two divisions in 1969 and the Red Sox began the season with a strong lineup that had a great chance to win the AL East division title. Tony Conigliaro was back and the Red Sox boasted a lineup that included

Reggie Smith	CF
Mike Andrews	2B
Carl Yastrzemski	LF (two-time defending AL batting champion
Tony Conigliaro	RF (youngest player to hit 100 HRs in baseball history)
George Scott	3B
Ken Harrelson	1B (Harrelson led the AL in RBI with 109 in 1968 and had 35 HR)
Rico Petrocelli	SS
Jerry Moses	C

They also had a pitching rotation that included Jim Lonborg, Ray Culp (16 game winner in 1968), Dick Ellsworth (also a 16 game winner in 1968), Jose Santiago, and either Billy Rohr or Dick Mills, a highly regarded minor league pitcher. With the exception of the catcher, everyone in the starting lineup was a key contributor.

The team got off to a slow start, however, and, on April 19, General Manager Dick O'Connell shocked the baseball world by trading Ken Harrelson, Dick Ellsworth, and pitcher Juan Pizzaro to Cleveland for right handed pitcher Sonny Siebert, catcher Joe Azcue, and relief pitcher Vicente Romo. The trade was very unpopular in Boston, since Harrelson had hit 35 HR and had 109 RBI in 1968 and was a real fan favorite.

Harrelson actually retired after the deal was made, not wanting to play anywhere but in Boston. After meeting with the Commissioner and Cleveland officials, however, he relented, and the trade was completed. The Red Sox were never the same. Siebert pitched OK, but was relegated to the bullpen at one point in the season. Azcue left the team in mid-season and wound up being traded for another catcher, Tom Satriano. Romo was not the pitcher that the Red Sox expected him to be. A season that began in promise wound up being derailed early. In addition, the powerful Baltimore Orioles were a very tough team to reckon with, as they began a string of three straight AL pennants with a 109-53 season. The Red Sox finished third.

1972 A strike by baseball players during spring training, primarily over the players' pension plan, caused the season to be shortened and not all teams played the same number of games. This especially hurt the Red Sox, who wound up in second place, one half game behind the Tigers. The Tigers played one more game than Boston, finishing 86-70 to Boston's 85-70.

The season started slowly for Boston. At the end of June they were 27-34 and in fourth place in the six-team AL East, seven and a half games behind the first place Detroit Tigers.

Despite the slow start, the Red Sox got themselves into the pennant race. It was another four-team pennant race (as was the case in 1967), this time with the Yankees, Tigers, and Orioles. The Red Sox actually moved into first place in September and might have won it all, except for an ill-conceived trade in which they sent ace reliever Sparky Lyle to the Yankees in exchange for first baseman Danny Cater. Cater hit only .237 for Boston, while Lyle kept New York in contention with a 35-save season.

The Red Sox went into the final weekend of the season, a three game series with the Tigers in Detroit, with a half game lead. Whichever team could win at least two of the three games would win the AL East pennant. The first game was lost by Boston in an odd way. Tommy Harper and Luis Aparicio were on base when Yastrzemski boomed a hit into the gap. Harper scored, but Aparicio fell rounding third. He scrambled back to third, but Yaz was already there and so he was tagged out and a potential rally ended. Oddly, this exact same thing had happened on opening day, also in Detroit. Harper had scored from second on a hit by Aparicio. Yaz hit a shot into the gap and Aparicio fell rounding third base so Yaz and Luis wound up at the same base that time as well. That Aparicio, one of the best baserunners in AL history, could fall rounding third twice to help the Red Sox lose a pennant was uncanny. These things only happen to the Red Sox. In any case, at the end of the year, the Red Sox lost the first two games in Detroit to give the Tigers the pennant. They won on the last day of the season to become the first and only team ever to lose a pennant by less than one game.

1973 It is hard to remember a lot about 1973 since this was a year of transition for me personally, being married in February and starting in the Air Force in July. We were in Texas from July-October, and so much of the AL East pennant race passed us by, giving way to a five-way pennant race in the National League Eastern Division (eventually won by the Mets with a pathetic 83-79 record) and the start of football season, which pushed all other sports into the background in Texas. However, I do remember 1973 as another year with a four-way pennant race among the Red Sox, Orioles, Tigers, and Yankees. It stayed that way through much of the season, but dissolved into a two-team race between Boston and Baltimore in September. The Orioles wound up getting very hot in September and winning going away. During one stretch the Red Sox won 8 in a row but could not gain any ground on the Orioles who were also winning 8 in a row.

1974 This year saw the second biggest collapse in Red Sox history. The team was in first place on August 24, leading by 7 games. Luis Tiant had just won his 20th game on a Friday night against the A's and everything was looking rosy for the Red Sox. However, the team just stopped hitting at that point and were shut out in big games over Labor Day against the Orioles. Despite the lack of hitting, the Red Sox refused for some reason to bring up and play minor league hitting stars Fred Lynn and Jim Rice or to claim Frank Robinson off waivers where he had been placed by the Dodgers. Robinson, one of the best players and team leaders in baseball history, could certainly have helped Boston down the stretch.

The Yankees and the Orioles both slipped past the Red Sox and Boston finished third, 7 games behind the Orioles. The Red Sox also were plagued by an injury to Carlton Fisk in June and a foolhardy decision to pitch Rick Wise in a cold April game in Boston. Wise, who had been acquired from St. Louis in the off-season after a very good career in the National League, hurt his arm that day and missed most of the season. The loss of Wise and Fisk and the loss of Boston's hitting led to a 14-game collapse for the Red Sox in 1974, from being in first place and 7 games ahead of their nearest opponent in late August to third place and 7 games behind the division winner at season's end.

1975 This was the year where it almost all came together. The Red Sox finally won in a year that the Yankees were also good. The Yankees added Bobby Bonds and Catfish Hunter and seemed to be the favorite to win the AL pennant. However, the Red Sox added the so-called "gold dust twins", Fred Lynn and Jim Rice, and welcomed back Carlton Fisk and Rick Wise after their injury-plagued years in 1974. Lynn was the first player to be both Rookie of the Year and MVP in the same season and finished with 21 HR, 105 RBI, and a .331 batting average. Rice had 22 HR, 102 RBI, and a .309 batting average. Fisk hit .331 in limited action. Wise came back from his injury to lead the team in wins with 19.

Unfortunately, just as the 1967 pennant-winning Red Sox had lost Tony Conigliaro to injury before the post-season, the 1975 team lost Jim Rice to a broken wrist after Rice was hit by a Vern Ruhle pitch late in the season, making him ineligible for the post-season.

The Sox upset the three-time defending champion Oakland A's in a 3 game sweep in the AL Championship Series, but went down to defeat to the powerful Cincinnati Reds in a thrilling 7-game World Series. The loss of Rice hurt. A decision by manager Darrell Johnson to pinch-hit for Jim Willoughby in the eighth inning of game seven also led to Cincinnati scoring the series-winning run in the top of the ninth. And a decision by Bill Lee to throw an eephus pitch to Tony Perez in the seventh inning of that seventh game cut a 3-0 Red Sox lead in that game to 3-2.

An inning after the Perez home run, Lee developed a blister and had to leave the game. Lee had shackled the Reds' great hitters in game 2 and game 7, but now, with Lee gone, the Reds came back to win 4-3.

This was the series that featured a game (game 6) that many believe to have been the greatest game in baseball history. The Red Sox, behind 6-3 in the bottom of the eighth, tied it on a pinch-hit three-run homer by Bernie Carbo. What followed then was a series of heroic efforts by players on both teams. Reds LF George Foster threw Denny Doyle out at the plate when Doyle was trying to score the winning run on a sacrifice fly in the bottom of the ninth. Dwight Evans made an outstanding catch to rob Joe Morgan of a potential series-winning home run in extra innings. The game was finally won in the bottom of the twelfth inning on a dramatic leadoff home run by Carlton Fisk. Fisk's blast has become one of the most famous home runs in baseball history, and the shot of Fisk waving his arms trying to will the ball to stay fair is a classic.

The Reds came back and won game 7 the next night to win the championship, but the Red Sox also hurt themselves throughout the series with bad base running and bad fielding. The base running especially took the Red Sox out of a lot of scoring opportunities, as the Red Sox kept running themselves into key outs on the base paths, such as:

- Dwight Evans thrown out shortstop to home in the bottom of the first, game 1

- Rick Burleson thrown out stealing in the bottom of the fourth, game 1

- Fred Lynn thrown out at home on a fly to short center, bottom of the sixth, game 1

- Cecil Cooper getting caught in a rundown between third base and home, bottom of the first, game 2

- Dwight Evans caught off second base (officially called out trying to steal third), bottom of the second game 2

- Fred Lynn out after slipping rounding first base in the top of the fourth inning, game 3

- Denny Doyle getting thrown out at home on a fly to shallow left with the bases loaded in the bottom of the ninth inning of a tied game 6

In the field, the key miscue was Denny Doyle misplaying a potential double-play ball that could have ended the seventh inning of game 7, just before Perez hit the home run that cut the lead to 3-2.

Given the tightness of the series, with 5 of the games (games 2, 3, 4, 6, and 7) each being decided by 1 run, these mistakes could easily have made the difference in the Reds winning and Red Sox losing. It's too bad that the Red Sox had fired Dick Williams. Perhaps with a little bit of fundamental baseball, they could have won this World Series.

1976 This may be a borderline year for inclusion in this list, but the Red Sox were coming off a pennant-winning season in 1975 and had strengthened their pitching rotation with the addition of former Chicago Cub Ferguson Jenkins, who had been one of the best and most consistent pitchers in baseball since 1967. Jenkins got the start on opening day and lost to the Orioles 1-0, a harbinger of what would be a tough year. An early 10-game losing streak dropped the Red Sox out of contention, and the loss of Bill Lee to a shoulder injury after a baseball brawl with the Yankees seemed to push the Red Sox out of it, but the team had cut the Yankees lead to 5 ½ games by June 15, when the Red Sox purchased the contracts of LF Joe Rudi and relief ace Rollie Fingers from Oakland. Fingers was the key acquisition. Commissioner Bowie Kuhn made the unfortunate decision to overturn the purchase and Rudi, Fingers, and Vida Blue (whom the Yankees had also purchased from Oakland) were forced to return to the A's. The pennant races were never the same.

Fingers could have really helped the Red Sox, who desperately needed bullpen help. Fingers won 8 games and had 12 saves for Oakland from June 15 to the end of the season. Those numbers could have been huge for getting the Red Sox back into contention. Columnist Leonard Koppett wrote in *The Sporting News* that it was Bowie Kuhn's decision to overturn these transactions that shaped the AL races that year.

Kuhn's decision was bad in June of 1976 and even worse when viewed in historical context. Oakland lost Rudi and Fingers to free agency at the end of the season anyway, and had nothing to show for them. Without Fingers, the Red Sox had to sign Bill Campbell as a free agent in 1977 instead of filling other needs. The Yankees won in 1976 and again in 1977 and 1978 having been helped in part by this decision and its aftermath. Also, the next year, Kuhn did not step in

The Possible Dream

when the Mets shipped all-time Met star and Met icon Tom Seaver to the Reds for very little value in a move that was as devastating to the Mets as the loss of Rudi and Fingers and Blue would have been to the A's. At least the Mets wound up with something for Seaver. The A's wound up with nothing for Fingers and Rudi. It was thought by many reporters and fans in 1976 that Kuhn made his decision as much to hurt long-time foe Charlie Finley, the A's owner, as for any other reason. Looking back, it is difficult to disagree with that contention.

1977 In some years, like 1974, the Red Sox had good pitching but not good hitting. In most years, it was the opposite, good hitting with little pitching. 1977 was perhaps the ultimate "good hit, no pitch" year for Boston. Eight Red Sox players hit 14 or more home runs, led by Jim Rice with 39. Five players had 95 or more RBI. However, there was no pitcher with more than 13 wins and the leading pitcher and winner was a relief pitcher, Bill Campbell, and for a time the staff ace was rookie Mike Paxton, who had not even started the season on the team's major league roster.

The team broke many hitting records and the lineup was feared throughout the league. One game that epitomized the season was a game against the Yankees in which the first two batters, Rick Burleson and Fred Lynn, hit home runs. After two outs were made, Carlton Fisk and George Scott also hit home runs. The four solo home runs off ace Catfish Hunter helped the Red Sox to a big victory.

The pennant race really came down to a decisive 3-game series with the Yankees at Yankee Stadium in mid-September. The Red Sox came in to the series 1½ games behind the Yankees. The Yankees won the first two games of the series (beating the Red Sox when the two teams met in a big series, as always seemed to be the case), stretching the lead to 3½ games. This series was marked by a lot of Red Sox players hitting into long outs in left field and left center, as the Red Sox right-handed power, in a team built for Fenway Park, turned into a liability in Yankee Stadium with its deep left field.

The Red Sox came back to win the third game of the series, but the damage had been done. The strong Red Sox hitting kept the team close and in contention until the last weekend of the season, but the Red Sox could not overcome those two September losses in New York. The Red Sox eliminated the Orioles on Friday night of that last weekend. The Orioles came back to eliminate the Red Sox with a home run barrage of their own on Saturday afternoon. The Red Sox came close. The Yankees went on to beat the Dodgers for yet another World Championship.

1978 There is no year in Red Sox history whose very mention brings as bad a taste to the mouths of any Red Sox fan who was alive at the time (and many who have been born since) as does 1978. There is no bigger collapse in the long history of baseball than that which the Red Sox brought onto their fans in 1978. The Red Sox had built a 10 game lead over Milwaukee and were 14 games ahead of the hated New York Yankees on July 18. The Boston Globe began doing a series of articles on "How the Super Team was Built" (in the words of the Pete Seeger song also made popular by Peter, Paul, and Mary, "When will they ever learn? When will they ever learn?"). Yet, through the terrible mis-management of Don Zimmer (as will be discussed in a later chapter), the Red Sox found themselves ahead of New York by only 4 games heading into a crucial 4-game series with the Yankees at Fenway Park in September.

The series was a complete disaster, which has since come to be known as "The Boston Massacre". The Yankees won the opener 15-3 and the second game 13-2, in both games having their leadoff man come up to bat for the third time before the Red Sox ninth-place hitter had batted once. Red Sox fielding was also terrible, as the team committed four errors in the first two innings of the second game.

Saturday's game started as a pitching duel between Dennis Eckersley and Yankee ace Ron Guidry, but a popup that landed between three Red Sox fielders in right-center field started a rally that led to a 7-0 Yankee win. The lead was down to one game.

Despite pleas from Red Sox pitchers Luis Tiant and Bill Lee to pitch the now-huge fourth and final game of the series, Zimmer decided to start rookie Bobby Sprowl. The results were predictable. The Red Sox lost 7-4 and now shared first place with the Yankees.

The entire series was embarrassing for Boston. The team trailed each game by big margins before they scored their first run – 12-0 in the first game, 13-0 in the second, 7-0 in the third game which ended in a shutout, and 6-0 in the fourth game. Don Gillis, a veteran sports reporter on Boston TV, talked about how the Red Sox had failed in the past, but that this was the worst that he had ever seen. A fan was quoted as saying that this was the first time he had seen a first-place team chasing a second-place team. The Red Sox had humiliated themselves completely. They were the laughingstocks of baseball. When they went to Baltimore after the Yankee debacle, an obscenity was burned into the grass of the infield at Baltimore's Memorial Stadium by an irate Red Sox fan who had somehow gotten into the Stadium. The team's horrendous play and the manager's pathetic performance earned them every insult that they received.

The Possible Dream

The weekend after the Boston Massacre, with Boston trailing the now first-place Yankees by 1½ games, the Red Sox went to Yankee Stadium for a three game series. The Yankees won the first game behind Ron Guidry and came back to win the second game on Saturday afternoon with a ninth inning rally. I still recall the ball being hit to left field to bring in the winning run in the Saturday game. Jim Rice didn't even bother to throw home. How can you not throw home in that situation? Maybe it's hopeless, but then players sometimes fall running the bases (see Luis Aparicio in the above description of 1972) and throwing it won't hurt, and even can help if that kind of thing happens. It was so typical of the Red Sox to not even try though. It was extremely frustrating to watch.

Somehow, the Red Sox and Yankees wound up tied at the end of the season and had a one-game playoff in Fenway the day after the regular season ended. Yankee ace Ron Guidry, who wound up the season with a phenomenal 25-3 record, was the New York starter. The Red Sox starter was Mike Torrez, who had pitched for the Yankees in 1977 and had never endeared himself to Red Sox fans. This game would make him one of the most disliked players in team history. The Red Sox took an early lead on a home run by Carl Yastrzemski off Guidry and the Sox extended the lead to 2-0 going into the top of the seventh. With two out and two on in the Yankee seventh, Bucky Dent fouled a ball off his foot. While Dent was walking it off, Torrez did not throw any tosses to the catcher to stay warm. When Dent stepped back up to the plate he then lofted a Torrez pitch into the screen for a 3-2 Yankee lead. Interestingly, earlier that season, Torrez had given up a similar home run to another weak-hitting Yankee shortstop, Fred Stanley (When will they ever learn …). A Thurman Munson double made it 4-2 and then a Reggie Jackson home run off reliever Bob Stanley made it 5-2 in the top of the eighth inning. The Red Sox struck back for 2 runs in the bottom of the eighth to make it 5-4, but a series of good defensive plays by the Yankees in late innings kept the Red Sox from scoring more. In particular, Lou Piniella saved some runs by making a stab of Fred Lynn's slicing hit to right field when the score was still 2-0 Boston.

What happened in the bottom of the ninth inning epitomizes the futility of Red Sox history. With one out and Rick Burleson at first, Jerry Remy hit a shot to right field that Piniella lost in the sun. However, Burleson, a notoriously bad baserunner, thought that Piniella might have been bluffing so he only made it to second base when he should have been at third. Frankly, Burleson should not have even batted first in the lineup and as such should not have been in the position on the basepaths. Remy, a better base stealer and with a better on-base percentage should have been, but Burleson insisted on batting leadoff.

Since the Red Sox manager, Don Zimmer, was really a non-manager, he let Burleson be his leadoff hitter. This cost the Red Sox dearly. Jim Rice was the next batter after Remy and he hit a long fly to right field. Burleson moved to third on the play but could have easily scored the tying run had he moved to third base on Remy's hit as most good baserunners and leadoff men would have done. Then with two out, Yastrzemski, who had had a good day at the plate, was jammed on a pitch by Rich Gossage and popped up to the end the playoff game, the season, and Red Sox hopes for years to come.

Our family had a ceremonial burning of Mike Torrez' baseball card in a fireplace after that game, but that was only because we didn't have a Don Zimmer card. Zimmer's bad managing caused this disaster. He buried players on the bench who could have helped him (such as Bill Lee). He kept playing players who were hurt even though they were hurting the team (Butch Hobson, Dwight Evans, George Scott). He banished Bernie Carbo in mid-season and therefore did not have him available to pinch-hit in the crucial playoff game. He pitched Bobby Sprowl in that crucial game in September against the Yankees even though both Luis Tiant and Bill Lee, each with great career records against New York, begged to pitch. He allowed Rick Burleson to bat leadoff even though that was not in the best interests of the team, and it cost him a tie in the playoff game. Zimmer is, quite simply, one of the biggest villains in Red Sox history. There will be much more in Chapter 3 about Don Zimmer's poor management of the team in 1978 and in other years.

1986 It took years after the 1978 disaster for the Red Sox to become a contender again. They won the pennant in 1986 led by a 24-4 season from new pitching ace Roger Clemens. They then came back from a 3-1 series deficit in the ALCS to defeat California and get into the World Series. The comeback in game 5 of the ALCS was particularly memorable. Trailing 5-2, a Don Baylor 2-run HR made it 5-4. With a man on and two outs and the Red Sox one strike away from elimination, Dave Henderson, a mid-season acquisition from Seattle, hit a 2-run HR to give the Red Sox a 6-5 lead. The Red Sox finally won the game in extra innings and then easily won the last two games of the series in Boston over a disheartened Angels team.

The World Series started out in great fashion, with the Red Sox winning the first two games over the Mets in Shea Stadium. Bruce Hurst handcuffed the Mets in game 1, winning 1-0. Game 2 was supposed to have been a great pitching matchup between young aces Roger Clemens and Dwight Gooden, but neither ace made it out of the sixth inning as the Red Sox won 9-3 to take a 2-0 series lead back home to Boston for 3 games.

The Possible Dream

The Mets started game 3 with a 4-run first inning off Dennis 'Oil Can' Boyd (the oil can in the nickname referred to beers, and Boyd had this nickname as he had been known for drinking many in his younger days). Then with the series 2-1, manager John McNamara started Al Nipper in game 4 and the result was a 6-2 Mets win and a 2-2 series tie. Bruce Hurst won again in game 5, 4-2 over Dwight Gooden, giving the Red Sox a 3-2 series lead and sending them back to New York where one more win would mean the title.

Game 6 was an absolute Red Sox disaster. The Sox took a 2-0 lead behind pitching ace Clemens but the Mets tied it in the fifth. Boston took a 3-2 lead with a run in the top of the seventh but the Mets tied it in the eighth and the game went on into extra innings. In the top of the tenth inning, Dave Henderson hit a home run off of Rick Aguilera and the Sox led 4-3. I remarked at the time that it's not always the shock but the after-shock that wins a game like this. Suddenly, and amazingly, the after-shock actually happened. Wade Boggs doubled and Marty Barrett singled him home to extend the lead to 5-3. I looked at my family incredulously. This is what the good teams do.

Could this finally be it?

The answer, of course, was no. The first two Mets batters in the bottom of the tenth inning, Wally Backman and Keith Hernandez, flied out. There were two outs and no one on. The Shea Stadium scoreboard flashed a note congratulating the 1986 World Champion Boston Red Sox (When will they ever learn …). Then Gary Carter got a single, Kevin Mitchell got a single, and Ray Knight got a single. Suddenly it was 5-4 with the potential tying run on third base and potential winning run on first base. With Mookie Wilson up, a pitch got past the catcher and the tying run scored. The pitch was called a wild pitch on Bob Stanley but anyone familiar with baseball knew that it was really a passed ball by catcher Rich Gedman. He should have caught it. He reached across his body to try to catch the inside pitch and it bounced off of his glove and back to the screen. A good catcher, especially in that situation with a championship on the line, would have moved his whole body in front of the pitch to make sure that the ball did not get behind him. Gedman did not do that. If Carlton Fisk had still been with the team, he would have caught it, but Fisk had been cut loose by the Red Sox in 1980 in a real bonehead move (the owners didn't send him a contract on time, making him a free agent), so Fisk was with the White Sox. After the tying run scored, Wilson then grounded a ball down the first base line. The ground ball went through the legs of Bill Buckner and the Mets won the game and tied the series. Buckner had usually been taken out of games in late innings, replaced by Dave Stapleton for defensive purposes, but manager John McNamara had decided to leave him in. It cost the team.

Game 7 was delayed a day by rain, and the Red Sox took and lost a 3-0 lead in game 7. The Mets won the game 8-5 and the Red Sox had another heart-breaking defeat for their fans to try to overcome.

Curiously, writers have bemoaned the fact that Boston's three World Series appearances during these years all came against the best National League team of that decade – the Cardinals in 1967, the Reds in 1975, and the Mets in 1986. What this misses is the point that there were 9 other years each decade in which the best team in the National League for that decade did not play. If the Red Sox were as good as they should have been, they would have won more than one pennant in each of those decades, and maybe won a title.

One other note – it is often the player who least deserves to make the last out who does so for the Red Sox. Marty Barrett had a great post-season for the Red Sox in 1986 and yet wound up making the last out of the World Series, not Rich Gedman or Bill Buckner who had bad series. Yastrzemski had a great day in the 1978 playoff game but wound up making the last out of that playoff game. Yaz also made the last out of the 1975 World Series (but did not make the last out of the 1967 World Series as baseball guru Peter Gammons has often claimed, George Scott did). Similarly, in 2003 Tim Wakefield had a great series against the Yankees but wound up on the mound giving up the series-winning home run to Aaron Boone. Not only did the Red Sox never win, there is no justice on who makes the final out when they lose.

1988 This was the year of Morgan magic in which the Red Sox won 19 of 20 games after Joe Morgan took over as manager from John McNamara and the Red Sox won the AL East by 1 game over Detroit. However, the Red Sox were overmatched in the ALCS against Oakland and were swept out in 4 games by the powerful A's.

1990 Again the Red Sox won the AL East. This time it was by two games over the Toronto Blue Jays. However, again they were swept out in four games in the ALCS by the powerful A's who were in the process of winning their third straight pennant. This was the series marked by Roger Clemens tirade against umpire Terry Cooney which got the classless and clueless Clemens ejected from game 4 and telling Cooney threateningly that he knew where he lived. Not a great moment in Red Sox history.

1995 The Red Sox won the AL East but were swept out in three games by the Cleveland Indians in the newly added playoff series, the AL Division Series (ALDS). The loss was in part due to

The Possible Dream

number 3 hitter Mo Vaughn and cleanup hitter Jose Canseco going a combined 0-for-27 at the plate in the series. The ALDS was added as this was the first year in which wild card teams were eligible for the post-season. In typical Red Sox fashion, though they finished first, they were upstaged by the Yankees who finished second and made the playoffs as the AL wild card team. Unlike the Red Sox, the Yankees actually won two games in their division series, before bowing to the Seattle Mariners 3 games to 2 in a thrilling 5th game finish in the Kingdome. I have never seen anyone run as fast around the bases as Ken Griffey Jr. did to score the winning run for Seattle in game 5 on a double by Edgar Martinez. If only Rick Burleson had run so fast on Jerry Remy's hit in the 1978 playoff …

1998 The Red Sox made it as the wild card team, and actually won a game in the ALDS versus Cleveland to break a 13-game post-season losing streak, dating back to the sixth game of the 1986 World Series. They lost the series to Cleveland 3 games to 1. The Yankees went on to win yet another World Series.

1999 The Red Sox went down 0-2 to Cleveland in the best 3 of 5 ALDS. However, they came back to win the third game 9-3 and then clobber Cleveland 23-7 in game 4 to send the series back to Ohio for a decisive fifth game.

Game 5 was a seesaw battle early. Boston led 2-0 then trailed 3-2. They trailed 8-7 after 3 innings but scored once in the top of the fourth inning to tie the game at 8. Then came the bottom of the fourth inning and Red Sox ace Pedro Martinez came out of the bullpen to pitch. It was eerie to see - Cleveland fans seemed to sense defeat even as Pedro was walking to the mound. It turns out that they were right. Despite an ailing arm, Pedro pitched 6 no-hit innings and the Red Sox wound up winning 12-8 to take the series.

The win put the Red Sox into the ALCS, playing for the pennant against the dreaded Yankees. New York won the first two games at Yankee Stadium 4-3 and 3-2 but Pedro came back to beat former Red Sox ace Roger Clemens in game 3, 13-1.

Game 4 was the turning point. With a chance to tie the series, the Red Sox lost with extremely bad umpiring costing the Red Sox a chance to win. In one instance, Yankee second baseman Chuck Knoblauch clearly dropped a throw at second base but the umpire ruled the runner out. In another, even more blatant play, Knoblauch fielded a grounder at second, took a swipe at the Red Sox runner Jose Offerman, who was going from first to second but missed him completely. The second base umpire called Offerman out anyway. He later claimed that he didn't see the play because his view was blocked but thought that Knoblauch had tagged him out by his motion. He "thought" that Knoblauch had tagged him out? Shouldn't you be sure? More to the point, Major League Baseball employs 6 umpires in post-season games. Couldn't one of them had said something like "uh, Al, he never tagged him; the runner is safe"? Or couldn't the second base umpire have asked the other umpires what they saw? Football officials get together after every penalty call. Basketball officials often overrule one another. Why couldn't these baseball umpires? It's not as if there was continuation on the play or that the call changed what happened next. The fielder missed the tag. The runner should have been safe at second. It's as simple as that. The Yankees won the game and the series and were clearly the better team, but the better team doesn't always win, and it's always a lot better to have an important game decided by the players and the play and not by a bad umpiring call. (It was good during the 2004 playoffs to see umpires conferring on bad calls and reversing decisions to get the calls correct on a number of occasions; too bad that common sense such as that and a desire to get things right in crucial games was not used in 1999 as well.)

2003 This could have been the year. The Red Sox had made some good moves in the off-season preceding the 2003 campaign, acquiring players such as Kevin Millar, David Ortiz, and Bill Mueller. The team had a togetherness about it that was greater than any other Red Sox team had had since the miracle team of 1967. Millar especially helped that togetherness with his play and his clubhouse style. It was Millar who coined the phrase "Cowboy Up" that became the rallying cry of the 2003 team. It symbolizes the desire of the players not to let obstacles get in their way, but to get psyched, get determined, and put in the extra effort to overcome those obstacles. It was also Millar whose video of his younger self playing air guitar and singing the Bruce Springsteen hit song "Born in the U.S.A" that became a rallying cry for the Red Sox when played on the video screen in late innings of games at Fenway.

The Red Sox gave the Yankees a little bit of a run for the division title before they settled into second place. They were able to win the wild-card spot, and faced the Oakland A's and their marvelous pitching staff in the AL Division Series. As they did in 1999, the Red Sox again came back from an 0-2 deficit to win the ALDS with a stirring comeback over the A's. Derek Lowe was a star in the series. After pitching in relief in game 1 (won by the A's on a surprise bunt in extra innings), Lowe won game 3 at Fenway with a gutsy performance. The Red Sox, on the brink of elimination after losing the first two games of the series in Oakland, won that third game 3-1 in extra innings. Lowe then came back in game 5, coming in in the ninth inning of that game with the Red Sox ahead 4-3 after Red Sox reliever Scott Williamson

The Possible Dream

had walked the first two Oakland batters. Lowe got out of the jam, striking out two left-handed batters with nasty pitches that broke from being inside to just catching the inside corner. The Red Sox hung on for the win that clinched the series 3 games to 2.

That win put the Red Sox into the ALCS against the Yankees. The Red Sox split the first two games of the series, winning the opener behind a brilliant performance by Tim Wakefield and losing to Andy Pettitte in game 2. I thought that in game 2 the Red Sox should have pulled starting pitcher Derek Lowe earlier than they did, since Lowe had pitched a lot in the Oakland series (appearing in game 1, starting game 3 and coming on to save game 5), and to allow themselves to bring him back in game 5 in Boston, where he had always pitched well during the season. Such forward thinking might have helped them.

Game 3 was Pedro versus Clemens again, and the Red Sox had a chance to break the game wide open in the first. With 2 runs in, one out, Manny Ramirez on first, and David Ortiz up with a 3-2 count, manager Grady Little called for Ramirez to run. This was despite the fact that Ramirez is not a fast runner and also despite the fact that Ortiz had been striking out a lot in the post-season. Predictably, Ortiz struck out, Ramirez was thrown out, and the threat ended. The Yankees wound up winning the game 4-3. This was also the game with the debacle of Pedro throwing at Karim Garcia, Clemens throwing close to Ramirez, both teams leaving their benches for an on-the-field confrontation and Don Zimmer, now a Yankee coach and 72 years old, embarrassing himself by charging Pedro Martinez. This was a low-light game for both teams.

After a rainout, Tim Wakefield again outdueled Mike Mussina to even the series and then each team won again to send the series to a decisive seventh game, with again the pitching matchup being current Sox ace Martinez against former Sox ace Clemens.

The Red Sox took a 4-0 lead over Clemens and the Yankees with a two-run HR by Trot Nixon and a solo HR by Kevin Millar accounting for 3 of the runs. The Red Sox actually had a chance for more runs with runners on first and third with nobody out in the fourth inning, but Mussina came in to take over for Clemens and got Jason Varitek to strike out and Johnny Damon to hit into a double play to end the threat. The Yankees pulled to within 4-2 on a pair of solo home runs by Jason Giambi, but Pedro held that lead after 7 innings. As Pedro left the mound with a 4-2 lead after 7, he pointed to his heart and to heaven as he left the mound, put on his warmup jacket in the dugout, and accepted congratulatory hugs from his teammates. It was clear that Pedro's night was over and that the game would be turned over to the bullpen that had pitched so well in the series thus far.

But Pedro's night was not over. He was sent back to the mound in the bottom of the eighth inning with the Red Sox now leading 5-2, thanks to a David Ortiz home run. This was OK. Starting the eighth with your best pitcher was an OK move, though he should have been told that this would have been the case so that he didn't expect the seventh to be his last inning. With one out, and the Red Sox now 5 outs away both from the World Series and from what would have been a great win over the Yankees, Derek Jeter doubled and Bernie Williams singled to make it 5-3. This was the time to take Pedro out and Grady Little came out to the mound, ostensibly to do just that. However, inexplicably, Grady left him in! The next batter, Hideki Matsui, doubled; still no change from Grady. The next batter, Jorge Posada, also doubled, tying the game. Now, finally, Grady replaced Pedro. But the damage had been done. The Yankee win was inevitable and happened on a leadoff home run by Aaron Boone off of Tim Wakefield. Once more the Yankees were going to the World Series and the Red Sox to an off-season of misery.

- - -

There you have it – 17 good opportunities to win it all and 17 failures. The positive feelings and optimism of the late 1960's turned into the hope of the 1970s. That hope was then dashed and turned into cynicism for many fans by the collapse of 1974, the loss of the 1975 World Series with bad fundamental play, the loss of the 1977 pennant by losing two key games to New York in September at Yankee Stadium, and then the absolutely abysmal collapse and loss of a 14-game lead and the playoff game in 1978. What has followed since has been the continued downward spiral of hope into cynicism and then into despair with the ball going through Buckner's legs in the 1986 World Series, and then even further into constant pessimism and expectations of defeat in the 1990's and through 2003. There is at least some optimism now for the future, as will be discussed later in this book, but this downward spiral and the history of losing opportunities such as these have certainly been depressing over the years for Red Sox fans.

Add to these 17 lost opportunities the World Series loss in 7 games in 1946 (when the Red Sox had a 3-2 series lead), the loss in the 1948 playoff to Cleveland when manager Joe McCarthy started Denny Galehouse instead of staff ace Mel Parnell, and the loss in 1949 when the Red Sox lost the last two games of the season when winning one would have one the pennant, and there are at least 20 times since the last Red Sox championship that they have had a good chance to win another. Yet it hasn't happened. Why? You would think that the law

The Possible Dream

of averages would have them win at least 1 of those 20 opportunities or at least once since 1918, yet it has not. Why? There has to be a set of reasons why this is the case. Now that we have reviewed their history (or, to use baseball terminology, now that we have set the table), let's start examining the reasons why the Red Sox had not been able to break this spell and had remained without a championship from 1919 through 2003.

Chapter 3 – Managers

First and foremost on the list of reasons why the Red Sox had not won from 1919 through 2003 is the set of on-the field managers that they have had over the course of their history. This then was a primary item that needed to change for them finally to win a championship.

Of all of the managers who are enshrined in the Baseball Hall of Fame, not one is there because of his work as a manager of the Boston Red Sox. Joe Cronin is in the Hall of Fame, but that is more for his exploits as a player than as a Red Sox manager. Joe McCarthy is in the Hall of Fame as a manager and had a stint as a Red Sox manager, but McCarthy is there for his success with the Yankees. While with the Red Sox, all McCarthy did was lose two pennants on the final days of two consecutive seasons. The 1948 pennant was lost when McCarthy surprised his entire team when he decided to pitch journeyman Denny Galehouse instead of staff ace Mel Parnell in the 1-game playoff with Cleveland. The 1949 pennant was lost when the Red Sox went to New York for the final 2 games of the season with a 1-game lead over the Yankees, and promptly lost both games.

There is no Red Sox manager in the Hall of Fame, yet, if there were a Hall of Infamy equivalent to the Hall of Fame, the Red Sox would have a number of entries – John McNamara, Don Zimmer, Grady Little, and others.

There have been many issues with Red Sox managers that make it easy to see why their ineffectiveness has been the most significant reason for Red Sox futility. In describing these, I will do so by once again focusing on the time since baseball first expanded in 1961, both to limit the focus of this investigation, and since it was at that time that I first became interested in baseball and began adding my name to the list of long-suffering Red Sox fans.

Rarely has it been more apparent that the manager is such an important cause for the on-going Red Sox failures than in the 2003 American League Championship series. The baseball manager's most important role is to put his team in the best possible position to win. Grady Little did not do that. In fact, the consensus among most Bostonians and Red Sox fans is that Grady Little did just the opposite, and that was the main reason that the Red Sox lost this series.

Start with the decisive game 7 against the Yankees. It is hard to argue with Grady sending Pedro out to start the ill-fated eighth inning. Pedro is the best pitcher on the team, and arguably the best in baseball. There have been many games that the Red Sox have lost after pulling Pedro from a game where he has been dominant, only to see the bullpen blow it (including at least 5 during the 2003 regular season). However, to all appearances, Pedro was done after seven innings. He pointed to his heart and to the sky as he left the mound after the seventh inning. He received the congratulatory hugs of teammates in the dugout between innings. It was clear that Pedro and his teammates thought that Pedro's night on the mound was done, as it has been so often after seven innings over the last few years. It has been reported that Little asked Pedro if he could still pitch, and that Pedro said he could do so. However, the fact that Little asked Pedro if he could still pitch beyond the seventh inning is extremely bad managing. The manager's job is to make decisions, not ask others to make them for him. What would he have expected Pedro to say – that he couldn't pitch any more? Joe Torre didn't ask Roger Clemens if he could still get people out when he went out to the mound in the 4th inning; he came to get Roger out of the game. Similarly, Grady Little should not have asked Pedro if he could still go, he should have thanked him for 7 tough innings and told him a reliever would be coming in to the game for the 8th.

Nevertheless, keeping Pedro in to start the 8th would have been fine had he told Pedro beforehand that he was going to go with him for as long as he could. Also, sending the best pitcher in baseball out to start the eighth inning is not a horrible decision or the worst decision that he made that inning (other than the fact that he rarely had done it with Pedro). It was keeping him in after the Yankees had gotten two hits and a run from Derek Jeter and Bernie Williams. Little went out to the mound at that point and just about everyone watching or listening had to believe that he was going to pull Pedro and bring in Alan Embree to pitch to the lefthand-batting Hideki Matsui and the switch-hitting Jorge Posada. This move made sense not only because Pedro had lost some of his effectiveness, but also because bringing in Embree would have caused Posada to bat right-handed in Yankee Stadium, a park geared for lefthanded hitters. After Matsui doubled, Little still could have brought in Embree to pitch to Posada, but did not. Posada's bloop hit that tied the game finally resulted in Little making the pitching change that everyone else expected earlier.

To make matters worse, Grady then claimed after the game that he did this because, as he put it, "Pedro Martinez has been our man all year long, and in situations like that, he's the one we want on the mound over anybody we can bring in out of that bullpen". This is

The Possible Dream

absolutely not the case. All season long, and for years before this, Boston's approach has been to pull Pedro no matter how well he has been pitching. There have been many times when they have pulled Pedro after he had just retired 10 or 11 men in a row and looked strong, and then brought in a reliever who blew the game. If what Grady said is correct, then why is it that Pedro left 5 games with a lead and wound up with a no-decision? If what he said was correct, then wouldn't it have made sense for Pedro to have been "on the mound in situations like that" during the season, so that he was ready to do this in the most critical game of the Red Sox season? Regardless, what Grady said was wrong. In the immortal words of Casey Stengel, "You can look it up".

It should be noted that beyond the baseball implications in that Grady had now put his team in position to lose instead of win, it was also a bad player decision for a man who is regarded in baseball as "a player's manager". Most managers – most good managers, anyway – would not have left Pedro in the game to put the winning run on base after he had pitched so valiantly all night. Little did. He could have set Pedro up to be the losing pitcher. The fact that his bullpen shut down the Yankees and prevented the Yankees from scoring Posada from 2nd base does nothing to diminish the poor game and player judgment that Grady showed with this move.

This was not however, Grady's only bad move in this pivotal game. Pinch-running for Jason Varitek after Varitek singled in the 9th was highly questionable. Yes, Varitek represented the potential winning run, but he had also been one of Boston's best hitters over the entire playoffs. As such, taking him out with extra innings looming is not what I believe that most good managers would have done in the same situation. Varitek should have been kept in the game so as to keep his bat in the lineup for extra innings. Pinch-running for David Ortiz in the tenth inning was, however, the right move, for different reasons. Ortiz had doubled and was therefore in scoring position. Varitek was not. Ortiz is extremely slow. Varitek is not fast, but he is a better baserunner than Ortiz. Varitek was having a good series at the plate. Ortiz was not. Ortiz' replacement, Gabe Kapler, was a man who would not have been a detriment batting later in the game. Varitek's replacement, Doug Mirabelli, was a non-hitter who would be an offensive liability in an extra-inning game. In fact, Mirabelli made the last out in the eleventh inning, and thus was the last Red Sox batter of the season. Would Jason Varitek have done anything different? I don't know, but I would have liked to have seen him try. Also, if Mirabelli had gotten hurt, who would have been catching for the Red Sox – Lou Merloni? How would you have liked to have had Merloni behind the plate with the pennant on the line? Grady did not think ahead, and it may have cost him.

Bringing in Tim Wakefield was also questionable. Tim Wakefield is valiant and always has been. A knuckleball pitcher though has a tendency to give up home runs – not something you want to see in an extra-inning game on the road. Wakefield didn't deserve to be put in this position and didn't deserve to lose after the series that he had had (and therefore this was another case of a supposed "player's manager" doing wrong by one of his players). The right move would have been to bring in Scott Williamson or perhaps sinker-baller Derek Lowe to hold the Yankees in the 10th and 11th, as Joe Torre did in pitching Mariano Rivera. If the game went on past the 11th, the Yankees would have been forced to pitch Jose Contreras, an ineffective Jeff Weaver (and we saw what the Marlins did with Jeff Weaver pitching in extra innings in the World Series), or a tired Andy Pettitte. The Red Sox could have been in position to have either Williamson or Lowe after that, and if the game continued beyond 13 innings, then bring in Wakefield.

It is not only the seventh game that gives Grady Little failing marks, however. Let's look at some of his moves earlier in the series. The most blatant is the ill-thought out move that he frequently made in starting the baserunner running from first on a 3-2 count on a batter with less than two outs. He did it in Game 1, and got a strike out-throw out double play. He did it in Game 2 when Gabe Kapler reached Andy Pettitte for a lead-off single and Bill Mueller, who has been struggling all post-season took a called third strike (and how do you take a called third strike in that circumstance?). Kapler was out at second by a wide margin. The worst such instance, however, was in the first inning of the pivotal Game 3. Manny Ramirez had just singled in two runs with one out to give the Red Sox a 2-0 lead over a struggling Roger Clemens. With a chance to maybe knock Clemens out with a big inning and get to New York's very unstable bullpen, another strike out – throw out double play on a 3-2 pitch to David Ortiz took the Red Sox out of the inning. The fact that Ramirez, a notoriously slow runner, was thrown out on a strike out of David Ortiz who had been striking out frequently in the post-season, could have easily been foreseen. Unfortunately, it should not have been allowed to happen. It was a bad managerial decision.

Little also inexplicably brought in Scott Sauerbeck to pitch in the second game of the ALCS. That game was played on October 9. The fact that Sauerbeck had not been in a game since September 27 made the move even more surprising. The Red Sox wound up losing that game.

Little's lineup moves were questionable. The Red Sox had already lost starting center fielder Johnny Damon for the first two games of the ALCS due to an injury suffered in an outfield collision in the Division Series with Oakland. Nevertheless, Little also chose to have Doug Mirabelli catch game 1 instead of regular catcher Jason Varitek, causing them to be two regulars down for game 1. This move was predicated by the fact that Little regularly had Mirabelli catch knuckleball pitcher Tim Wakefield, the Red Sox game 1 starter, during the season, but this move showed no imagination, and put his team in a difficult position. The Red Sox did win that game, but lost the next game when Little again decided to rest a second regular, sitting down the red-hot Todd Walker against lefthander Andy Pettitte. This made starters of Gabe Kapler and Damian Jackson, who did not help the Red Sox at all in a 6-2 loss that evened the series.

The list could go on. Joe Torre dropped an ineffective Jason Giambi from the third spot in the Yankees' batting order to the seventh spot for Game 7. Little never did drop an equally struggling Nomar Garciaparra from the same third spot in the Red Sox' batting lineup. With Varitek and Trot Nixon hitting well in this series, perhaps it would have been good to move one of them up to bat third, the other to fifth in place of David Ortiz, and try to bunch some hits and runs together. Also, with Johnny Damon out for the first two 2 games of the series due to injury as just described, having another regular sit out (Varitek in game 1, Todd Walker in game 2 when Walker was in a hot streak) and having two regulars on the bench for each of the first two games of the series, is not the best way to set your team up to win.

In any case, letting Grady Little go after moves like this was a very good decision by the Red Sox. What type of manager should manage the team in the future is a question that will be addressed in a later chapter.

One thing that is hard to debate, however, is that in the history of the Red Sox since 1918, there has been exactly one manager who has done a consistently good job of putting his team in position to win – Dick Williams. Williams was an excellent baseball manager and strategist. The first year that Williams was Boston's manager was THE best year in Red Sox history, 1967. The team that had been moribund for 17 years suddenly became the darling of Boston. Williams had them playing excellent fundamental baseball, a trait rarely seen under any other Red Sox manager before or since. He benched people who did not produce and sent sore-armed pitchers down to the minors. He was willing to make unpopular moves, such as benching George Scott in a crucial game because Scott was overweight or starting rookie Gary Waslewski in Game 6 of the World Series instead of "going by the book" and pitching Gary Bell or another veteran.

Of equal importance was Dick Williams' attitude and leadership. When writer Al Hirschberg asked Williams in the red-hot 4-team 1967 pennant race how he thought things would work out, Williams answer was that of a leader: "We'll win it". Interestingly, when Hirschberg asked the same question of Joe McCarthy during the 1948 3-team pennant race, McCarthy's answer was "We do it or we don't". Williams was aggressive and set the positive tone for his team. McCarthy was basically was telling the team that it was fate that would decide the race, not their play. Which of these men would you prefer managing your team? Actually, only one managed the team, the other was just keeping a seat warm in the dugout.

The Red Sox should have never let Williams go, but they did after 3 years, primarily because owner Tom Yawkey did not like him (as will be discussed in more detail in a later chapter). All Williams did after being fired by the Red Sox was manage the Oakland A's to two World Series championships, the San Diego Padres to 1 of only 2 World Series appearances that that franchise has had, and almost manage the Montreal Expos to a pennant in the strike-shortened 1981 season.

Dick Williams was, quite simply, an excellent manager whose stay in Boston should have been as long as that of Tom Kelley in Minnesota, Tony LaRussa in St. Louis, Tom Lasorda in Los Angeles, and other managers who were good at their craft and whose longevity really helped the team's development and provided continuity and stability to their teams.

If Dick Williams was the best, then who was the worst? That is a question that is extremely easy to answer. It is not Grady Little or Joe McCarthy, though they were certainly contenders. It is Don Zimmer. Zimmer's performance in 1977-78, especially 1978, was simply horrible. He stopped playing players that he didn't like, even though they could help the team. The most obvious of these was Bill Lee, who was pretty much a forgotten man in the 2nd half of the season as the Red Sox were blowing a 14-game lead over the Yankees. Lee had one of the best won-lost marks of pitchers against the Yankees, but Zimmer's personal issues with Lee led him not to use Lee down the stretch of what turned into a tight pennant race. Lee could have helped them win. Zimmer wouldn't let him.

Yet another man exiled because of Don Zimmer's petty dislike for him was Bernie Carbo, a serviceable pinch-hitter and utility outfielder. Carbo was let go in mid-season, sold to Cleveland. I remember saying at the time that it was a bad move since Carbo could help them win one game in the 2nd half of the season and one game could make the difference in who wins the pennant. As it turns out, that was indeed the case. With the two teams tied at the end of the season,

The Possible Dream

the pennant came down to a 1-game playoff. Late in the game, facing New York's fireballing righthander Rich Gossage, the Red Sox had to send up a pinch-hitter. This would have been a great spot for Carbo, a left-handed batter who had hit a memorable pinch hit home run in the 1975 World Series. However, because of Zimmer's pettiness, Carbo was no longer on the team. As a result Zimmer instead sent up Bob Bailey to pinch hit. Pinch stand is a better way to describe it, as Bailey took three strikes from Gossage, and went back to the bench. The at-bat was so bad that if Bailey hadn't even brought his bat up to the plate and had just stood there, it would have been hard to tell the difference. Would Carbo have done any better? Who knows, but (a) I would have liked to have seen him available to at least try, and (b) my guess is that he would have at least gone down swinging instead of standing.

Bailey was on the team only because he was a National League friend of Zimmer's. I remember him being interviewed a few weeks after joining the team and he kept referring to the team in the 2nd and 3rd person plural, as in "You have a good team here with a chance to win it all". Nothing like showing that you are not part of the team. Most often players will say something like "It's nice to be here where we have a good chance to win it all". That interview told fans a lot about both Bailey and Zimmer and how they view a team.

Zimmer was called "The gerbil" by Bill Lee, who actually made the comparison to Billy Martin, whom Lee described as "The rat". Nevertheless, the nickname stuck, and turned into a pejorative comment, as Zimmer, an overweight man with puffy cheeks could have been said to resemble a gerbil. According to baseball writer and guru Peter Gammons, Zimmer was also referred to by pitcher Ferguson Jenkins as a buffalo, since buffaloes are among the planet's ugliest animals. Thus a group of Red Sox players became known as "The Buffalo Heads". These were good players, but players with whom Zimmer had issues due to clashes in style and beliefs. The Buffalo Heads included pitchers Bill Lee, Ferguson Jenkins, Rick Wise, and Jim Willoughby and outfielder Bernie Carbo. Zimmer, a vindictive man, stopped using these players out of spite, even though all could contribute to the team.

Ultimately, the team got rid of these players, and got little in return. Carbo was sold to Cleveland in 1978 and, thanks to Zimmer's shortsightedness, was gone when they needed him. Lee was buried in the bullpen and not used against the Yankees in 1978 when he could have helped. He was traded after the 1978 season for Montreal utility infielder Stan Papi, an unbelievably bad trade for Boston. Lee wound up with a solid 16-10 record for Montreal in 1979, while Stan Papi hit a meager .188 in 50 games for Boston. Lee, who appeared in 33 games for the Expos, almost played as many games as a pitcher as Papi played for Boston that season. Papi appeared in only one other game for Boston, in 1980, so Lee wound up appearing in 2/3 as many games in one season as Papi did for his entire stay in Boston. These numbers help to show the absurdity and one-sidedness of the deal.

Jenkins, a big winner throughout his career, was traded for John Poloni, another bad trade. As was the case in the Lee for Papi trade, the Red Sox came out the worst in the deal. Poloni did nothing for the Red Sox. Meanwhile, Jenkins, a forgotten man on the Red Sox pitching staff thanks to Don Zimmer went on to have an 18-8 record for Texas in 1978 and followed that with a 16-14 record for Texas in 1979.

Willoughby was sold to the Chicago White Sox early in the 1978 season and was second on the White Sox in saves with 13 that season.

Wise was the only traded player of this group for whom the Red Sox actually got real player value in return. In spring training in 1978 he was included in the trade that brought Dennis Eckersley from Cleveland. Eckersley was a 20-game winner for Boston that season. Unfortunately, Eckersley was the only player of value that the Red Sox got back for five very good players. Zimmer was more interested in getting rid of them than in using them to help the team or in getting value for them in trades.

Zimmer's managerial moves and his hand in personnel moves helped ruin what had been a very promising Red Sox team in the 1970s.

These personnel moves were not the biggest reason why Zimmer stands at the bottom of Boston's managerial rankings. Zimmer starting Bobby Sprowl in the 4th game of the September series versus New York that has become known as the Boston Massacre, stands as perhaps THE worst decision a Boston manager has ever made. The Yankees had come into that 4-game series having cut Boston's lead over them from 14 games to 4. The Yankees then destroyed the Red Sox in the first three games of that series by scores of 15-3, 13-2, and 7-0. Now the only thing standing between the Yankees and a first-place tie was a Sunday afternoon game at Fenway Park. Bill Lee, owner of a great career record against the Yankees, was available to pitch, but was bypassed. Luis Tiant, the team pitching leader for 7 years and another pitcher with a great career record against the Yankees, was begging to pitch (and no pitcher in Red Sox history could hold a lead better than Luis). Tiant was told that he was pitching the next day against Baltimore because that was a big game too. Tiant's reaction was "Bull ----. This is against the Yankees." Too bad that Tiant was a

The Possible Dream

better judge of the situation than the man who was being paid to manage the team. In any case, Zimmer started Sprowl, whom he described as having "f---ing icewater in his veins". As was predictable to everyone except the so-called Red Sox "manager", Sprowl was blasted and out of the game early, the Yankees won 7-4, the two teams were tied for first, and the Yankees went on to win the pennant.

The bad moves continued even after the disastrous 1978 season. Relief pitcher Bill Campbell, who had pitched well for Boston in 1977 after signing as a free agent, had since developed arm problems. In mid-season of 1979, Campbell was ready for work to test out his rehabilitated arm. Zimmer kept him out of a blowout win in a mid-week game against Baltimore (a perfect opportunity to give Campbell some work), but then brought him in during a Saturday afternoon game against the Yankees. At the time the Red Sox were leading 3-2. An inning later, they were trailing 4-3. It is inconceivable how Zimmer could pitch Campbell in a tight game versus the arch-rival Yankees after not giving him work in the more appropriate blowout game in which he could not cost the team a win.

The examples could go on, but suffice to say that, at least until Grady Little, no Red Sox manager did more to ensure the success of the New York Yankees than Don Zimmer, and I don't believe that anyone in Boston was sorry to see Zimmer fired when management finally made that decision.

Having reviewed the best, the worst, and the most recent, a natural next step for this review would be to do a brief analysis of other Red Sox managers. This will now be done for every Red Sox manager since 1961. Each such analysis will also conclude with a rating for that manager, using a scale of 1-6 as follows:

6 – Outstanding
5 – Very Good
4 – Good/Promising
3 – Average
2 – Fair
1 – Poor

The first Red Sox manager during this stretch was Mike "Pinky" Higgins. How Higgins got this job, I'll never understand. He was a bad manager, more interested in drinking than succeeding, and not a good person. Peter Golenbock, in his book "Fenway", for example, describes Higgins as having been violently opposed to having black players on the team. The fact that the Red Sox were the last of the original 16 teams to integrate says a lot about them and about Higgins. Under Higgins, the players were undisciplined and they played terrible fundamental baseball. Higgins believed that major league players did not need instruction or work on fundamentals, so he did not provide any. As a result, his teams played badly and were losers in all senses of the term. Higgins' rating: 1/Poor.

Johnny Pesky followed Higgins in 1963 but had the unenviable position of having Higgins as his boss, as Tom Yawkey inexplicably made Higgins the General Manager after the 1962 season. Pesky had done a great job as a manager in the Red Sox minor league system, and in developing good players for the team. His first season as a manager also started well. The Red Sox were actually in third place behind the Yankees and White Sox at the All-Star break, and were getting strong years out of hard-hitting Dick Stuart and Carl Yastrzemski, and also from pitchers Bill Monboquette and Dick Radatz. Stuart would lead the league in runs batted in and contend for the home run title until late in the season. Yastrzemski would win the batting championship. Monboquette became a 20 game winner for the first and only time of his career. Radatz was the best reliever in baseball.

The team stayed in contention for the pennant through the first half of the season. They were tied for second place on July 6, five and a half games behind New York. They were in third place on July 21, seven and a half games behind the Yankees, but just a half game behind the second-place Chicago White Sox. However, the bottom fell out for the Red Sox in the second half of the season, and they finished in seventh place in the ten-team league, 28 games behind the pennant-winning Yankees. Pesky received no help from Higgins during the season that might have kept the Red Sox in the top half of the standings. For example, Pesky kept asking his GM for players to bolster what he had on the roster; Higgins got none. Pesky was also being undermined by Dick Stuart. As Stuart kept subverting Pesky's authority, nothing was done about it by either Pesky or Higgins. Eventually, dissension arose and the team dropped. Higgins hardly spoke to Pesky. What had started out as a promising season had ended sourly. Pesky has been a beloved member of the Red Sox organization for decades, and remains so today. He deserved far better than he got. Pesky's rating: 4/Promising.

Billy Herman was next and hated to play young players. This is unfortunate, since at the time the Red Sox farm system was starting to produce a group of very good youngsters, like Tony Conigliaro, Rico Petrocelli, Dalton Jones, and Jim Lonborg. Herman practically pushed the high-strung Petrocelli out of baseball with his treatment of him. Petrocelli was a young player with a lot of insecurities who needed encouragement and proactive management in order to succeed.

Herman's view was to let the players play and not work with them. That didn't help Petrocelli or any of the other up-and-coming young players. The worst situation that I remember was a day when Petrocelli left the park early because he felt that his wife needed him. It turns out that she did, because she had collapsed on the floor at their house. Instead of compassion, Herman dealt with this with anger and almost caused Petrocelli to quit. Petrocelli stayed (having been convinced by the team's veteran players not to quit because of this situation), and later became an All-Star under Dick Williams and a solid player for the Red Sox pennant winners of 1967 and 1975. However, for him and the rest of the team, any hope for player development and Red Sox improvement was dashed by Herman's ineptitude. Herman's rating: 1/Poor.

Dick Williams was next and we have already discussed him. Williams' rating: 6/Outstanding.

Following Williams was Eddie Kasko and results were mixed. Kasko at least played some young players, such as Cecil Cooper and Ben Ogilvie, but had a very sour relationship with reliever Sparky Lyle that ultimately resulted in the Sox trading Lyle to the Yankees (!) for Danny Cater, which was a disastrous move. Lyle went on to be a great reliever for the Yankees, culminating in his winning the AL Cy Young Award in 1977. Cater did nothing for Boston, and the Red Sox lack of a reliever of Lyle's category haunted them for years. They could have used Lyle in the 1975 World Series. Although Dick Drago did a fine job in that series, Lyle was at the top of his games in those years. With Lyle, the Red Sox would not have needed to sign Bill Campbell as a free agent in 1976, and could have looked to strengthen the team elsewhere (Bert Campaneris as a shortstop and a basestealing threat at the top of the order perhaps? Bobby Grich? Joe Rudi?). In any case, Kasko rates an OK 3/Average.

Darrell Johnson managed the Red Sox from 1974 into 1976 and won the American League pennant in 1975. Darrell Johnson also gets positive marks for the way that he helped Carlton Fisk develop into a Hall of Fame player. Fisk has credited Johnson for a lot of his success. On an interview show in late 2003 that was hosted by Tim Russert, the excellent host of NBC's "Meet the Press", Fisk was a guest along with three other men who were among the best catchers in baseball history: Yogi Berra, Johnny Bench, and Gary Carter. When the guests were asked to name the person or people who were the biggest influences in their lives, Fisk's answer was his father "and a man named Darrell Johnson". Johnson managed Fisk in the minor leagues and really helped him develop his game. Fisk had been struggling previously, but turned into an outstanding player, the AL Rookie of the Year in 1972, and a perennial All-Star.

Despite these positives, however, Johnson's managerial stint in Boston was not as successful as had been hoped. A year before winning the 1975 pennant Johnson presided over the second biggest Red Sox pennant race collapse during this era (second only to the 1978 catastrophe perpetrated by Don Zimmer). In 1974, the Red Sox led the AL East by seven games on August 24 and wound up third, seven games behind. All of the hitters went into slumps, many due to sickness. Although Johnson had young players like Fred Lynn and Jim Rice available, he didn't play them, even as the shutouts mounted, the slump continued, and the pennant was frittered away. That Lynn and Rice were so good in 1975 and beyond makes not playing them in 1974 even more incomprehensible.

Earlier that year, Johnson pitched Rick Wise, a very good pitcher whom the Sox had acquired from St. Louis during the off-season, in a very cold, rainy game in early April. Wise pitched a complete game and pitched well, but ruined his arm for the season. Wise, who had been a solid performer for Philadelphia and St. Louis, was wasted for a meaningless April game.

In 1976, after a very slow start, the Red Sox started making a move on the first place Yankees. On June 15, GM Dick O'Connell acquired outfielder Joe Rudi and relief pitcher Rollie Fingers from the Oakland A's, purchasing each of their contracts for $1,000,000. The acquisition of Fingers seemed an especially good one, as the Red Sox had a very weak bullpen that year. Although both players were available to Johnson that night, he decided not to use either one. That decision would have drastic ramifications. The next day Commissioner Bowie Kuhn put the transaction on hold and then later reversed the deal, returning the players to Oakland. Many baseball experts expressed the belief that Kuhn would not have made that decision if Johnson had played either player that first night, as he very well could have done, and should have done, to solidify that deal.

Lastly, it was Johnson who pinch hit for Jim Willoughby in Game 7 of the 1975 World Series after Willoughby had been very strong in relief. However, with two outs in the bottom of the 8th, Johnson pinch hit for Willoughby, sending up Cecil Cooper, who had been having a horrendous World Series at the plate (1 hit in 18 at bats). Cooper went out, and the Cincinnati Reds scored in the top of the 9th to win the World Series.

Given all of this, Darrell Johnson's rating as Red Sox manager then is a 2/Fair.

The Possible Dream

Don Zimmer was next, and we've already rated him as the worst manager in Red Sox history. It's tempting to rate Zimmer a 0 on our scale of 1-6, but let's put him at 1/Poor, and the lowest of the low.

The Red Sox manager after Zimmer was Ralph Houk. In hiring Houk, the Red Sox did what they have done many a time and recycled an old Yankees' manager who was past his prime. What did he bring to the team? It's not clear that the Red Sox were any better or worse under Houk than they would have been under any other manager. Houk's rating: 3/Average.

John McNamara won a pennant in 1986 and came within one strike of winning that elusive World Championship. He gets credit for getting them there and so close, but also takes the blame for leaving Bill Buckner in to make the infamous error that cost the Red Sox Game 6 to the Mets. McNamara had frequently replaced Buckner with Dave Stapleton for defensive purposes in late innings during the season. He did not in Game 6 and it cost him. It was reported at the time that McNamara chose to keep Buckner in the game since Buckner had said that he wanted to remain in the game, and because McNamara felt that Buckner deserved to be on the field when the Red Sox won the title. However, as pointed out earlier, it is the manager's job to put his team in the best possible position to win, and replacing Buckner with Stapleton would have been a move that did put his team in the better position to win. The fact that he did not is something that McNamara will rue for years to come.

McNamara's handling of the pitching was also questionable. He used most of his bullpen sparingly during the series, underutilizing Sammy Stewart for example though Stewart had been effective in the playoffs. Starting Al Nipper in Game 4 at Fenway with a 2-1 series lead was tantamount to giving away a series-tying game. Leaving an obviously tiring and valiant Bruce Hurst in game 7 with Hurst going on what was short rest for him also helped turn a 3-0 lead into a 3-3 tie. The most interesting pitching move was pulling Roger Clemens in Game 6. It still is not clear if McNamara decided to pull Clemens or if Clemens begged out of the game himself with a blister. Each claims that the other decided it. Who knows who did what other than these two, but it is the manager's job both to make the decision and to handle this type of controversy and make it a non-issue. McNamara did not, and the issue and controversy linger today.

McNamara was also set in his ways. In 1987, when injuries occurred, McNamara substituted players right into the batting order for the player that they were replacing. This resulted in such oddities as Ed Romero replacing an injured Wade Boggs at third base, but also in Romero stepping into Boggs' third spot in the batting order. This makes no sense. It is non-managing. A manager should be more creative in juggling his lineup in such circumstances. Romero should have been batting ninth, not third. The lineup should have been adjusted to accommodate the players who were actually in the lineup, not just keeping the spots warm until the injured players returned.

Lastly, when the Red Sox reported to camp for the 1987 season he told them to forget the 1986 World Series. Why? Shouldn't getting within a strike of winning the World Series be something to remember and use as motivation? Would Red Auerbach have wanted the Celtics to forget losing to the Hawks in 1958? Would Vince Lombardi have wanted the Packers to forget losing to the Eagles in 1960? Admittedly, there is more emotion in basketball and football than baseball, but it also sometimes would be good to see more emotion from the Red Sox, as in "we're mad and sick and tired of losing to the Yankees and are not going to let that happen this year". Emotional baseball managers like Earl Weaver and Billy Martin have helped their teams win many pennants … and I doubt that Earl Weaver told the Orioles to forget losing the 1969 Series to the same Mets franchise before they came back and won it all in 1970.

All in all then, McNamara, like pennant-winning Darrell Johnson before him, is not rated highly. He gets a 2/Fair as did Johnson.

Joe Morgan from Walpole, MA took over for Johnny Mac in the middle of 1988 and the team promptly went on a streak in which they won 19 of 20 games and took over first place. Morgan was the second-best manager the Red Sox have had in this interim. The team played well for him and won two division titles. They lost both ALCS appearances to the powerful Oakland A's of Jose Canseco, Mark McGwire, and Dave Stewart, but that does not detract from their accomplishments. Joe had some unique ways about him, including a tendency to bring an outfielder in to become a fifth infielder in some situations (but it is at least nice to see a Red Sox Manager actually doing something proactively to try to win games), and some curious phrases, like "6, 2, and even" (it's still not clear what this means), but was a good manager. He rates a 5/Very Good on our rating scale.

Joe was removed as manager so that the Red Sox could promote Butch Hobson from managing their Triple A Minor League team before any other team took Hobson as manager. What a waste. Hobson was not a good manager at all, and has not managed elsewhere since leaving Boston. Hobson's rating: 1/Poor.

After the Hobson debacle, the Red Sox hired Kevin Kennedy as manager. Kennedy won a division title in 1995 and certainly seems knowledgeable as a baseball broadcaster on Fox. Here again, though, changing the lineup as Mo Vaughn and Jose Canseco went 0-for-27 in the AL Division Series would have been called for. Nevertheless, we'll rate Kennedy a 4/Good.

Jimy Williams managed the Red Sox to two wild card playoff appearances, losing to Cleveland in 1998 and then beating Cleveland and losing to the Yankees in 1999. He gets high marks for doing that, for managing the turbulent Carl Everett, and for resisting the pleas to pitch Pedro on 3 days rest in game 4 of the 1998 playoff with Cleveland. Even if they had won that game (and a well-pitched game by Pete Schourek almost let them do so), they would have had to win another, so having Pedro pitch a possible game 5 with full rest was much preferable to pitching a game 4 on short rest. He gets especially high marks for saying, with the Sox down 0-2 to Cleveland in the 1999 ALDS, that the Indians had better win the next game because if they don't they might not win again. It was almost reminiscent of that other Williams (Dick) saying "We'll win it" when asked about the Red Sox chances in the 1967 pennant race.

However, Jimy Williams also left Tim Wakefield off the roster for the ALCS versus New York in favor of Bryce Florie, and we saw how effective Wakefield could be against New York in 2003. He also had a habit of pushing Pedro back in the rotation when it was his normal turn to pitch but there had been a rainout or a day off. It seems to me that if you have the best pitcher in baseball, you'd want to get him out on the mound as often as possible to help your team win as many games as possible. In 2000, for example, this resulted in Tomo Ohka pitching on days when Pedro could. Which of these pitchers would you rather have pitch for you? The answer is obvious.

Jimy also had a habit of resting players at the wrong time. It was frustrating, for example, to see Nomar Garciaparra benched for a rest in the opener of a Yankee series, when he could have been rested before or after the series with New York.

Finally, Williams persisted in playing Scott Hatteberg as a catcher. Now Hatteberg is a great guy for getting on-base (there is a whole chapter about this in the book "Moneyball" by Michael Lewis), but he simply cannot catch. I have pointed out many times that there are two positions in all of sports that define exactly what you are supposed to do – tackle in football (defensive tackle that is) and catcher in baseball. Hatteberg could not do a good job catching. Oakland has been successful with him as a first baseman, and I wish him all the best of luck, but Williams did him and the team a disservice by continuing to catch him.

Overall though, we'll rate Jimy Williams as a 4/Good.

Joe Kerrigan took over for Jimy Williams when Jimy was fired. Joe was a very good pitching coach, but not a good manager. His rating: 1/Poor.

Grady Little was discussed in detail earlier, but now let's rate him as a 3/Average.

There you have it. Of the 15 men who have managed the Red Sox since 1961, only 1 was outstanding (and he was let go after 3 very successful years as we will discuss in the Chapter 6), and 1 was very good. 5 were poor, 2 fair, 3 average and 3 good. Not a very good score card, but then, it is certainly easy to understand why the Red Sox have not won a championship during this time. The on-the-field management has to take the lion's share of the blame.

The Possible Dream

Chapter 4 – General Managers, Bad Trades, Questionable Player Personnel Decisions

While on-the-field management is the primary reason why the Red Sox had not won a championship, a close second is the series of trades, free agent signings, and player acquisitions and non-acquisitions made by the team's General Managers over the years.

Heading into the 2004 season there was actually hope for the future, however, based on the early decisions and moves made by Theo Epstein, the current Sox GM. His acquisitions before the 2003 season of Kevin Millar, Bill Mueller, and David Ortiz were instrumental in making the 2003 Red Sox season a success. His in-season addition of Scott Williamson helped the bullpen, and his acquisitions of Scott Sauerbeck and Jeff Suppan, although they did not pan out as well as had been hoped, were the right moves to be made at the time.

Despite the good moves made by Epstein, there were still questionable ones that he made which are the types to be avoided for the future if he wanted to build on the success of 2003. Before the 2003 season, rumors were rampant of a trade in which the Red Sox would give up a good left-handed pitching prospect, Casey Fossum, and starting third baseman Shea Hillenbrand, and acquire right-hand pitcher Bartolo Colon. With Colon having been one of the best pitchers in the American League while with Cleveland and still very good with Montreal, this is a trade that should have been made. One thing the Red Sox have not learned over the years (and the Yankees have) is that old baseball adage that you cannot have enough pitching. Imagine, for example, a 2003 rotation that could have included Pedro Martinez, Bartolo Colon, Derek Lowe, Tim Wakefield, and John Burkett. That is a very strong rotation. This could have meant Colon pitching in game 2 against the A's in the ALDS or Game 1 or 2 of the ALCS. Perhaps a win by Colon earlier in the ALCS could have even allowed the Red Sox to win the series without the need of a seventh game. Who knows what would have happened, but, again, it would have been fun to try.

Instead of that move, Epstein and the Red Sox early in the season sent Hillenbrand to Arizona in exchange for Byung-Hyun Kim. This was not a good move. To be sarcastic, the only advantage that this had is that Kim already knew how to blow big games against the Yankees having blown leads in 2 consecutive World Series games to them in 2001 by giving up late-inning home runs. Kim was not effective against the Yankees, and, in fact, was even left off of the roster for the Yankees playoff series. The official explanation was injury, although it was not clear that the Red Sox had any confidence in having Kim pitch against New York. The obscene gesture that Kim made to Red Sox fans when being introduced before game 3 of the Oakland series (the fans were booing him for his blowing the lead in game 1) also did not put him in good stead with management or fans. It may be too early to give a final judgment on the Kim acquisition, but the early returns show that this was disastrous.

Before the 2003 season, Epstein also allowed Brian Daubach to leave. Daubach was a decent player and a streak hitter who can help carry the team when he is hot. Again this shows a weakness that the Red Sox have had and the Yankees have not over the years – the building of a good bench. The Red Sox mentality seems to be that if you have two players who can play a position, it's time to get rid of one since one player won't be happy on the bench. The Yankees' mentality is 'let's get all the good players that we can get, and that way if someone gets hurt or goes into a slump, we can replace him with someone who can be productive'. In the 2003 playoffs, with Ortiz, Millar, and Mueller all in slumps, there was no one who could really be summoned off the bench to try to substitute for any of these players and give the team a spark. Daubach could have helped. At least having him come in for Ortiz or Millar would have been a good option.

Unlike Epstein, who at least seems to have a plan and philosophy (a philosophy similar to that of Billy Beane in Oakland), the man who served the longest as Red Sox GM since 1961, Dick O'Connell, never did seem to have a plan. Trades were made with no long-term view or sometimes even short-term reward. It was O'Connell, for example, who made the ill-fated trade of Sparky Lyle for Danny Cater. Lyle was one of the best relief pitchers in the game. Cater was a journeyman. O'Connell's explanation of the trade was that Cater always hit well in Fenway Park. Of course he did – he was facing Red Sox pitching! As described previously, Lyle went on to have a great career with the Yankees, while Cater never did do much of anything in Boston.

The Possible Dream

Another highly inexplicable move by O'Connell was the trading of Earl Wilson for Don Demeter in 1966. Wilson was a good right-handed pitcher, Demeter another journeyman (I'll try not to overuse that term, but it is surprising how often the Red Sox make a trade for just that type of player). Wilson was just coming into his own in 1966 and in fact would have a 22-win season in 1967 for Detroit. Just as it was interesting to imagine a Martinez-Colon combination in 2003, just imagine what it would have been like having 22-game winner Jim Lonborg and 22-game winner Earl Wilson in the rotation in that magical 1967 season. Perhaps the pennant could have been won before the final day of the season. Perhaps having Lonborg and Wilson would have been enough to offset the great Bob Gibson in the World Series against the Cardinals. But Wilson was gone, having been traded for Don Demeter who was a non-contributor to the Impossible Dream team one year after being acquired. It's also not clear why the Red Sox wanted Demeter. He was an outfielder coming to a team that had budding outfield stars in Carl Yastrzemski and Tony Conigliaro and a coming star from the minors in Reggie Smith. There was no reason to trade for Demeter. Could the reason have been to get rid of Wilson? If so, why? Could this have been a case of racism? Wilson, a black player had been involved in an incident in a bar in Winter Haven, the Red Sox spring training facility in Florida. The incident involved Wilson not being served a drink because of his race, so he and the others with him left the bar. The Red Sox never liked bad publicity, particularly bad publicity that involved black players, and Wilson wound up being traded in June to Detroit with Joe Christopher (another black player) for Demeter and a non-descript pitcher who never pitched for Boston. What a waste and what a bad move by the GM.

These were not the only bad moves of the O'Connell era. In April of 1969 he traded Ken Harrelson, and pitchers Dick Ellsworth and Juan Pizzaro to Cleveland for pitchers Sonny Siebert and Vicente Romo and catcher Joe Azcue. Harrelson had been the American League RBI leader in 1968 and Ellsworth had won 16 games for Boston in 1968. Siebert was a good acquisition, but the Red Sox gave up too much. Harrelson's popularity in Boston also led to a fan uproar about the trade. Acquiring Azcue again showed that the Red Sox had no plan, as they had a good young catcher already on the team, Jerry Moses, and an intriguing prospect in the minors by the name of Carlton Fisk. Although Fisk's minor league numbers were not great, the potential was there, so acquiring Azcue was not a good strategic move. By the end of 1969, Azcue and Romo were both unhappy (Azcue was eventually traded for another catcher, Tom Satriano), so Siebert was the only real value that the Red Sox got from this trade.

After the 1970 season, it was clear that the Red Sox were going to make some moves. On October 11, they traded Tony Conigliaro, catcher Jerry Moses, and pitcher Ray Jarvis to California for second baseman Doug Griffin, pitcher Ken Tatum, and outfielder Jarvis Tatum. Conigliaro had returned from a scary beaning in 1967 to have a productive year in 1969 and his best year ever in 1970 (36 home runs). To trade him essentially for a minor league second baseman (Griffin) who was a good fielder with some speed does not seem like equal value. Conigliaro's eye problems stemming from being hit by that disastrous pitch in 1967 caused him to leave the game in 1975 (after a final stint as a Red Sox Designated Hitter), but they could have gotten more for him in 1970.

One year to the day after that trade, they also made another trade in which they seemed to give up too much for what they got. On October 11, 1971 they bundled Jim Lonborg, the pitching hero of the dream 1967 season; first baseman George Scott, another star in 1967; Ken Brett, a lefthanded pitcher with potential; Joe Lahoud, a lefthand-hitting outfielder; Billy Conigliaro, a righthand-hitting outfielder; and Don Pavletich, a backup catcher, in a trade with Milwaukee. In return, the Red Sox acquired speedy outfielder Tommy Harper, right hand pitchers Marty Pattin and Lew Krausse, and minor leaguer Pat Skrable. All of the Red Sox players involved in this deal had been rumored to be on the trading block after the season, and Red Sox fans wondered what trades would be made with them. That's "trades", plural. To bundle all of the tradeable players into one deal was not a desirable way to proceed. This is especially true given the number of star players who changed teams during that off-season. Frank Robinson was traded by the Orioles to the Dodgers. Joe Morgan was traded from the Astros to the Reds in exchange for Lee May, Ken Holtzman was traded to the A's by the Cubs for Rick Monday. Sam McDowell was traded to the Giants for Gaylord Perry. Couldn't the Red Sox have used some or all of the players that they traded to try to acquire someone in this group? Pattin was a solid pitcher in the Red Sox rotation and Harper brought speed and base-stealing to a team that sorely needed it, but this was not an equitable trade.

O'Connell also was at the center of a storm on June 15, 1976, which was then the trading deadline. He acquired Joe Rudi and Rollie Fingers from Oakland for cash at the same time that the Yankees acquired Vida Blue from Oakland also for cash. Rudi and Fingers were with the team the night of the trade but were not played. This later proved shortsighted as commissioner Bowie Kuhn the next day put the deals on hold and later overturned them as not being "in the best interests of baseball". Had the Red Sox played Rudi or Fingers this would have been harder for Kuhn to do and may have resulted in

Kuhn's just fining Oakland owner Charlie Finley instead of returning the players to Oakland. It is also interesting that the Red Sox, always in need of pitching, did not go for Blue and Fingers. They also needed a third baseman and could have tried to purchase Sal Bando from Oakland. In fact, when Red Sox owner Tom Yawkey was told about the deal he questioned why they didn't get Bando. I guess it was not only the fans who were second-guessing O'Connell.

O'Connell also was the GM who presided over the team as the era of free agency began. As noted previously, by having traded Sparky Lyle in 1972, the Red Sox first free agent signing was Bill Campbell. Campbell had one good year for Boston and then turned around and convinced other players (most notably Rod Carew) not to consider Boston when their turn came up in free agency.

To be fair, O'Connell did make a few good moves and was very helpful in reversing the racist trends of the previous Red Sox regime. It was under O'Connell's leadership that good black players such as Reggie Smith and George Scott became regulars. It was also O'Connell's trading for Gary Bell, Jerry Adair, and Elston Howard in 3 separate deals during the 1967 season that helped make the Impossible Dream season possible. Trading minor league outfielder Bill Schlesinger for pitcher Ray Culp after 1967 was one of the three best trades the Red Sox have made since 1961 (the others being the trade of Carl Pavano and Tony Armas, Jr. for Pedro Martinez in 1997 and the trade for Curt Schilling in 2003). However, he also made the other bad deals described above, passed on a chance to acquire relief ace Tug McGraw in 1974 for Juan Beniquez when the Red Sox needed a good relief pitcher and the Mets were shopping for an outfielder and high on acquiring Beniquez, fired Dick Williams after Williams had had three very successful seasons as Boston manager, and, as stated earlier, never seemed to have a plan as to where he was taking the Red Sox.

A decade after O'Connell, Lou Gorman did an all right job as GM – not outstanding, but not horrible. He made some good moves and positioned the Red Sox to get into the World Series in 1986. His acquisition of Don Baylor helped provide some needed leadership for that team, and acquisitions of Tom Seaver, Dave Henderson, and Spike Owen also helped to solidify the team. Henderson almost won the 1986 World Championship for Boston with a 10th inning home run in game 6 against the Mets.

Gorman also traded Curt Schilling and Brady Anderson to Baltimore for Mike Boddicker to help win another division title. It was difficult to part with Schilling, who went on to a great career with Philadelphia and a championship and World Series MVP with Arizona (and, ironically, was re-acquired by Boston for the 2004 season) and

Anderson, who went on to have a 50 home run season in Baltimore. However, this was trading value for value and getting Boddicker was a good move that did result in the desired AL East championship.

There is another trade, however, for which Gorman will always be remembered. That was the ill-advised trade of minor league prospect Jeff Bagwell for journeyman (there is that word again) long-relief pitcher Larry Anderson in 1990. This trade made no sense at the time or since. A long-relief pitcher is not going to help you win a pennant, and the Red Sox wound up having Anderson only for a few months and he pitched just over 20 innings for the team for the entire season. Bagwell, meanwhile, has gone on to have over a decade of success as one of the most feared hitters in the National League. As has been the case so many times in Red Sox history, if they decided to trade Bagwell, they could have definitely gotten more value for him.

Another memory that Gorman probably wishes we did not have is his comment about "where would we play him?" when asked about the possibility of acquiring former NL Batting champion Willie McGee. Again, unlike the Yankees, the Red Sox never think of having depth, which has hurt them often in the past, and will continue to do so unless and until that lesson is learned.

The other prominent GM during these 43 years has been Dan Duquette. Duquette is the man who allowed team leader Mo Vaughn and star pitcher Roger Clemens to leave as free agents, getting nothing in return. The more annoying of these was Vaughn, with whom the Red Sox were clearly unhappy. Yet, though Mo Vaughn was unhappy in Boston and Mark McGwire was unhappy in Oakland, the Red Sox never pursued what was an obvious trade possibility. The A's wound up trading McGwire to the Cardinals, where he promptly hit 70 home runs to shatter the then-record of 61. The Red Sox would up getting nothing for Vaughn. Maybe McGwire wouldn't have hit 70 HRs for Boston, but it sure would have been nice seeing him hit with the wall in Fenway being as close to the plate as it is.

Letting Clemens go was not the worst idea. He did seem to be losing it. However, letting him go and getting nothing in return was unnecessary. Even a couple of minor league players, perhaps from the Astros or Rangers in Clemens' home state of Texas, would have been better than the whole barrel of nothing that the Red Sox wound up with, and may have helped prevent him from going to the intra-division rival Blue Jays and then Yankees.

Haywood Sullivan and Buddy Leroux deserve mention here as well, though these individuals will be treated more fully in the chapter on ownership. These guys were inept at running the ballclub and it is

The Possible Dream

incomprehensible to me that these are the people to whom Jean Yawkey wanted to sell the team after the death of long-time owner Tom Yawkey. Again, we'll leave many of the Sullivan-Leroux shenanigans to their ownership, but their work in player personnel decisions has to be mentioned. It was they who knowingly and purposely neglected to send a contract extension to Carlton Fisk before the required December 20 date in 1980, making Fisk a free agent. When it was announced at a press briefing, Sullivan followed that with an announcement that the bar was open, making him look like a complete buffoon. Fisk, the best catcher in the team's history, a team leader since he was a rookie in 1972, a native New Englander who always hustled and would dive into the stands to catch foul balls, was let go because of the complete ineptitude of these individuals. It was that day that I decided that the Red Sox didn't care about winning and didn't care about their fans, so why should I care about them. I doubt that I was the only fan who felt that way.

No talk of Red Sox GM's and bad player moves can be complete without mentioning the selling of Babe Ruth to the Yankees in 1920. Has there been any worse move in the history of professional sports in America? I don't believe so. Neither team has been the same since. Through 2003, the Yankees had won 26 World Series, the Red Sox had only appeared in 4, losing each time. Selling Babe Ruth? Unbelievable.

Equally unbelievable is the fact that the Red Sox could conceivably have had both Jackie Robinson and Willie Mays. Robinson was one of 3 black players given a tryout at Fenway in 1945. From what has been written, a voice, sometimes described as being Tom Yawkey, sometimes Joe Cronin, yelled "Get those n_____ off the field". The tryout was a sham, and none of the three players was offered a contract by the Red Sox. The derogatory comment that was yelled, and the non-tendering of a contract to a player who was as obviously skilled as Jackie Robinson, is all too believable given the racist history of the Red Sox, the last of the original 16 teams to field a black player. Robinson went on to have a stellar career with the Brooklyn Dodgers, appearing in 6 World Series. Another of the players involved in the tryout along with Robinson, Sam Jethroe, was later signed by the Boston Braves as well, so it was clear that these players had talent. It's too bad, to say the least -- and disgusting, to state the obvious -- that the Red Sox were not colorblind enough to see the obvious talent of these players and not just the color of their skin when they tried out for the team in Fenway.

Mays was available to the Red Sox through their affiliation with the Birmingham minor league team and their affiliation with the

Birmingham Black Barons, with whom Mays played. There was a related story of the Red Sox sending a scout to see Mays play, having been tipped off about Mays by the manager of the Black Barons. The scout, Larry Woodall, was reportedly not happy about being sent to scout a black player, even one with as much talent as Mays. This was compounded by the fact that the scout left after three days of rain without ever seeing Mays play, and reportedly provided a fictitious and less than positive scouting report about Mays. The Red Sox, at that time under the leadership of Joe Cronin, did not pursue signing Mays as they could have and should have done. Mays is probably the best ballplayer that most living fans have ever seen, and, with the death of Joe Dimaggio, is now acknowledged as being the "greatest living ballplayer". In any case, the opportunity to sign Mays was real. Years later, Mays was talking to Ted Williams and told him that he thought they'd be playing together. They should have been.

Imagination is sometimes all that Red Sox fans have, since Red Sox reality is so stark, but imagine a 1950's Red Sox lineup that would include Ted Williams, Willie Mays, Jackie Robinson, Bobby Doerr, Johnny Pesky, Dom Dimaggio, and all. They might have actually won something.

Boston's basketball team, the Celtics, was famous for breaking racial barriers. The Celtics were the first team to draft a black player (Chuck Cooper from Duquesne). They were the first to field an all-black starting lineup (Bill Russell, Willie Naulls, Tom Sanders, Sam Jones, and KC Jones in 1965). More importantly, they were the first team in the 4 major sports leagues to hire a black man as a head coach, when they hired Bill Russell in 1966. The Celtics are a team to be proud of for their racial stances; the Red Sox are a team to be abhorred for its history. When they couldn't even see past their prejudices to sign players as talented as Willie Mays and Jackie Robinson, they didn't deserve to win.

Ruth, Robinson, Mays, then later Sparky Lyle and not sending Fisk a contract is a pathetic litany for the Red Sox general managers. Add to that the fact that the Red Sox, with all of their money declared themselves "conscientious objectors" not wanting to sign free agents, making them the equivalent of the Pittsburgh Pirates and not ready to compete with the Yankees and other teams when they had the resources to do so. Add to that the signing of free agents like Mike Torrez and Bill Campbell (before the conscientious objector days) when better players were available. Add to that moves such as trading Dick Stuart after two season of 100+RBI and 75 home runs for a sore-armed left-handed pitcher, Dennis Bennett, who never did much of anything for Boston. Add to that leaving Jim Fregosi unprotected before the expansion draft in 1960, leaving Don Buddin as their starting shortstop and giving the Angels an All-Star shortstop of their own. Add to that General Manager Bucky Harris picking Billy Jurges to manage instead of Gene Mauch, a manager in the Red Sox farm system who was described by Al Hirschberg as "one of the brightest young managers in baseball" – Mauch went on to have a stellar career managing in the big leagues (though he never had as good a team as he would have had in Boston) while Jurges' managerial record in Boston was abysmal. This list could go on and on, but suffice to say with all of these examples that the Red Sox front office has done a poor job of player acquisition and trades.

It was hoped going into 2004 that Theo Epstein would build on his successes of 2003 and learn both from his mistakes and from the many mistakes of his predecessors, so that the Red Sox could reach their ultimate goal.

Chapter 5 – Players and Playing Style

After Game 1 of the 1967 World Series, which the Red Sox lost 2-1 to the St. Louis Cardinals, Carl Yastrzemski took extra batting practice. This surprised members of the media and members of the Cardinals team, many of whom had never seen anything like it. What was particularly surprising about it was that:

- Yaz had just come off a triple-crown season, so he was clearly in a hitting groove all year

- Yaz had finished the season by going 7-for-8 in the final two games of the season, against the Minnesota Twins with the pennant on this line, so he certainly had been performing well in the clutch

- It was only one game into the World Series

- The loss was to Bob Gibson who has only been one of the two best pitchers in baseball over the last half century (only Sandy Koufax was better), a pitcher who could make anyone look bad

Despite all of this, there was Yaz taking extra batting practice. Yaz knew that his team depended on him and didn't want to embarrass himself. The extra work paid off the next day as Yaz hit two home runs to account for 4 of the 5 runs in the Red Sox 5-0 win over the Cardinals. Yaz went on to bat .400 for the series (going 10-for-25 in the 7 game series).

In 2003, Nomar Garciaparra was having a very bad post-season, not just one game. He knew the team depended on him and he was definitely embarrassing himself by turning himself not into a Mr. October, but into a Mr. Popup. Yet there were no reports of Nomar taking extra batting practice or doing anything different to try to regain his batting touch.

Nomar is by all reports a good player, a good teammate, and a guy with a lot of class, but this shows something either about him, the Red Sox, or the state of the game. Maybe it shows something about all three.

The Red Sox have rarely had that fiery team leader that lifts the rest of the team by both his actions and his words. Yaz was a private man who led more by example. Nomar is the same. Their history includes no one like Frank Robinson, who showed the Orioles how to win when he joined them in 1966. The Orioles went on to win the World Series in 1966 and were in the World Series again in 1969, 1970, and 1971, winning a second title in 1970. There is no Reggie Jackson, who was a leader on both the A's and Yankees of the 1970's. There is no Pete Rose, who was the fiery leader of the Cincinnati Reds. These men burned to win and led their teammates any way that they could. The closest that the Red Sox have come is with two players: Don Baylor, who was a leader in 1986, and Carlton Fisk, who was a leader in 1972 and later. But neither was "the straw that stirs the drink" as Reggie used to refer to himself.

With one exception, neither have the Red Sox had the fiery manager, the Billy Martin or Earl Weaver type who drove their team to win. The exception was Dick Williams, and all he did was awaken what had been a moribund franchise for many years.

Instead of these leaders, the Red Sox have had many of the most selfish baseball players in history. Ted Williams, the man generally thought to be the best player in franchise history, was also one of baseball's most selfish players. One example was his refusal to hit to left field against the famous Williams shift, where opposing teams moved the shortstop to the 2nd baseman's side of 2nd and the 3rd baseman way to his left. A few well-placed bunts would have undone that shift forever and wound up helping the team, but Williams was too stubborn and self-absorbed to do so.

If Williams was the best player in history, the man thought by many to be the best pitcher in franchise history, Roger Clemens, shared the same traits. In fairness, Roger was sometimes a warrior who would go out to the mound and pitch well after an injury, but he was also a whiner, who often came up with some medical excuse after a bad outing that was never mentioned beforehand. He also held out in 1987 when he had a contract, hurting the team when it needed a good start to put the disastrous 1986 World Series behind them. In contrast, catcher Rich Gedman was vilified for not being with the team at the start of the 1987 season, but Gedman did not have a contract. Clemens did have a contract but chose not to honor it. It is generally felt that Clemens was out of shape for the last few years of his Red Sox stay, again a disservice to his teammates.

Clemens also kept talking at the end of his Red Sox career about playing for a team closer to his home in Texas. He wound up signing with the Toronto Blue Jays and then playing for the Yankees, neither of which is appreciably closer to Texas than is Boston. If that is not hypocritical, it's not clear what is. Clemens went where the money was, not to get closer to Texas.

Clemens best showed the type of person that he is with his approach to the Mets' Mike Piazza after Clemens joined the Yankees. After Piazza had hit Clemens well the first few times that they faced each other, Clemens hit him in the head with a pitch. That was not only foolhardy, it was dangerous. It also put the team in the position where they usually from that point on had to avoid pitching Clemens in Shea Stadium since he would have to bat for himself there (no Designated Hitter is used in National League parks), and might face retaliation from the Mets' pitchers. This handcuffed his manager and forced his team to have to work around him when they went to Shea. Then, in the 2000 World Series, when Piazza broke his bat on a grounder early in game 1, Clemens picked up the broken end of the bat and threw it at Piazza as Piazza was running down the first base line. This is an egregious act, and Clemens should have been immediately thrown out of the game for it. It's also a selfish act in that his team would have then had to scramble to replace him after he was ejected. However, for some reason that is a mystery to this day, the umpires did not eject Clemens as they should have. The Yankees were lucky that Clemens' selfishness did not hurt them as it should have.

Clemens may have been a good pitcher, but his act over the years was classless. He will not be missed.

Wade Boggs is the person who wins the award as the most selfish baseball player I have ever seen. In no way was Boggs a good teammate. Examples of his selfishness abound. When asked once why he failed to swing at a pitch when his manager called for a hit-and-run, causing the runner to be easily thrown out at second, Boggs replied that he was "not accustomed to swinging at the first pitch". I guess it was easier for Boggs to embarrass his teammate, embarrass his manager, cost his team an out, and eliminate a baserunner than to do something that he was not "accustomed" to doing. On another occasion, Boggs called the official scorer to have him reverse an error that was charged to him. The scorer did so, costing the pitcher (it happened to be Roger Clemens) an earned run in a year when Clemens was in the running for the league ERA title. The error would have meant nothing to Boggs, but he was too selfish to swallow his pride and help his teammate.

Boggs was on off-the-field disaster as well. His long extra-marital affair with Margo Adams helped split the team apart when it was revealed. Adams talked about how she and Boggs would photograph other Red Sox players with women who were not their wives either, sometimes bursting into hotel rooms to do so (in something that they called "Operation Delta Force"). It is unknown why they would do that, but that certainly got a lot of Boggs' teammates upset and concerned and probably strained a few marriages. Boggs missed time one season for hurting his back while pulling on his cowboy boots, certainly one of the oddest injuries and injury causes in baseball history. Boggs also claimed one year in spring training that he was being hijacked in his pickup truck but saved himself by, as he put it, "willing myself invisible".

Boggs was a good hitter, but not a good teammate on or off the field. In the history of the Red Sox there is no player that I found to be more despicable than Wade Boggs. It was good to see him leave, even if he went to the Yankees.

There are other players in Red Sox history who exhibited selfishness. Another example was Rick Burleson who "had" to bat leadoff in 1978 even though the speedy Jerry Remy would have been a better choice as a leadoff hitter. As described in the yearly summary in chapter 2, this may have helped cost the Red Sox a pennant as Burleson's tentative running in that playoff game prevented him from being in position to score the tying run in the bottom of the 9th.

For years, the Red Sox were described as being a team of "25 players, 25 cabs" meaning that when they went on the road, the players had no togetherness, no team identity. This "25 players, 25 cabs" mentality was epitomized by players such as Williams, Boggs, and Clemens.

The Red Sox have also been a lumbering team of good hitters, but players who were not fast, not good on the basepaths, and not all that they should have been defensively. What team other than the Red Sox could boast a collection of such infamous players and plays as

- Bill Buckner not getting his glove down and costing the Red Sox game 6 of the 1986 World Series

- Luis Aparicio falling while rounding 3rd base twice in one season against Detroit in a year in which the Red Sox would lose the pennant to the Tigers by ½ game.

- Bob Bailey taking three called strikes from Rich Gossage in the 1978 playoff game

- Rick Burleson not going to third on a hit to right that Lou Piniella lost in the sun in that same 1978 playoff game

- Jim Rice talking about wanting to be judged only on his "numbers", meaning of course his personal numbers/statistics (hits, home runs, etc.) when the only numbers that matter are how many wins the <u>team</u> has, not how many hits and home runs a player has

- Denny Doyle being thrown out at home in game 6 of the 1975 World Series because he thought he heard 3rd base coach Don Zimmer (there's that man again) yell "Go, go, go" instead of "No, no, no" on a fly ball to left – could this ever happen to any other team?

- Rich Gedman not moving his body to block an inside pitch by Bob Stanley in game 6 of the 1986 World Series, allowing the ball to get behind him and the tying run to score in the 10th inning of what should have been a series-clinching Red Sox win

In addition to the selfishness and lack of leadership, the Red Sox have also had a string of players who did not understand or appreciate the intensity of the desire to beat the Yankees. The Dodgers-Giants rivalry in the National league was very intense and marked by players who desperately wanted to beat the other team. In fact, when Jackie Robinson was traded from the Brooklyn Dodgers to the New York Giants he chose to retire from baseball rather than play for the hated Giants. Yet, unlike the Dodgers and the Giants, the Red Sox seem to go out of their way to help the Yankees.

Mo Vaughn, for example, offered Jim Leyritz his protective arm armor after the Red Sox were eliminated from the 1995 playoffs by Cleveland in three games while the Yankees' series with Seattle was continuing and eventually became a five-game series. Would a Yankee player have done anything to help a Red Sox player? How would Steinbrenner have reacted if any Yankee did? In contrast, after a meaningless Yankee loss to the Red Sox in a 2003 mid-season game, Steinbrenner was quoted as saying "they haven't won anything yet". It is readily apparent that the Yankees have burned with a desire to beat the Red Sox, while the Red Sox have been all too willing to accept their defeats at the hands of the Yankees.

Just once it would be good to see a Red Sox player, a team leader, stand up and say "We're not going to take this anymore". Instead what we see are things like Nomar Garciaparra fraternizing happily with Derek Jeter, and Manny Ramirez having dinner with Yankee Enrique Wilson in 2003 when he was too sick to play for the Red Sox. It is also seen in Manny's doing an interview with broadcaster Joe Morgan in which he claims that he would love to play for the Yankees before his career is over. This is a far cry from Jackie Robinson's refusal to play for the Giants when traded to them. But then

Manny Ramirez is a very far cry from Jackie Robinson in many, many ways … competitiveness and team leadership are at the top of that list.

The Possible Dream

Chapter 6 – Ownership

Tom Yawkey was the beloved owner of the Red Sox for 43 years, from the time that he purchased the team in 1933 until his death in 1976. Fans saw him to be a real fan of the game, as they were themselves. They also saw him as an owner who would do anything he could to help the Red Sox, including buying the contracts of key players such as Jimmie Foxx and Lefty Grove to try to give the Red Sox a chance to win a title.

However much good Yawkey did, or appeared to do, the Yawkey regime was marked with a great deal of cronyism, incompetence, and meddling. It was Yawkey, for example, the South Carolina plantation owner, who helped to keep the Red Sox from bringing in black players. Many writers blame Yawkey as the person who yelled "Get those n____ off the field" when Jackie Robinson and two other black players (Sam Jethroe and Marvin Williams) were getting tryouts in Fenway Park in 1945. The feeling was that Yawkey wanted no part of black players and also wanted to get on the field himself for the batting practices that he frequently took at Fenway while the team was on the road.

If it was not Yawkey who yelled that unfortunate slur, it was one of his cronies. Yawkey had a tendency to hire people that he liked, not necessarily good baseball people. Thus, people like Eddie Collins, Joe Cronin, and Mike Higgins ascended to heights within the Red Sox hierarchy that they did not earn and that they probably would not have with any other team. The other person generally thought to have yelled that yell during the Robinson tryout was Joe Cronin. Stories written since have Cronin facing away from the field, not even watching the tryout, so it was most likely Yawkey who yelled that out, but it was also clearly a farce to even have these players in for a tryout since the Red Sox had no intention of hiring them. Mike "Pinky" Higgins (the nickname might also reveal his favorite skin color) is also known for having said that "there will be no n____s on the Red Sox as long as I'm here" and then backed that up by sending Pumpsie Green to the minors before the 1959 season when Pumpsie had clearly made the team. Green later joined the team after a managerial change. If Yawkey was serious about building the Red Sox into a powerhouse, he would not have entrusted the care of the team to men such as Collins, Cronin, and Higgins, and he would definitely have looked to bring in talent regardless of color. It worked for Walter Brown, Yawkey's counterpart as owner of the Boston Celtics. It could have worked for Yawkey had he let it.

Joe Cronin was in charge during the ill-fated opportunity to sign Willie Mays, and was also "credited" with passing on the opportunity to acquire Pee Wee Reese because he was afraid that Pee Wee might take his job as shortstop when Cronin was a player-manager for Boston. An earlier chapter has already speculated as to how good a Red Sox team with Ted Williams, Jackie Robinson, and Willie Mays might have been. Put Pee Wee Reese on that team and you have to wonder how many pennants the Red Sox might have won. The Brooklyn Dodgers dominated the National League in the late 1940's and 1950's with Reese and Robinson as their keystone combination. Put them together with Ted Williams and the others and perhaps the Red Sox would have won at least half as many pennants as the Dodgers of that era (who won pennants in 1947, 1949, 1952, 1953, 1955, and 1956 while the Red Sox were winning exactly zero).

Cronin was not the only incompetent signing of Yawkey. The afore-mentioned Mike Higgins was another. Mike bombed as Red Sox manager in the late 50's and early 60's, then, when it was clear that Higgins was not the right manager for the Red Sox, what did Yawkey do? Did he fire him? No. He promoted Higgins to the position of General Manager, the most influential position in the organization. As GM, Higgins was the boss of his replacement, Johnny Pesky. If Higgins did not knowingly undermine Pesky (and I believe that he did), he certainly did nothing to help Pesky. Red Sox fortunes turned around when Yawkey finally saw what he had in Higgins and fired him for good in 1965, coincidentally on the day that Dave Morehead pitched a no-hitter over Cleveland.

Dick O'Connell took over as GM that September day when Higgins was fired and, though he had his faults (see Chapter 4), he also finally brought the Red Sox into the real world and began building a real team. It was O'Connell who, while Yawkey's interests in the team were waning, made trades to bring in black players such as John Wyatt and Jose Tartabull in 1966 and helped elevate George Scott and Joe Foy to the major leagues. A year later, 1967, another black joined the team from the minors, Reggie Smith, and in mid-season the Red Sox acquired black catcher Elston Howard from New York to help bolster the drive for the pennant. It was clear that under O'Connell, the prejudiced days of the Yawkey-Cronin-Collins-Higgins Red Sox were finally over.

Yawkey in general exhibited bad ownership and business skills. His regime was marked by the hiring of his friends, not competent baseball businessmen. Thus, the Yawkey era saw key jobs going to people like Joe Cronin, Mike Higgins, Bucky Harris, Eddie Collins, Billy Jurges and others. The result of this cronyism was a legacy of failure. It was only after Yawkey finally brought in a baseball man like Dick O'Connell that the years of failure ended. It's too bad that this did not happen until 1965, 32 years after Yawkey first took control of the team.

With the return to glory brought on by the Red Sox Impossible Dream season of 1967, Yawkey's level of interest in the team also increased. That was unfortunate, as Yawkey began then to undermine the authority of Dick Williams, the best manger that he ever had. Williams had to ask Yawkey to stop letting players come to him when they had problems with what Williams was doing. Yawkey did not stop. Ultimately, it was Yawkey who decided to fire Dick Williams near the end of the 1969 season. All Williams had done by that time was

1) turn a bunch of perpetual losers into the darlings of New England for their style of play

2) won the Red Sox first pennant in 21 years, in 1967

3) kept the Red Sox in contention in 1968 despite

    a) the loss of cleanup hitter Tony Conigliaro for the entire season due to the injury to his eye and vision stemming from that horrible beaning on August 18, 1967

    b) the loss of Jim Lonborg to an off-season skiing injury; Lonborg had been honored with the Cy Young Award as the best pitcher in the American League in 1967

    c) the loss of Jose Santiago to an elbow injury early in the season, just as Santiago was showing himself to be one of the best pitchers in the league

    d) the ineffectiveness of George Scott who had hit .303 in the pennant-winning year of 1967 but who slumped to .171 in 1968

That Williams was able to keep the team in contention given this string of problems was near miraculous. Some felt in fact that Williams did a better job of managing in 1968 than he had done in winning the pennant in 1967.

Williams also did a good job in 1969, handling a team that was very strong but not strong enough to challenge the very powerful Baltimore Orioles. The Red Sox finished 3rd behind Baltimore and Detroit and were winding down the season when Williams was fired.

General manager Dick O'Connell was against the firing of Williams, but could not go against the wishes of the team owner.

After Williams was fired by the Red Sox he went on to Oakland and won the AL West Title in 1971 and the World Series in 1972 and 1973. He also won a pennant in San Diego in 1984 and was a successful manager everywhere that he went. The problem is that he should have never had to go anywhere. He should have stayed in Boston. The only reason that he left was Tom Yawkey.

Tom Yawkey's death on July 9, 1976 sent the Red Sox franchise into turmoil. Tom's widow, Jean Yawkey, took over the team, but wanted to sell it. Her main target for that sale was a group headed by former Red Sox player Haywood Sullivan and former Red Sox trainer Buddy Leroux. Other suitors included a group headed by Dom Dimaggio, which also included his more famous brother Joe. Another group was headed by Jack Satter of Colonial Provision Company, which, among other things provided Fenway Franks, the hot dogs sold at Fenway Park. In reality, as Dimaggio and others found out, there was no real bidding. Jean Yawkey was determined that the Sullivan-Leroux group would get control of the storied franchise. The first attempt to sell the team to them failed, since the other American League owners were rightly concerned about the way that Sullivan and Leroux were financing the purchase and the amount of loan debt that they were incurring. The sale finally went through when Jean Yawkey made herself part of the arrangement, and so the Sullivan-Leroux ownership took over the team in early 1978.

The Sullivan-Leroux era was a complete disaster. It was under this regime that the Red Sox became conscientious objectors in the free agent process, making them unable to sign any quality free agents. The Sullivan-Leroux combo, in fact, had no idea how to deal with free agency. For example, before they became conscientious objectors in free agency, the Sullivan-Leroux Red Sox made another personnel blunder, refusing to draft free agent pitcher Tommy John in 1978. Haywood Sullivan explained the decision by saying "We know something about his arm." Sullivan never revealed what they supposedly knew, but apparently it was not the fact that it had a lot of major league wins still left in it.

They also did not know how to handle the personnel that were on their team. For reasons known only to him, for example, Sullivan kept making negative comments to and about Carlton Fisk, one of the team's best players and the best catcher in the team's history. One of the most ridiculous comments came from Sullivan when Fisk was hurt, as he often was during his career due in large part to his aggressive, "win at all costs" style of play, more of which from more players would

The Possible Dream

have been exactly what the team needed. Sullivan's comment that "Fisk's contract hurts him more than his arm" insulted Fisk. Additionally, in 1976, Fisk had been told that the Red Sox wouldn't renegotiate his contract because they did not do that. Fisk was told that if anyone else renegotiated, then he could too. However, after the Red Sox renegotiated Jim Rice's contract and Fisk brought up the agreement, he was asked to show where it said in writing that he could renegotiate. Fisk, a native New Englander who felt that a man's word was his bond, never forgave Sullivan for going back on this verbal agreement.

It was under this regime that one of the biggest personnel blunders in the team history was made – the worst at least since the sale of Babe Ruth to the Yankees. Carlton Fisk was not tendered a contract by the December 20, 1980 deadline, making the best catcher in team history a free agent. This blunder, which also included not sending a contract to Fred Lynn, incredibly was done on purpose. Sullivan believed that, had he sent contracts to Lynn and Fisk, the players could take the team to salary arbitration, and had he not sent the contracts he would have nothing to lose. Unfortunately, he had plenty to lose. By not sending them contracts, this resulted in both Lynn and Fisk becoming free agents. Why Sullivan didn't at least send a contract to them and then trade each or both of them for value has never been explained. Lynn was happy to reach an agreement and get himself traded to the Angels, but Fisk, having been slighted and insulted often by Sullivan during Sullivan's ownership, understandably would not do anything to help Sullivan out of this ludicrous predicament. Fisk signed with the Chicago White Sox and went on to have many productive years with Chicago. Fittingly, in fact, the White Sox beat the Red Sox on opening day the next year, 1981, thanks in large part to an eighth inning home run by Fisk. Revenge for Fisk must have been sweet. A healthy Fisk also might have made the difference for Boston in the 1986 World Series, but the utter incompetence of Sullivan and Leroux had already caused the exile of Fisk to the Windy City.

Another personnel disaster perpetrated under Sullivan and Leroux was the treatment of Luis Tiant. Tiant was not only the pitching leader of the Sox in the 1970s, he was the team leader, and the man that Carl Yastrzemski described as "the heart and soul of the team". Luis kept everyone loose in the clubhouse. He was beloved by the fans, who regularly chanted "Loo-ee … Loo-ee" when Tiant strode to the mound in big games. In 1972, Tiant's first big year in Boston, he would get standing ovations when he walked in from the bullpen after warming up before his starts, an unprecedented and phenomenal situation at the time. The fact that Tiant was a black, Hispanic player who was so beloved was a sign that the Red Sox fans were truly colorblind.

Most importantly, Tiant wanted to pitch big games and he thrived in pitching in big games. There has been no pitcher in Red Sox history who defended a lead in a big game with the tenacity and iron will of Luis Tiant. It was Tiant whose great pitching in game 1 of the 1975 ALCS against Oakland set the tone that the Sox could beat the three-time defending World Champions. It was Tiant who shut out the powerful Cincinnati Reds, the Big Red Machine, in game 1 of the 1975 World Series to give his team confidence in that series against a very strong opponent. It was Tiant who was given a 5-4 lead over the Reds in the 4th inning of game 4 of that series and defended it in one of the grittiest pitching performances in Series history, a 163-pitch complete game victory. Tiant kept pitching out of trouble for the last 5 innings of that very tense game. It was Tiant who pitched the final regular season game in 1978 with the Red Sox one game behind the Yankees and trying to get into a playoff who said that the only way that the Red Sox would lose that game to the Blue Jays was "over my dead body", and then went out and shut them out 2-0. And it was Tiant who, when the Red Sox 14 game lead over the Yankees in 1978 was cut to 1 during the infamous "Boston Massacre" in September, begged to pitch the last game of the series against NY but was told that he was pitching the next day against Baltimore because that was a big game too. Luis' response "Bull ___. This is against the Yankees." showed that he knew more about baseball and the Red Sox than did his manager, Don Zimmer, whose failings have been discussed in detail previously.

All of this meant that Tiant was well deserving of a new contract extension when he was eligible in 1979. However, Haywood Sullivan and Buddy Leroux didn't think so. They also thought that they could intimidate Tiant into taking less money than he was worth. All Tiant wanted was a two-year contract. They wouldn't give it. Leroux crowned this lowlight by telling the proud Tiant "Luis, think about your age". Insulted, Tiant refused to re-sign with the Red Sox. Watching all of this a few miles south was George Steinbrenner, the owner of the Yankees. Steinbrenner has his faults, but he is always willing to do whatever he can to improve his team. He also will do whatever he can to show up the Red Sox or cross-town rival Mets. Seeing both a public relations win and a chance to simultaneously help his team and hurt the Red Sox, Steinbrenner swooped in and signed Tiant to the two-year deal that Luis coveted. Carl Yastrzemski was quoted as saying "When they let Luis go, they tore out our heart". Tiant went on to have a good season for the Yankees in 1979, finishing with a 13-8 record. The Red Sox, one of the best teams of the 1970s, would not contend again for years to come.

Yet there was more to come. Probably the worst transgression of this regime was the buffoonery involved in the infamous coup of June 5, 1983. The Red Sox were in the midst of celebrating a reunion of the magical Impossible Dream Team of 1967. This celebration was also put together to help raise money for the on-going care of Tony Conigliaro, the former Red Sox slugger, who had suffered a severe heart attack/stroke in 1982 while heading to Logan Airport in Boston after interviewing for a Red Sox broadcasting job. During the celebration, a press conference was hastily called by Buddy Leroux at which he announced that he, and some of the limited partners had merged their shares to form a majority ownership. Leroux announced that he was taking over the team, firing Sullivan, and returning Dick O'Connell to the position of General Manager from which he had been fired when this group took over the team. Sullivan later that same day called his own press conference announcing that the Leroux takeover was invalid, and that he and Jean Yawkey, with a 2/3 vote of the principal owners, were blocking the deal. Needless to say, the issue had to go to court. Equally needless to say is that the 1967 reunion and fund-raiser was a shambles, completely upstaged by the buffoonery of the team's owners. The courts ultimately ruled that the takeover was invalid, but the damage to the team's psyche and the franchise's reputation had already been done. The Red Sox were the laughingstocks of baseball.

Noted Boston Sportswriter Ray Fitzgerald at one point in the Sullivan-Leroux era started referring to Haywood and Buddy as Dumwood and Shoddy. Given the above history, the descriptions may have been very appropriate.

Inept, bumbling, characterized by buffoonery -- the Sullivan-Leroux regime was all of that, and more.

The Sullivan-Leroux team ultimately gave way to John Harrington. Harrington was pretty much an absentee owner who seemed more interested in his position within the league than in doing a lot to help the Red Sox. Not much was accomplished in the Harrington regime and not much of note came from it.

Truth be told, this is also the period after Fisk was let go by the Sullivan-Leroux team that I lost all interest in the team, and so have few first-hand memories or observations to relate of what was occurring at this time. There were free agent pursuits of Kirby Puckett in 1992 when the Twins star and a favorite of baseball fans everywhere was available, and of Yankee centerfielder Bernie Williams when he became a free agent in the late 1990s, but most fans felt that there was little chance of the team signing either player. This indeed turned out to be the case, as Puckett re-signed with the Twins and Williams re-signed with the Yankees. All the Red Sox involvement had done was to drive up the salaries that the players would receive when re-signing with their original teams.

Harrington ultimately sold the team to the trio of John Henry, Tom Werner, and Larry Lucchino and Red Sox fortunes appear finally to be in good hands. These men seem genuinely interested in improving the ballclub and doing what it takes to provide Boston with a winner. Unlike the previous owners, they are actually seen at the games, including attending the playoff games in the hostile territory of Yankee Stadium. They are willing to spend money and bring in talent, and are also willing to cut their losses, as they showed by quickly deciding not to have Grady Little return as manager after the disastrous 2003 playoff loss to New York. They also understand that beating the Yankees is very important to Red Sox fans. Lucchino took some criticism for referring to the Yankees as "the Evil Empire" in the spring of 2003, but that is exactly the attitude that will endear him to Red Sox fans. You have to want to beat the enemy, and these guys do. The Red Sox franchise now appears to be in good hands. Finally there is hope for the future.

No treatise on Red Sox ownership would be complete without mentioning Harry Frazee. It was Frazee who sold Babe Ruth to the Yankees in 1920, marking the pivotal point in the history of both franchises. Ruth is a player who transcended the sport, and is one of the most recognizable figures in all of sports history. To sell him was a colossal mistake. Frazee's deal also included his receiving a loan and giving ownership/collateral of Fenway Park to the Yankees. The money from the sale and loan ostensibly went to help Frazee finance the play "No No Nanette". I hope that Frazee enjoyed the play on the stage. The play on the field has not been the same since.

Chapter 7 – External Factors: Fans, the Media, and the Ballpark

During game 7 of the 2003 ALCS a picture was shown of workers at Fenway Park painting the World Series logo behind home plate. My guess is that at that very point thousands of Red Sox fans were screaming a long and loud "NO-O-O-O-O" at their television sets. Why would the Fenway workers do this? Why then? Not all Red Sox fans are superstitious, but enough are that they saw this as the wrong thing to do. It tempted fate and fate has not been kind to the Red Sox over the past 8 decades. There is no reason that the sign/logo could not have been painted on Friday IF the Red Sox had actually held on and won the game on Thursday night. It certainly was not painted at Yankee Stadium until Friday, the day after the game. More to the point, it also was absolutely ludicrous to allow a picture to be taken of this at Fenway, given the Red Sox propensity to turn potential victories into crushing defeat. It is tempting to say again "When will they ever learn?", but let's suffice to say that it simply made no sense.

The day after game 7, we also heard from Manny Ramirez that he had called his father during the fifth inning of that seventh game to tell him "we're going to the World Series". If Red Sox fans had yelled "NO" when seeing the World Series logo being painted on the Fenway grass, they probably yelled "WHAT?" when hearing that Manny did this. Along the all too familiar lines of "When will they ever learn?" why would Manny have done this? First of all, doesn't he understand that this is baseball, and that the game is not over until the last man is out (and that the last man is not out in the fifth inning)? Secondly, doesn't he understand that no lead is ever big enough for the Red Sox, especially against the Yankees? Lastly, why was he on the phone at all in the fifth inning of such an important game? Shouldn't he have been concentrating on the game at hand, a game that would decide the pennant?

Looking at all of this, especially something like the logo incident, one can conclude that it is not only the players who have helped to keep the championship drought going. That is true. The ballpark, the media, and the fans have also contributed.

Yes, the fans are a part of this too. Why wasn't there a hue and cry about Manny calling his father during game 7? There should have been. Unfortunately, Boston fans have been all too tolerant of their Red Sox heroes over the years.

Many fans also just don't get it. The Yankees opened their 2003 playoffs a day before the Red Sox, and lost that first game to the Minnesota Twins. Some fans calling the Boston radio talk shows the next day were lamenting the fact that the Red Sox wouldn't have a chance to beat the Yankees since the Yanks would lose to the Twins. This is ludicrous. First of all, the Yankees had only lost 1 game and were clearly a better team than the Twins. The Yankees in fact came back to win the next 3 games to win the series, 3 games to 1. Secondly, the Red Sox still had not played the first game of their series, and there was no guarantee that the Red Sox would beat a very tough Oakland A's team in that series. Oakland boasted an outstanding pitching staff and had home-field advantage. The A's in fact took a 2 games to none lead, and very much could have won that series. Thirdly, there is nothing in the last 85 years of Red Sox and Yankees history to indicate that the Red Sox could beat the Yankees with the pennant on the line.

As another example, on the morning of game 3 of the ALCS, while walking past Fenway Park, I saw a man in a Yankee sweatshirt walk past the fans who were lined up hoping to get tickets to that game. The fans immediately starting booing the man and yelling that ridiculous "Yankees Suck" chant that some Boston fans seem to yell at every opportunity, no matter how inane. Maybe Red Sox fans should really wait until their team actually wins something, or beats the Yankees in an important game or series before yelling things like that. The team always makes fans like this wind up eating crow, and Yankee fans always get the last laugh. If fans wait until they win, they can then yell whatever they want (up to a point), but until then, they should keep comments like this to themselves.

Most importantly, though, Red Sox fans don't demand enough of the Red Sox organization. It doesn't matter to most Red Sox fans if the Red Sox win or lose. They are "the lovable" Red Sox who play in a "lyrical bandbox" of a ballpark. In the eyes of most fans, if they don't win this year, then next year will be the year. But those eyes are myopic. It is inevitable that, if the Red Sox start a season well, we'll be hearing that "Pennant Fever Grips Hub". Over the years, the hopes of April, May, June, and July have all too often turned into the disappointments of August, September, and October, and yet still the fans drool about the Red Sox and any early season win. The fans should be more demanding, much more demanding given the

The Possible Dream

exorbitant prices that they pay for tickets. If the Red Sox are not committed to winning, STOP GOING! I say this with the realization that the current team ownership does seem committed to winning, but previous regimes have not been. I took the stance in 1980, after the fiasco with the Red Sox not sending Carlton Fisk a contract on time, thus making him a free agent, that if they didn't care, why should I. They didn't care about winning. They didn't care about the fans. So there was no reason to care about them.

The park has also been a factor in Red Sox failures. The inviting left-field wall, just 315 feet from home plate, had for years caused the Red Sox to build a team of righthanded sluggers and look for home runs as the key to winning. Thus players such as Dick Stuart were brought in. Stuart was a terrible fielder and a divisive force in the clubhouse, but the Red Sox saw him as someone who could hit home runs in Fenway, so he was brought in. Similarly, the Red Sox brought in players such as Roman Mejias (after one good year in Houston), Jack Clark, and others, whose main purpose was to hit home runs. Unfortunately, the Red Sox play half of their games away from Fenway, and some of their key games are played in Yankee Stadium where the distances are deep to left field. Those fly balls that are Fenway Park home runs become long outs in other parks, and the team was not built to win any other way.

Building the team around home runs also kept it from being built for speed. Never was this more graphic than in the 1986 off-season. After losing to the Mets in the seventh game that year, the Red Sox should have been adding what they needed to win it all the next year. A key ingredient would have been speed and a free agent that year was speedy Tim Raines from Montreal, one of the best leadoff hitters in the game. The Red Sox made no attempt to sign Raines despite the fact that his speed could help the team. However, the mentality of Boston was that speed was not important, and so they have not pursued players like Raines who can help them win with speed.

The other factor that the left field wall has created is the lack of reliance on good lefthanded pitching. The Red Sox have shied away from lefthanders in the past, fearing that that would give righthanded batters even more of an advantage in Fenway. Thus, the Red Sox have had only a couple of good lefthanded pitchers over the past 43 years. Bill Lee in the 1970s and Bruce Hurst in the 1980s were the only lefthanders who pitched for a few years in Fenway and were solid contributors over those years. Other lefthanders, such as Bob Ojeda, John Curtis, Rogelio Moret, Ken Brett, and John Tudor were not given much of a chance and were shipped out of Boston too soon.

One other comment about the Park: it is not as good a place to watch a game as its reputation says that it is. If you have ever tried to sit in the right-field boxes or grandstand seats, for example, you would be surprised to find out that the seats face the left-field wall, not home plate. It is incomprehensible that a park built for baseball, as Fenway Park was, would not have all seats facing in toward the pitching mound and home plate. That's where the action is. Yet, this is not the case for right field in Fenway. Fans sitting in those seats have to turn to their left and sit at an awkward angle to watch the game that they have paid good money to attend. It should not be this way. Those seats may be good for watching a Bruce Springsteen concert in center field but they are not good for watching Pedro Martinez pitch to Derek Jeter, or any other such matchup in baseball. Tearing down Fenway and building a new park is not as bad an idea as many of the locals would have you believe. It would improve things for the fans, and maybe even help things for their championship-starved team.

The local print and broadcast media is the last external factor that has not helped the Red Sox. Local sportswriters are too quick to criticize anything that the Red Sox do, even after they have called for it. Thus we see the media call for the firing of managers like Jimy Williams and Grady Little and then lament that they were fired. Immediately after the firing of Grady Little, for example, we heard criticism of the move because Little had won over 90 games in each of his two years at the Boston helm. That's not the point. The point is that Little lost the games that really counted the most. Little's managing, or mis-managing may be a more appropriate way to describe it, was one of main factors that the Yankees, and not the Red Sox, wound up going to the 2003 World Series. If Grady Little deserved to be fired, and he did, then these sports reports should say so and then stick by that statement. If he did not deserve to be fired, then say it before it happens and while it is being considered, not after the fact in the "Jimy, we hardly knew ye" style that is all too common with writers such as Dan Shaughnessy, who is the biggest frontrunner among the local media. Shaughnessy will be quick to write a book when the Red Sox are successful and also quick to write a front-page story when they fail. I stopped reading Shaughnessy years ago and have not missed him yet.

There are some good writers, past and present that are worth noting, however. The late, great Ray Fitzgerald was one of the best sportswriters in Boston history. His columns were always cleverly written and a joy to read (if you have the opportunity to get one of Ray Fitzgerald's books I would strongly encourage that you do so – you will enjoy his writing). Larry Claflin was another good writer in the past. In the present day, Peter Gammons knows his stuff and writes it very well. He is consistent. Jackie MacMullan is an outstanding writer. She is excellent at baseball, and her column the day after the Red Sox lost game 7 to the Yankees was a classic; it described the $1 bet that she has with her father every year about whether the Yankees or Red Sox will go further, and how she felt as things were progressing during the night of that seventh game. Her excellent baseball writing is exceeded only by her writing about basketball over the years, however, and we still miss her on the Celtics beat.

On the broadcast side, there is no one who could top the radio duo of Ned Martin and Jim Woods. They painted a verbal picture of what was going on so well that you could really see in your mind what was going on on the field. The words and descriptions that these broadcasters provided were outstanding. I particularly remember a call from Jim Woods on an April night in 1975 where he describes a long drive by Tony Conigliaro, then a Red Sox designated hitter as being "Over everything, into the blackness of the night. Home run, Conigliaro, 4-0 Boston." What a great description. Contrast that with the current Red Sox broadcasters Joe Castiglione and Jerry Trupiano who spend more time with ads and inane chatter and often don't update the score or situation and often will yell "long drive" when it's an easy fly ball and it's easy to see that the verbal descriptions are not there any more. Their descriptions too often reveal their hopes and wishes, not what actually is happening. You can hear the voice drop in sadness when the Red Sox make an out and hear the hope that a fly ball hit by a Red Sox player will get out of the park. Martin and Woods wanted the Red Sox to win but called the game in a way that made you feel that you were there and could not only picture what was happening but almost exactly where it was happening. No fly was a "long fly" ball unless it really was. Baseball on the radio used to be much better than it is now. Red Sox fans have been lucky in having announcers like Ned Martin, Jim Woods, Curt Gowdy, Sean McDonough, Ken Coleman, and Jerry Remy, and writers such as Ray Fitzgerald, Larry Claflin, and Jackie MacMullan.

It was also time to stop referring to "The Curse of the Bambino" or any other curse as being the cause of the Red Sox woes. That was a media creation that the media and many fans have kept alive. There was no curse that caused the Red Sox not to win a championship through 2003. It was bad management, bad ownership, bad general management and player personnel decisions, and not having enough of the right players to win. Until those things were addressed, the Red Sox would not win. Address these problems and championships (more than one) will follow and there would be no more talk of the fictitious curse.

Red Sox fans need to be more demanding of their broadcasters and writers, of the park that they visit, and the team that they support. If they demand more, they may get more.

Chapter 8 – A Tale of Two Cities (the differences between the Yankees and Red Sox)

On November 28, 2003, the Red Sox did something almost unheard of in Red Sox history. They actually outmaneuvered the Yankees and signed ace pitcher Curt Schilling to a contract for the 2004-2006 seasons (with an option for 2007). Schilling was one of the best pitchers in baseball. *Sports Illustrated* magazine, in fact, in its 2003 baseball preview, had rated Schilling as the 2nd best pitcher in baseball, behind only his Arizona Diamondback teammate Randy Johnson, and ahead of Red Sox ace Pedro Martinez, who was ranked fourth.

The signing of Schilling is memorable for a number of reasons. Schilling had been one of the primary targets of George Steinbrenner and the New York Yankees to acquire during the off-season. New York saw Schilling as someone who could come in and help rebuild the Yankee pitching rotation, replacing the "retiring" Roger Clemens and the soon to be released David Wells. Also, earlier in the 2003 off-season Schilling had agreed to waive the no-trade clause in his contract, but only for a trade to either the Yankees or Philadelphia Phillies. He specifically said that he did not want to be traded to the Red Sox, since he felt that Fenway Park was not conducive to a pitcher who gave up as many fly balls as Schilling did.

According to all reports, the Yankees had in fact offered Arizona 2B Alfonso Soriano and/or 1B Nick Johnson in exchange for Schilling, but Arizona owner Jerry Colangelo had turned down the deal. Rumors had it that Colangelo did this for two reasons:

(1) He was still upset with the Yankees for stealing David Wells from the Diamondbacks when it appeared that Wells was ready to sign with Arizona for the 2003 season.

(2) He had received a new trade offer from the Red Sox for Curt Schilling.

The offer from the Red Sox was LHP Casey Fossum, RHP Brandon Lyon, minor-league pitcher Jorge De La Rosa, and minor league outfielder Michael Goss in exchange for Schilling. Arizona agreed to the Red Sox deal but now Theo Epstein and the Red Sox owners had to convince Schilling to agree to a trade and were given a 72 hour period to do so. This is where Red Sox fans fully expected the negotiations to break down, Schilling to refuse a trade to Boston, and the Yankees to swoop in and get Schilling after all. However, Red Sox owners did a remarkable job of carrying out the negotiations, including having Theo Epstein spend Thanksgiving with the Schilling family instead of his own, and addressing any concerns that Shilling and his family had (for instance, showing that Fenway was a more difficult park in which to hit home runs than he had thought). The negotiations also got a boost when Schilling was involved in discussions with fans in an on-line chat room. These on-line interfaces also helped convince Schilling that Boston was well worth considering. Schilling did wind up signing with Boston, much to the surprise and delight of Red Sox fans. This gave Boston a starting rotation headed by Martinez and Schilling, 2 of the 5 best pitchers in baseball. In one fell swoop the new Red Sox owners and GM had beaten the Yankees to the punch and had finally shown that they understood that old baseball adage that you can never have enough pitching. Yes, there is finally hope for the Red Sox.

The acquisition of Schilling was the first time in recent memory that the Red Sox have bested the Yankees in such a player move. It would still behoove the Red Sox however to look back on that history to understand that they should not rest on their laurels. The Yankees will strike back and the Red Sox should be prepared for it, and keep doing what they now have started by acquiring Schilling.

Prior to the Schilling deal, the Yankees had always out-maneuvered the Red Sox in player moves, and wound up with the best players available. In 1974, Oakland A's pitcher Catfish Hunter was awarded free agency as MLB ruled that A's owner Charlie Finley had violated Hunter's contract. Stories abounded that the Red Sox were willing to open their checkbook to acquire Hunter, and had the inside track because, supposedly, Red Sox owner Tom Yawkey had developed a very good relationship with Hunter. Catfish signed instead with the Yankees and helped the Yankees to 3 World Series in 1976, 1977, an 1978 and 2 World Championships, in 1977 and 1978. The Red Sox got the headlines; the Yankees got the player.

Also in 1974, Red Sox writers reported that the team was hot on the trail of Bobby Bonds, the very talented outfielder for the San Francisco Giants. There were stories for days about the possible trade with San Francisco. Then suddenly came the news that the Yankees

The Possible Dream

had acquired Bonds in a 1-for-1 deal for Bobby Murcer. This was typical of the two teams' histories. The Red Sox were talkers and got the headlines, the Yankees were doers, and got the players.

There are numerous other examples. When Jose Contreras was a free agent in 2003, the Red Sox and Yankees were the top suitors for his services. Contreras naturally signed with the Yankees. When Mike Mussina was a free agent, stories were reported of the Red Sox interest in the Oriole pitcher. This included Peter Gammons reporting that with a starting rotation headed by Pedro Martinez and Mike Mussina, the Red Sox would be favored in any post-season series in which they participated. Mussina signed with the Yankees. The Red Sox wooed Bernie Williams when Williams' contract with the Yankees expired and Williams was a free agent. The Red Sox made a generous offer to Williams and hoped to get him, but all that their negotiations had wound up accomplishing was to get Williams a better contract with the Yankees than he would have otherwise received. Many people felt that Williams had had no intention of signing with the Red Sox or anyone but the Yankees. That is certainly what did happen.

The only previous time that the Red Sox had seemingly out-maneuvered the Yankees in a player deal was when they signed pitcher Mike Torrez away from the Yankees after the 1977 season. Haywood Sullivan and Buddy Leroux were pleased that they had lured Torrez away from the Yankees. What they didn't realize was what they had gotten in Torrez, a pitcher who was not good in the clutch and whom the Yankees were not really interested in re-signing. Instead, the Yankees used the money that they saved by not signing Torrez to sign free agent relief ace Rich Gossage. When the 1978 season came down to that infamous 1 game playoff, Torrez was the goat for giving up the key home run to Bucky Dent and Gossage was a hero for getting the save with two innings of relief work. Once again the Yankees had topped the Red Sox both on and off the field.

Player moves between the two teams had always gone in favor of the Yankees, starting with Babe Ruth and moving on through Sparky Lyle and others. The Red Sox thought that they hurt the Yankees by signing Torrez away from them. They did not. In fact, they helped the Yankees to another title. However, a year later, when Red Sox ace Luis Tiant was a free agent, the Yankees saw a legitimate opportunity to hurt the Red Sox by signing him. They did sign Tiant, the heart and soul of the Red Sox team from 1972-1978, and the Red Sox were not the same for years to come. The Red Sox team that had finished with 99 wins in 1978 and in a 1 game playoff, fell to third in 1979 without Tiant and were non-contenders in 1980-1985. Steinbrenner had indeed done the damage that he had hoped to do.

When the Red Sox made a move in 1976 to purchase Rollie Fingers and Joe Rudi from the cash-strapped A's for $ 1,000,000 each, the Yankees did them one better by purchasing LHP Vida Blue from the same A's for $ 1,500,000. The Red Sox could have used pitching (over the years they always could have used more pitching), but wound up not getting Blue, who at the time was one of the best pitchers in the game. Commissioner Bowie Kuhn overturned the deals, returning all three players to the A's, which also only helped New York, as the Yankees went on to win the AL East title easily.

The Yankees on-the-field play also always outdid the Red Sox, not just in results, but also in style of play. For example, in the fifth inning of game 4 of the 2003 ALCS, Derek Jeter hit a grounder that bounced off the third base bag. Nomar missed it, the ball went into left field, scoring David Dellucci (who would have scored anyway), but sending Soriano to third base and Jeter to second instead of keeping them at first and second base. It was hard to shake the feeling that, if the roles were reversed, Jeter would have slid to keep the ball in front of him and would have prevented the runners from taking the extra bases.

This was also reminiscent of a key play that Jeter made in the 2001 playoffs against Oakland. With the Yankees down in the series 0-2, he raced well into first base foul territory and backhanded a throw to the plate to get Jeremy Giambi out at the plate and help preserve a 1-0 Yankee win in game 3. That play was a key factor in turning that series around in favor of the Yankees, and New York wound up winning the series in 5 games. I doubt that Garciaparra or any Red Sox player would have made the same play.

Similarly, in the pivotal eighth inning of game 7 of the 2003 ALCS, with the Yankees trailing 5-3, Jorge Posada looped a hit to center field, scoring two runs and tying the game. Posada, representing the potential winning run, went to second when no Red Sox player covered the base. Both shortstop Garciaparra and second baseman Todd Walker had raced into the outfield to try to catch the ball, so it was up to first baseman Kevin Millar to cover second and make sure that Posada did not advance into scoring position. He didn't do it. Once again, this demonstrated that one team, the Yankees, always played good fundamental baseball, whereas the other, the Red Sox, did not. This had to change if the Red Sox were to win a title.

The tale of two cities extends to the managers of both teams as well. In the same 2003 series the third-place hitters for both teams were in slumps – Jason Giambi for New York and Nomar Garciaparra for Boston. Despite Nomar's extended slump, Manager Grady Little kept Nomar batting in the third spot of the Red Sox batting order and thus in the spot where he killed many potential rallies. Meanwhile NY Manager Joe Torre dropped Giambi from third to seventh in the New York batting order for the crucial seventh game. Giambi responded with a pair of home runs and the Yankees won the game, as they always do when the games between these two teams are most meaningful.

The differences between these two franchises also extend into the front offices. Until the Schilling move, the Red Sox always felt (erroneously) that they had enough pitching. The Yankees on the other hand always kept getting more pitching. Again, as described above, one team talks, the other does. The Red Sox have also always looked to trade a player when they got another good player who played the same position. The Yankees on the other hand, would always accumulate as many good players as they could and thus had good depth for pinch-hitting purposes or for overcoming injury. The best example of this was in 2000. Needing a leftfielder, the Yankees got three, obtaining Glenallen Hill and Jose Canseco before they finally acquired and settled on David Justice. This mentality of getting what the team needs when they need it and building depth on the roster is yet another reason why the Yankees always win and the Red Sox always lose.

So what does this all mean? The Red Sox-Yankees matchup has been referred to as one of sports' best rivalries. Through 2003, it had not been. It is not a rivalry when one team always dominates the other. Nebraska-Iowa State is not a rivalry in college football, neither is Michigan-Northwestern. Army-Navy is a rivalry in college football, since the teams are evenly matched, each looks forward to playing the other, and it is unknown who will win in any given year. Duke-North Carolina is a rivalry in college basketball. Chris Evert and Martina Navratilova was a great rivalry in women's tennis. Harvard-Yale is another real rivalry in college football, as is Notre Dame-Southern California and USC-UCLA. In baseball, Los Angeles Dodgers-San Francisco Giants and before that Brooklyn Dodgers-New York Giants was a real rivalry. Through 2003 Red Sox-Yankees was not a rivalry, and I have not referred to this as a rivalry anywhere in this section of the book. It was not a rivalry because the Yankees have dominated it. It would not be a real rivalry until the Red Sox finally broke the bonds of dominance in which the Yankees have held them since 1918 and finally beat the Yankees when it counts. It would also not be a rivalry until the Red Sox had at least one title of their own to match up against the 26 that the New Yorkers have won since 1920. That finally happened in 2004.

The acquisition of Curt Schilling was the first step in that direction.

Chapter 9 – $$$ (Money makes the world go around)

After defeating the Red Sox in the 2003 ALCS the New York Yankees went on to play the Florida Marlins in the World Series. On paper this was a mismatch in every possible way. The Yankees have won 26 World Series titles, the Marlins 1. The Marlins have never even finished first, having made the World Series both in 1997 and 2003 as a wild-card playoff team. The Marlins had, in fact, only had two seasons with over a .500 winning percentage in their ten year history. Oddly, they made it to the World Series and won it in both of those years.

The biggest discrepancy between the two teams however, was a financial one. The Yankees had baseball's biggest payroll (as they have most years) at $180,000,000. The Marlins payroll was in the $45,000,000 range. In most years the teams with baseball's largest payrolls are the ones that are the most successful, especially since the watershed year of 1994, when baseball's labor problems saw the cancellation of the season in August and no World Series for the first time since 1904. Since that strike, it has been the richest teams that have won, beginning with the Atlanta Braves in 1995, the Yankees in 1996, 1998, 1999, and 2000, the one-year-wonder Marlins in 1997 (the team was broken up and most of the regular players discarded for financial reasons after the 1997 title in another black eye for baseball), the Arizona Diamondbacks in 2001 and the Anaheim Angels in 2002.

That the Marlins actually beat the Yankees in 2003 was a surprise. The main reason that the Marlins won was the reason that most teams that get to the World Series and win it usually win, specifically, the fact that, in a short series, good pitching will almost always win out. The Marlins, with Josh Beckett, Carl Pavano (former Red Sox pitcher), and Brad Penney, had too much pitching for the Yankees to overcome.

Nevertheless, the specter of money deciding who plays for the championship remains one of baseball's biggest problems. The Yankees have the most money, stemming in large part from getting the most revenue from broadcast rights and extremely high ticket prices, and so therefore they are odds-on favorites every year to get to the World Series. On the other hand, small market teams with significantly less revenue, such as the Pittsburgh Pirates, Montreal Expos, Milwaukee Brewers, and Kansas City Royals, go into each baseball season with virtually no chance to get into the World Series. Fans of these teams have virtually no hope of seeing their team get into the World Series. This is not right.

The disparity in revenues has meant that there is no competitive balance in baseball. Going into each baseball season, there are maybe 4-5 teams that have a legitimate chance for a championship, and it is almost a foregone conclusion that the Yankees will be there. For one thing, if they find themselves a player short, they will simply go out and buy the player that they need. They do this in the off-season by signing some or all of the top free agents (players such as Reggie Jackson, Dave Winfield, Mike Mussina, and Jason Giambi). They do this during the season when they find that they are weak, and so bring in players such as Jose Canseco to play left field when that position is weak, or Aaron Boone to play third base when third base is a problem. Most other teams don't have the luxury of just going out and getting whatever they need, whenever they need it. With their large bank account the Yankees can pretty much do that whenever they want.

Contrast baseball's situation with the National Football League. It has been a fair assumption in November of every year since 1994 that the Yankees and maybe the Braves would be in the next World Series eleven months later, even when the first pitch of that season was months away from being thrown. However, in that same November, which is the halfway point of the football season, no one knows who will be in the Super Bowl in January. In many cases, it is not even known who will be in the playoffs a month later. Football has competitive balance, and most teams have a chance to win. Baseball does not.

The biggest difference in the two sports is that the NFL has revenue sharing among all teams. Baseball does not. It was the wisdom of NFL Commissioner Pete Rozelle in the early 1960s that the best way for the league to survive and succeed and for all teams to have an equal chance to win, was for all teams to share revenue equally. Thus, unlike baseball, a team in a major media market like the New York Giants, with millions of dollars available for broadcast rights in the media capital of the world, would not have an unfair advantage over a team like the Green Bay Packers, in one of the smallest markets in all of pro sports. In football's world, the Packers have won 6 championships since 1960 and the Giants 2. If these teams were in baseball or following the revenue rules of baseball, the Giants would probably have as many titles as the Yankees (8) and the Packers far fewer, if any.

In 2000, Bob Costas, one of the best sports announcers in history and a man who is extremely knowledgeable about baseball, wrote a book entitled "Fair Ball", and subtitled "A Fan's Case for Baseball". He touched upon a number of topics, but one of the things that was most interesting was a set of tables that he included that showed the discrepancies in broadcast revenues for the Major League teams for the 1999 season. The Yankees topped the list with an estimated 73 million dollars in such revenue. The Red Sox were tenth with an estimated 36 million dollars, less than half of the Yankees' total. The Montreal Expos were last with an estimated 18 million dollars, which is less than a quarter of the Yankees' figure. This is not putting these teams on an equal playing field, literally or figuratively. The Yankees can stockpile their team with talented players. The Expos, on the other hand, sign and develop good young players, but then see them leave to sign lucrative contracts with the richer teams of the sport. The Red Sox can afford a few good players. The Yankees can afford as many as the roster can hold.

This is seen in free agent bidding year after year. Mike Mussina becomes a free agent and there are really only two teams competing for him – Boston and New York. Similarly with Manny Ramirez, there were only two teams competing for him. The 2003 off-season was filled with stories of the Red Sox signing Curt Schilling and relief pitcher Keith Foulke and pursuing Texas superstar Alex Rodriguez, and the Yankees acquiring Atlanta outfielder Gary Sheffield, Montreal pitching ace Javier Vasquez, and Dodger pitching ace Kevin Brown, and pursuing White Sox pitching ace Bartolo Colon, and perhaps Montreal superstar outfielder Vladimir Guerrerro. Hardly any other team is mentioned as a possibility of signing any of these players. Why is it that a team like Minnesota, which has finished first in the AL Central in each of the last two years and which could use some help to get further in the playoffs than they have, cannot pursue these players? Or the Houston Astros, who finished second to the Cubs in the NL Central and could use some help to try to overcome the Cubs? The answer is simple – they do not have the incoming revenue, and therefore the money to compete with the rich teams. For that matter, who is the last good free agent that the Twins have signed, or the Detroit Tigers, or the Pittsburgh Pirates? All teams are not competing equally.

The answer is obvious – baseball needs to adopt the same type of revenue sharing that has made football as competitive as it is and helped football surpass baseball as the real national pastime. Revenue sharing will allow all teams to compete on an equal basis and help keep the same team from dominating year after year, primarily because they have the largest bank account. It makes sense to do this, but it is unlikely that it will happen. The Yankees will never go for it and neither will Major League Baseball. It makes too much sense.

Chapter 10 – How Major League Baseball Itself was to Blame

We have already seen a number of ways that Major League Baseball itself has contributed to the Yankees string of championships and the Red Sox decades of futility. Financial disparity between teams and the lack of revenue-sharing among them was discussed at length in the last chapter. That is not the only way that MLB has perpetuated the Yankee dynasty and Red Sox' problems, however.

Let's be fair though - the Red Sox themselves had been the main reason for the Red Sox' 86-year championship drought, for all of the reasons described in earlier chapters. Bad managers, general managers, and ownership, and the Red Sox players and playing style have all been the primary reasons why the Red Sox have always found a way to lose. However, Major League Baseball has not helped over these years.

The rules of baseball prior to 1967 favored a team like the Yankees. There was no common draft of amateur talent, as there has been for years in football and basketball. Teams were free to bid for any good college player or high school phenom. The Yankees, with the highest revenue in baseball, could afford to sign the best players. With the best players came a series of championships, and the process then became a self-perpetuating one. The Yankees could go in to a meeting with the top prospects, tell them that if they play with the Yankees they have their best chance to win championships (plural), and then lay out a contract proposal with a higher dollar total than any other team. In this way, the Yankees could get just about any player that they wanted. When baseball instituted a common draft, the playing field was leveled and there was competitive balance for a number of years.

Competitive balance evaporated again when the era of free agency began in 1976. With the first set of free agents, the Yankees' money again came into play, and they were able to sign the best free agents. This began with Catfish Hunter in 1974, Reggie Jackson, the top free agent available in 1976, and continued through Don Gullett, Dave Winfield, and so on, through Mike Mussina before the 2001 season, Jason Giambi before the 2002 season, Hideki Matsui and Jose

Contreras before the 2003 season, and Gary Sheffield before the 2004 season. Once again this is self-perpetuating, as the fact that the Yankees have signed these players means that they have been successful. Their success means that good players want to play with them so that they can have a chance for a championship, and so on. Thus it is that a Curt Schilling initially waives the no-trade clause in his contract only for being traded to the Phillies (the team where he first had success, and where he hopes ultimately to have his family live) or the Yankees, because playing with the Yankees would give him his best chance for a championship. He ultimately and surprisingly signed with the Red Sox, but the lure of the Yankee dollars and the chance to play for a championship has brought players such as Wade Boggs, Roger Clemens, and Jason Giambi to New York.

As discussed at length in chapter 9, the continuing lack of revenue sharing has been a significant factor in perpetuating the Yankee dynasty. The Yankees get the most money and can therefore spend the most money. Unless and until baseball adopts the same type of revenue sharing as is used in professional football, the Yankees will continue to dominate baseball. If baseball wanted competitive balance, they could make it happen. If they want to keep the Yankees as the dominant team in baseball, all they need to do is to continue what they have been doing.

Beyond the financial aspects of the game, key decisions that have been made by Major League Baseball over the years have always also favored the Yankees more than any other team. When baseball had their first in-season strike in 1981, many people felt that the decision of how to handle the resumption of the season favored the Yankees. Commissioner Bowie Kuhn decided that the season would be split into two halves. The teams that were in first place when the strike began would automatically qualify for the playoffs. The teams that had the best record in the second half, after the season resumed, would also make the playoffs. This decision went against the collected history of baseball which said that the best teams over the course of an entire season would be the ones to get into the postseason. However, with that decision, baseball ensured that the Yankees and Dodgers would be in the playoffs. Since the Yankees and Dodgers represented the two top media markets in the country, New York and Los Angeles, this did not seem like mere coincidence. There would be nothing better for baseball or better suited to generate interest in the game after the strike than having the teams in the top media markets in the playoffs. The decision ultimately meant that the teams with the best records in baseball, the Cincinnati Reds and St. Louis Cardinals, did not even make the playoffs. This was unfair. Would Kuhn have made the same decision if the Milwaukee Brewers or Cleveland Indians and not the

The Possible Dream

Yankees were in first place in the AL East and Houston Astros or San Diego Padres and not the Dodgers were in the lead in their division when the strike began? The answer is unknown, but the cynic would doubt it.

It was also Bowie Kuhn who decided to overturn the sales of Joe Rudi and Rollie Fingers to the Red Sox and Vida Blue to the Yankees in 1976 as being "not in the best interests of baseball". Yet baseball had seen the sales of many players by many teams over the years and no other such move was overturned. The biggest such transaction in baseball history was the selling of Babe Ruth by the Red Sox to the Yankees and that was not overturned. Jimmie Foxx was sold by the A's and that was not overturned. Kuhn himself did not overturn the thinly-disguised sale of Tom Seaver by the Mets to the Reds the year after the Rudi-Fingers-Blue decision (the Mets received players but far from equal value for Seaver), even though that deal had as devastating an effect on the Mets as the A's deals had on the Oakland franchise. As Leonard Koppett described in a column in *The Sporting News*, that decision shaped the 1976 race as the Red Sox with Fingers could have made a run at the Yankees. Without Fingers on the Red Sox, the Yankees coasted home to the division title and made it to the World Series.

It is also unfortunate that Kuhn made that decision, since it left the team with no alternative. Had the Red Sox known that this deal would not have been allowed, they could have perhaps gone in a different direction and acquired a different player, or maybe two. As it turned out, however, Kuhn's reversal decision was made after the trading deadline, so the Red Sox were handcuffed and not in position to make any other deal that could have helped the team make the pennant race tighter. The right decision would have been no decision to reverse the deal. The second alternative, also better than what Kuhn decided, would have been to preemptively state that no other cash transactions would be made without his prior agreement and approval. By making the decision that he did, at the time that he did – after the fact and after the trading deadline, Kuhn effectively decided the 1976 pennant race in the Yankees favor. The Yankees may have won the division that year anyway, but Kuhn's decision made it extremely easier for them to do so.

Major League baseball has also continued to favor the Yankees in recent days, sometimes overtly (as we will describe when discussing umpiring shortly) and other times not. An example of the latter could very well be the Yankees acquisition of Montreal star pitcher Javier Vasquez. During the 2003 season, Major League Baseball, which, because of the Montreal Expos' financial woes in recent years, actually owns and runs the Montreal Expos, put a moratorium on deals involving either Vasquez or Montreal superstar outfielder Vladimir Guerrerro. They could not be traded to another team. Yet, after the season ended and after the Red Sox had acquired Curt Schilling from Arizona, Vasquez was traded by Montreal to the New York Yankees. Why Vasquez could not be traded during the season but could be traded to the Yankees after the season is unclear. It is also interesting to note that, as owners of the Expos, it is Major League Baseball that traded a player to the Yankees that helped rebuild the Yankees' pitching staff after the losses of Roger Clemens, Andy Pettitte, and David Wells. It is curious then that Major League Baseball had swung a deal that helped the Yankees and may help to perpetuate the Yankee dynasty. This may very well have been done unintentionally, but given the favoritism that baseball has shown the Yankees over the years, it certainly is curious.

Umpiring has always curiously favored the Yankees over the years. This may in part be due to the fact that the American League and Major League Baseball offices have traditionally been in New York City, and umpires do not want to look bad or be booed in front of their supervisors. Whether this is true or not, a lot of questionable decisions have been made in favor of the Yankees, many/most of them at Yankee Stadium, adding credence to that theory.

The first game of the 1996 ALCS provides an interesting example of this situation. With the Yankees trailing the Orioles 3-2 in the 8th inning of that game, Derek Jeter hit a long fly to right field. As the Baltimore outfielder settled in to make the catch at the wall, a young Yankee fan named Jeffrey Maier reached over the right field wall and caught the ball before it could reach the Oriole outfielder. In any other park and with any other team, this would have been called fan interference and Jeter would have been called out. However, this was Yankee Stadium and these were the Yankees, so the play was called a home run, despite the vigorous (and valid) arguments of the Orioles. It is worth noting that, in the postseason, baseball uses 6 umpires instead of the usual 4, so the call was made by the man umpiring the right-field line. In other words, he was right there and still made the wrong call. It was highly suspect.

Contrast that with a regular season game between the Red Sox and Yankees in Yankee Stadium a few years earlier. With the Red Sox leading and two out in the bottom of the ninth, a popup seemed to end the game. However, a fan had run onto the field as the last pitch was being made so the play was ruled a non-play and the batter was allowed back up to bat, even though the fan in no way interfered with the play. Needless to say, he got a hit and the Yankees wound up

The Possible Dream

winning the game. It is hard to see the logic in this. The play was underway when the fan came out of the stands and he did not interfere with the play. The Yankees were thus rewarded for not being able to control their own fans. It is a wonder that other fans have not done the same in similar situations to help give their team a second chance to win. It is not a wonder that this decision favored the Yankees. That is the way that it is in Major League Baseball.

A pivotal play in the 1975 World Series also cost the Red Sox dearly. With the series tied at one game apiece after the first two games at Fenway, the Red Sox and Reds moved to Cincinnati's Riverfront Stadium for the next three games. The Reds were ahead 5-3 in the 9th, but a 2-run homer by Dwight Evans tied the game and gave the Red Sox new life and momentum. In the bottom of the tenth inning, with a runner on at first base, Cincinnati pinch-hitter Ed Armbrister attempted a bunt to sacrifice the runner to second and into scoring position. The bunt bounced right in front of home plate, and when Fisk went to field the ball, he was obstructed by Armbrister who had just stood at the plate and made no move to first and no move to get out of the way. Fisk fielded the ball but his throw to second was affected by the bumping with Armbrister and sailed into center field. The runner on first thus made it to third base, and scored from there on a fly to center to win the game for the Reds. The Red Sox argued (correctly) that Armbrister should have been called out for interference, which it clearly was, as Armbrister did interfere with Fisk as Fisk attempted to make the play. In that case, Armbrister would have been out, and the runner returned to 1st base. That would have been the correct call. However, home plate umpire Larry Barnett, although acknowledging the bump, did not call interference. His explanation was that there was no "intent" to interfere. Now, that is particularly ridiculous, since there is nothing, nor has there ever been anything, in the baseball rule book about there having to be intent to interfere in order for interference to be called. It makes sense that intent is not a requirement. If an infielder gets in the way of a baserunner when trying to field the ball and prevents the runner from getting to the next base by doing so, it is interference. He simply interfered with the runner's ability to get to the base. The same thing applies with Armbrister preventing Fisk from being able to make a play. Intent has nothing to do with it. In basketball, if a defender bumps into the player with the ball as both are moving to the basket, it is a foul. Intent has nothing to do with it. In football, if a player trips another player, there is no question of whether it was accidental or intentional, a penalty is called. The same should have been true with this play. It is hard to believe that the umpires were biased against the Red Sox, although it is interesting to speculate what would have happened had the Yankees and their catcher Thurman Munson been victimized by this play instead of the Red Sox and Fisk.

The umpiring decisions in the 1999 Red Sox-Yankees ALCS playoffs, especially the out call on the phantom tag by Chuck Knoblauch of Jose Offerman, also in Yankee Stadium, which the umpire later explained that he did not see, is another example of undue favoring of the Yankees (and it was good during the 2004 playoffs to see umpires conferring on bad calls and reversing decisions to get the calls correct; too bad that bit of what one might call common sense was not used in 1999 as well). Similarly, in game 4 of the 1978 World Series, Reggie Jackson, having been forced out at second in a game also at Yankee Stadium, stayed in the basepath and threw his hip into the throw to first on an attempted double play, knocking the ball into right field and helping the Yankees come back to win the game and tie the series at 2 games apiece.

What was clear to thousands of eyes at all of these games and millions of eyes watching these games on TV was apparently not clear to the six men who had the responsibility for umpiring these games and for ensuring that the rules were followed. It is possible that these are all coincidences, but odd that most of these decisions favored one team and only one team, the New York Yankees.

In actuality, the Red Sox have had their chances to beat New York and have not done so. It is not umpiring and Commissioner decisions that have prevented the Red Sox from doing so, or that have kept the Yankees on top, but these decisions have not helped, and have often given the Yankees the opportunities that they have needed to win a key game or win a championship. With a good team, that opportunity is all that is needed.

The Possible Dream

SECTION 2 – 2004: REDEMPTION!

Chapter 11 – 2003 Season Wrapup and Off-season Positioning

With the Red Sox having come whisper-close to beating the Yankees in the 2003 playoffs, the off-season between 2003 and 2004 saw a rapid series of changes by both teams:

Curt Schilling: The acquisition of Curt Schilling by the Red Sox was an excellent move. Schilling is one of the best pitchers in baseball, and has been one of the best post-season pitchers in baseball, as witnessed by his work in the 1993 World Series for the Phillies and the 2001 World Series for the Diamondbacks. He also was a team leader and one of the people to whom reporters went for quotes and reactions. This was seen early on by Schilling's appearing at the Red Sox ticket sales in December and mingling with the fans (would Nomar ever do something like that?). It was also seen in his being involved in e-mail and chat room discussions with Red Sox fans and calling a radio talk show both (a) to defend his and John Henry's communicating with fans over the internet and (b) to denounce the ruling of Gene Orza and the Major League Baseball Player's Union disapproving the trade of Alex Rodriguez to Boston. Schilling was a very welcome and absolutely refreshing addition to the Boston Sports scene.

Terry Francona: Terry Francona was hired as the new Red Sox manager on December 4, 2003. My preference as manager would still have been Frank Robinson, for reasons given elsewhere in this book, but we gave Francona the benefit of the doubt. The press conference held to announce the signing of Francona as manager and to introduce him to the media and fans was positive. Francona said all of the right things about wanting to get his team prepared, wanting to get to know all of the players, and even described getting a tingling feeling when Epstein called to offer him the job. At least this says that managing the Red Sox is a position that Francona really wanted (a far cry from previous managers like Mike Higgins who just saw this as their next job). For their part, the Red Sox management seems to feel that Francona is their man. They were impressed with him during the interviews, and did enough background/reference checks to address any concerns that they had (e.g., that he could and would be tough on players when he needed to be). The hope was that they were right and that Francona will be as successful in his role as Dick Williams was when he joined the Red Sox in 1967.

Keith Foulke: The Red Sox signed Oakland relief ace Keith Foulke as the team closer in the bullpen. Given Foulke's statistics for the preceding five years, including his having an AL-leading 43 saves in 2003, this was an excellent upgrade from the closer-by-committee approach that the Red Sox tried for much of 2003. One reason that Foulke cited for joining the Red Sox instead of staying with Oakland was that he, a big hockey fan, had gotten a call from Bobby Orr, former Bruins superstar. Orr called to help convince him to come to Boston, telling him that if a player wins in this town, he will be idolized forever. It is great to finally see the Red Sox using former players and local celebrities to help bring in free agents. The Yankees have done it for years, with Derek Jeter and Joe Torre, for example, calling free agents to convince them to come to New York. It was nice to see the Red Sox finally catch on to how to deal with and attract quality free agents to Boston.

Yankees acquisitions: The Yankees acquired starting pitchers Javier Vasquez and Kevin Brown, relievers Tom Gordon and Paul Quantrill, and outfielders Gary Sheffield and Kenny Lofton. The Yankee acquisition of Kevin Brown for Jeff Weaver is one that raises the eyebrows – how could the Dodgers trade a key starting pitcher and get only Jeff Weaver, whose stock has dropped dramatically since he came to New York? Why is it that the Yankees can always get a player like Kevin Brown for a player that seems to be far less than equal value?

Vasquez and Brown were meant to offset the losses of key starters from the 2003 Yankees staff, but they did not have the same reputations or strengths that those pitchers had. Gordon and Quantrill, both former Red Sox players, were brought in to help the Yankees' middle relief, which was abysmal in 2003. These moves certainly did not seem to match the Red Sox acquisitions of Curt Schilling and Keith Foulke.

Kenny Lofton will move into center field and thereby move Bernie Williams into the DH role that Jason Giambi had last year. Giambi was to play first (though it turned out that he was disabled for much of 2004), replacing the very promising Nick Johnson, who went to Montreal for Javier Vasquez. Sheffield moved into the right-field spot that was so problematic for the Yankees in 2003. However, Sheffield has always been a selfish player, who doesn't seem to exude the type of class that New York Yankees had always seemed to have. It was Sheffield who, when he was a shortstop with Milwaukee a few years ago, was deliberately making errors like throwing grounders into the right-field stands on purpose, in order to get the Brewers to trade him. It was Sheffield who demanded more money from Steinbrenner and the Yankees after they had agreed to the deal; Steinbrenner originally refused, but then the signing was finalized. It may very well be that in years to come George will regret signing Sheffield and passing on Vladimir Guerrerro, who is younger, a better player, and nowhere near as selfish as Sheffield.

Andy Pettitte: Meanwhile, surprisingly, the Yankees lost a key free agent for the first time in memory, with the signing of Andy Pettitte by the Houston Astros. It is almost inconceivable that the Yankees would lose a free agent of the magnitude of Pettitte. Perhaps the Yankee charm was starting to wear off.

Alex Rodriguez: The Red Sox and Rangers pursued a trade of Alex Rodriguez to Boston for Manny Ramirez, and a related deal of Nomar Garciaparra to the White Sox for Magglio Ordonez. All sides wanted this deal to be made, and apparently a deal was struck that would have had the Red Sox sending Ramirez, a pitching prospect, and millions of dollars to Texas in exchange for A-Rod, and Rodriguez and his agent having restructured A-Rod's contract to make it more acceptable to Boston. All sides were happy with the deal, until Gene Orza, of the Major League Baseball Player's Union, spoke up and said that he wouldn't allow it.

Baseball's Collective Bargaining Agreement has provisions against a player renegotiating and taking less money and allowing the union the right to refuse to accept a deal or contract change. The deal is meant to protect players from being forced to accept less money to keep playing, but this seems ridiculous and one-sided. In this case, with both sides having agreed to the deal, and the deal being in excess of $200,000,000, it seems that no one is being asked to perform in servitude. A-Rod would have gotten enough money to still be the highest paid player in the game, would have had a chance to play for a winner, with a team and in a city to which he wanted to come, and would have had a chance to earn much more in endorsement fees in Boston and with a post-season contender than he would in Texas. The ability for the Union to turn down a deal is described as being possible unless the Union believes that the player is getting something of value in return. A-Rod would be getting plenty of value in return. Given the observations in the earlier chapter about how Major League Baseball itself is to blame, one had to wonder what the situation would have been if the Yankees had been the team looking to restructure A-Rod's deal. Too bad the Yankees had already traded Jeff Weaver – the Rangers would have probably taken Weaver and some of Don

Zimmer's old chewing tobacco for A-Rod, and restructured his contract to suit them, without any whining from the baseball union.

While the Union gets primary blame for this deal not occurring, second on the list of villains in this deal not being completed is Texas owner Tom Hicks. Hicks wanted to get rid of A-Rod and A-Rod's contract, but then tried to hold the Red Sox up for more money in addition. This is greed at its ultimate. He was already going to save something on the order of $80,000,000 by taking Manny instead of A-Rod, and he still wanted to get another $25,000,000 from the Red Sox? Does the phrase highway robbery come to mind? Beyond that, wasn't there a high level of probability that Hicks would turn around and trade Manny to the Yankees within the next twelve months? If any deal had been made, the Red Sox would have been wise to have added a provision either that Manny could not be traded to the Yankees or that Hicks would have had to return to the Red Sox any money that he got from Boston in the deal (and additional dollars as a penalty) if he was traded to the Yankees.

Unfortunately, more bad news regarding A-Rod was to come during spring training.

Magglio Ordonez: The Ramirez-Rodriguez deal would also have resulted in the Red Sox trading Nomar Garciaparra to the White Sox for outfielder Magglio Ordonez. There were rumors that the White Sox would then have traded Nomar to the Dodgers for pitching prospects. Whatever the White Sox would do afterward, these two trades would have helped the Red Sox. As described previously, A-Rod was widely considered to be the best player in baseball and an upgrade to Nomar defensively and in the clubhouse. Similarly, by all accounts, Ordonez is a very good team player and good in the clubhouse. He was not signed for longer than 2004, but then neither was Nomar.

Roger Clemens: With Andy Pettitte going to Houston, Clemens decided to un-retire and join the Astros. This came as no surprise to Red Sox fans, who were always skeptical that Clemens would really go through with retirement. This is the same man who didn't honor his signed contract in 1987 and who wanted to leave the Red Sox to be closer to his home in Texas, and then signed with Toronto. Now that he was ready to retire and spend more time with his family, he rescinded that retirement before the off-season was three months old. It was good, however, to consider the idea of Roger pitching in the National League, since now he would also have to bat. The thought was that maybe in some Mets game, down the road, with the Astros blowing out the Mets, the Mets could bring Mike Piazza to the mound to face Clemens ...

Additionally, Texas Rangers owner Tom Hicks then claimed that he wanted Roger to play for his team instead of the Astros. Wait a minute. Didn't Hicks say that he was financially strapped, which is why he had to get rid of A-Rod and still get $25,000,000 from the Red Sox. If Hicks was financially strapped, how could he have the money to pay Clemens? What a joke. Maybe these two deserve one another.

- - -

In any case, the Red Sox were at what was both an interesting and crucial crossroads in their history. As has been noted previously, the ownership of John Henry, Tom Werner, and Larry Lucchino, and the work of general manager Theo Epstein seem to have the Red Sox moving in the right direction for the first time in decades. There is finally some real hope that this long championship drought and long-time fan nightmare may actually have a chance of ending.

Chapter 12 – Spring Training:
A New Team Leader Emerges

Optimism may have been higher than ever as the Red Sox opened their 2004 spring training camp in February. The near-miss of 2003, when the Sox had a three-run lead over the Yankees with just five outs to go in the seventh and deciding game of the ALCS, had really fanned the hopeful flames of Red Sox fans. In the eyes of most of those fans, the Red Sox had not lost that series, Grady Little's managing had lost it for them. These fans were overlooking the baserunning blunders that the team had made during that series, the terrible slump that engulfed Nomar Garciaparra (and, to a lesser extent, David Ortiz) during that series, and the fact that Pedro Martinez, the pitching ace, could not close out the Yankees in that seventh game. Yes, Grady should not have kept Pedro in after he gave up consecutive eighth inning hits to Derek Jeter and Bernie Williams, but isn't this game the reason that the Red Sox had gotten Pedro in the first place? In other words, didn't they get him with the idea that HE was the guy that they would want on the mound in a key/deciding game with the Yankees? The fact that he had failed in exactly the position that the Red Sox would want him to be in was lost on the ever-optimistic Red Sox fans.

Nevertheless, there were some positive signs as spring training started. The most positive of them all was the attitude of new pitching ace Curt Schilling. Schilling was a breath of fresh air for the usually reserved and staid Red Sox. He actually spoke his mind, openly and intelligently, and seemed to want to interact with the fans. He mingled with fans who had come to get tickets on the first day that tickets were available. He continued to interface with fans on web sites. He also called sports talk shows more frequently than expected, or than any of his teammates. He also seemed like a sportswriter's dream in that he was a quote machine. Whether it was giving his views of the Alex Rodriguez situation, or the steroid crisis that hit baseball during spring training, it was clear that Schilling would be a player to whom the writers could go after any game for quotes on that game. It was also clear that Schilling would be a new and vocal leader for the team itself.

Schilling was well-prepared for spring training. He followed his usual off-season training regimen and was in great shape when camp began. He also made the unusual, and logical, request that the Red Sox not pitch him against any AL East opponent during the spring exhibition season. Schilling did not want them to get any experience against his pitches in games that did not count. He felt that in this way he would have an edge on them when he first faced them during the regular season. This made perfect sense, and the Red Sox did indeed honor that request.

Things were not as upbeat for the team's other stars in spring. Contract issues swirled around a number of key players who were in the last year of their existing contracts – Nomar Garciaparra, Pedro Martinez, Jason Varitek, and Derek Lowe. Nomar was coming into spring training after an off-season in which he was whisper-close to being traded in the deals that could have involved Alex Rodriguez and Magglio Ordonez coming to Boston. Manny Ramirez was also involved in those talks, but came into camp seemingly without that bothering him. He was also talking about setting up a web site for communicating with fans, which seemed very un-Red Sox like. Derek Lowe was making noises about being convinced that the Red Sox would not resign him. Pedro was late coming to camp (which is an almost annual occurrence for him), but once he did, was his usual smiling self. To his credit, Varitek did not say a word publicly about his contract situation, but just went about his business of getting ready for the season. This was in keeping with the strong work ethic that he had displayed throughout his entire career in Boston. This work ethic has helped him to become a favorite of Red Sox fans.

Another Red Sox fan favorite, Trot Nixon, was struggling for other reasons. Nixon's contract was also coming into its last year, but he signed a new contract with the Red Sox in the spring for less than he potentially could have gotten elsewhere. He wanted to stay with the Red Sox, which was a welcome change for fans from past players who seemed to jump at the opportunity to leave Boston. Unfortunately, Trot also was developing back problems, and on March 20 it was announced that he would miss perhaps the first month of the season, and possibly more. This was not a good omen. The Red Sox planned to fill the void by using either Gabe Kapler as Trot's replacement, or moving Kevin Millar from first base to right field, David Ortiz from designated hitter to first base, and one of the two recently-reacquired players – either Brian Daubach or Ellis Burks – as designated hitter. It was a series of moves that would weaken the team defensively and which did not bode well for the Red Sox.

On the same day that the Red Sox announced that Nixon would be out for a month or more, they also announced that Nomar

The Possible Dream

might miss the season opener due to problems with his Achilles tendon. This necessitated even more shifts, this involving moving Pokey Reese from second base to shortstop to replace Nomar, and Terry Shumpert to second base. This again was a series of moves that would weaken the team on the field and at the plate.

It is worth contrasting these shifts with the reaction of the Yankees to what could have been similar problems. At one point in spring it was feared that Yankee outfielder Gary Sheffield, signed by the Yankees as a free agent in the off-season, had broken his thumb and would be out for 2-3 months. The immediate reaction was news that the Yankees were pursuing acquiring either Magglio Ordonez from Chicago or Ken Griffey Jr. from Cincinnati to replace Sheffield. Once again, the Yankee approach was to get an All-Star, or a stable of All-Stars, to replace an injured player or fill a key hole in the lineup. It was similar to their acquisitions in 2000 of David Justice, Jose Canseco, and Glenallen Hill to replace their struggling leftfielder. When you have the money that the Yankees have, these moves are easier, but it was not clear why the Red Sox would not have pursued either of these players as potential replacements for Trot Nixon when they learned of Nixon's injuries. It was evidence yet again of the glaring differences between these two teams and why the Yankees had won 26 championships in the last 80+ years while the Red Sox had won none.

Spring training, as it always is, was a leisurely way for the players to prepare for the new season. Center fielder Johnny Damon arrived in camp with long, flowing hair and a full moustache and beard. It was a somewhat biblical look as viewed by some (and by the 3rd home game of the regular season a group of people showed up at the game calling themselves "Damon's Disciples" and wearing fake bards and long-haired wigs). Schilling arrived for workouts each day wearing the uniform shirt of some other player and from other sports (the John Hannah jersey was a nice salute to one of the all-time great offensive lineman for the NFL's local entry, the New England Patriots); once the games began he was all business. His first workout on 2/28 was described as outstanding. Schilling was very sharp in the 45-pitch outing, displaying a good fastball, curve, slider, cutting fastball, and his usual excellent control. Boston fans were ecstatic about their new star.

Convinced (finally) that you can never have enough pitching, the Red Sox were one of many teams interested in a workout conducted by former Yankee pitcher Orlando Hernandez. There seemed to be some interest on Boston's part, but the expectation was that "El Duque", as he was known, would pitch for the Yankees if he could pitch for anyone.

One of the biggest spring stories was a March 2 story in the San Francisco Chronicle about widespread use of steroids in baseball. A number of star players were implicated, most notably slugger Barry Bonds of the San Francisco Giants, Jason Giambi of the New York Yankees, Gary Sheffield of the New York Yankees, Bill Romanowski (former NFL Player), and others. This story was yet another black eye for baseball and raised questions about the legitimacy of some of the home run records established in recent years, including the current one-season record of 73 set by Bonds. Unlike the Yankees, no Red Sox player was implicated, so this was not as much of a distraction for The Olde Towne Team as it was for their counterparts from New York.

Despite the injuries, these happenings had spring looking very positive for the Red Sox … until Valentines' Day. On that day, the Yankees acquired Alex Rodriguez in a trade. The trade was precipitated by Yankees thirdbaseman Aaron Boone injuring himself in a basketball game. Playing basketball was prohibited by his contract, but, for some reason, that didn't stop Boone. To replace Boone at third base, the Yankees went out and got the best shortstop in baseball, Alex Rodriguez, and convinced him to move the third base. The primary player that that Yankees traded to the Texas Rangers to acquire A-Rod was secondbaseman Alfonso Soriano. Once again, the Yankees had swooped in and acquired a player that the Red Sox had coveted and had tried themselves to get. In A-Rod's case, the Yankees acquired him by giving up less than the Red Sox would have (Alfonso Soriano versus Manny Ramirez AND Nomar Garciaparra), by convincing A-Rod to play a position other than shortstop, which he would not do for Boston, and by getting the Major League Baseball Players' Association to agree to changes in A-Rod's contractual arrangements, which they would not do for the Red Sox. Anyone who still feels that the competitive playing field in Major League Baseball is even for all teams needs to open their eyes – there is one set of rules for the New York Yankees, another for the other set of teams who have money and influence (like the Red Sox, Mets, and Dodgers), and still a third set for the have-nots who won't be competitive for years to come (like the Pirates, Brewers, or Tigers).

The A-Rod signing led to some harsh and childish interchanges between Red Sox and Yankee management. John Henry, in an e-mail to fans stated that "We have a spending limit, and apparently the Yankees don't." The ever-classless George Steinbrenner, an arrogant bully if there ever was one, responded that "We understand that John Henry must be embarrassed, frustrated, and disappointed in his failure in this transaction. Unlike the Yankees, he chose not to go the extra distance for his fans in Boston." First of all, it was time for the Red Sox to shut up and not say anything. They had been bested (once again) by the Yankees, and until they finally wind up on top where and when it counts – in late October – they should focus their efforts on beating the Yankees on the field, not out-debating them in the press. Secondly, it was time for the Yankees to shut up and not say anything. They had bested the Red Sox (once again), and a gracious winner would keep his or her mouth shut and not denigrate the loser. Unfortunately, George Steinbrenner has never been gracious either when winning or losing. It was up to Bud Selig to be the voice of reason in telling the two teams to stop such comments; the fact that Bud Selig was the voice of reason says tons about how out of touch the Red Sox and Yankee ownership was. The only class that was shown in this regard was by new team leader Curt Schilling, who stated simply and correctly "If one guy is going to stop us from winning it all, then this team is not put together right, and I don't believe that. I firmly believe that from top to bottom this is going to be the best team that I've ever been on." Schilling went on to reiterate the claim that he made after agreeing to the trade to the Red Sox, that he felt that the team not only had an opportunity to win the World Championship in 2004, but "multiple championships". This is the attitude of a leader, and Schilling more and more was becoming a spokesman for both the team and its fans.

The games during spring training were highlighted by the two Red Sox-Yankees games during the exhibition season. The Yankees won both times (be it ever thus).

On Sunday, March 7, the Yankees won 11-7 in a game at the Red Sox Spring Training facility in Fort Myers, Florida. The hero of the game was Tony Clark, who had played for the Red Sox in 2002, where he was a miserable failure. Just signed by the Yankees after the 2003 off-season, Clark led the Yankees to victory with 2 home runs and 5 RBI. The fact that a Red Sox castoff had come back to beat them in a Yankee uniform seemed almost too fitting and ironic, given these teams' histories. The Red Sox wasted a solid pitching performance by starter Bronson Arroyo, who pitched 3 shutout innings, allowing only 1 hit. Arroyo had been locked in a battle with Byung-Hyun Kim for the position as the team's fifth starter, though, if truth be told, most Red Sox fans would have wanted Arroyo as the 5th starter over the shaky Kim. Arroyo had proven his worth with a solid post-season for the Red Sox in 2003, after a very good season with the Red Sox at their Triple A minor league team in Pawtucket, Rhode Island, including a perfect game.

The second game was played at the Yankees' Spring Training facility in Tampa, but the results were the same. The Yankees won 8-6, with journeyman Donovan Osborne out-pitching Boston veteran Tim Wakefield. A Red Sox highlight was a three-run home run by David

McCarty, who was struggling to make the team as a combination hitter-pitcher: a right-handed bat off the bench and a left-handed relief pitcher. The Yankees received a scare when Alex Rodriguez was injured and had to leave the game. The injury was a freak one, as a throw from Yankee leftfielder Hideki Matsui to third bounced off the foot of sliding Red Sox base runner Brian Daubach and hit Rodriguez under the left eye. A-Rod's injury was not serious, however, as he wound up with just a bruised swelling under his eye, and he was able to accompany the team to Japan the next day for exhibitions and the Yankees' season-opening games with Tampa Bay.

On March 27 came word that Nomar Garciaparra's Achilles tendon injury was worse than expected, and it was doubtful that he would be ready for the opening game of the season. In fact, the report indicated that Nomar may miss the first week of the season. A few days later, on March 31 it was diagnosed to be even worse than had been originally thought, and the projection was that Nomar would be out for the entire month of April. This was a major setback for the Red Sox. It also illustrated again that perhaps the trade that they should have made in December was not Manny Ramirez for Alex Rodriguez, but the proposed three-way swap that would have sent Nomar to Anaheim, David Eckstein and others to Texas, and A-Rod to Boston. While costing Boston more in salary (for both Ramirez and Rodriguez), this trade may have been more palatable to Texas owner Tom Hicks than his taking on Manny's huge contract, and would have strengthened the team. To Red Sox fans, Nomar's injury was another reason to worry going into the regular season.

That regular season began oddly, in that, while 28 teams were still playing exhibition games, the Yankees and Tampa Bay Devil Rays opened the season with two games in Japan. They then flew back to the US to play more exhibition games before resuming the regular season. The Devil Rays, with a payroll of $29 million, among the lowest payrolls in all of baseball, shocked the Yankees, with their major league payroll high $ 183 Million, 8-3 in the opener. The Devil Rays were led by former Yankee Tino Martinez, who hit a big two-run home run, the 300th home run of his career, to put the game away in the seventh inning. Alex Rodriguez had an inauspicious start in his regular- season debut for the New Yorkers, taking called third strikes in his first two at-bats, and colliding with relief pitcher Paul Quantrill on an infield roller, causing Quantrill to leave the game. The Yankees won the second game 12-1 with Jorge Posada hitting a pair of three-run homers and Hideki Matsui also homering in his return to his homeland.

Other than the injuries to Trot Nixon and Nomar Garciaparra, the biggest concerns that the Red Sox had during spring training were the ineffectiveness during the spring of Keith Foulke, the team's new closer, and the drop-off in pitch speed that Pedro Martinez was experiencing. Pedro was only hitting 85-90 MPH with his fastball on the speed gun, as opposed to 95-99 that he had been hitting in previous years.

Spring Training ended on April 3, with one of the biggest positives being the performance of Curt Schilling. In his last spring training start, Schilling allowed catcher Jason Varitek to call every pitch, wanting to see how in synch the new pitcher and veteran catcher were. Although manager Terry Francona pointed out that this could be the only time all year in which Schilling did not get the last word, this was a classy and smart move by Schilling. It was clear that Schilling was indeed a team leader. Even if the team had some question marks and not everyone might have been ready for the season to start, it was clear that their new star pitcher was ready.

It was time to head to Baltimore for the season opener.

Chapter 13 – April: The New Season Starts Slowly but the Month ends very well

The 2004 Red Sox season opened with a Sunday night, nationally televised game with the Orioles in Baltimore. The Red Sox opening day lineup was

Johnny Damon	CF
Bill Mueller	3B
Manny Ramirez	LF
David Ortiz	DH
Kevin Millar	1B
Gabe Kapler	RF
Jason Varitek	C
Mark Bellhorn	2B
Pokey Reese	SS

Pedro Martinez was the opening night pitcher. He was opposed by Oriole righty Sidney Ponson.

The Orioles struck first with three runs in the second inning. New Oriole catcher Javy Lopez, just signed in the off-season as a free agent from Atlanta, led off the inning by hitting the first pitch that he ever saw in the American League for a home run. Pedro, who had not given up a home run to a righthanded batter at all in 2003, had given up one to the fourth batter of the season in 2004. Also, according to Red Sox TV analyst Jerry Remy, it was off an 88 MPH fastball from Martinez, continuing the concern about Pedro's arm and pitch speed. The Orioles wound up winning 7-2, with the Red Sox leaving 14 runners on base. The bright spots for the Sox were 3 hits each by Mueller and Kapler, and 2 (plus a near-miss home run) by Mark Bellhorn. This was offset by 0-for-5 nights by Johnny Damon (5 groundouts) and Jason Varitek, and another of those infernal 1-out 1-on strike-out (Varitek) throw out (Kapler) double plays to douse a potential Red Sox rally. Another negative for the Red Sox was a 2-out bunt by Pokey Reese with runners on second and third late in the game. Reese's bunt was easily fielded by Ponson and Reese was thrown out to end the inning. Manager Terry Francona later indicated that he would have preferred to have seen Reese swing away in that situation … as would any right-thinking Red Sox fan.

The lowest of the low-lights of the opener, however, was the fact that Pedro Martinez left the game and the stadium after he was removed from the game, before the game was over. This was a breech of etiquette as well as an affront to his teammates and manager. Terry Francona put the blame on himself for not explaining the rules, but it seems like this is a rule that logic dictates should not have had to be explained to a veteran Major Leaguer. Had Frank Robinson been the manager (as was my preference), I believe that this message would have gotten through forcefully, even if it had to be given after the fact. It seemed like the Red Sox were in mid-season form already (or, perhaps more appropriately, in September-swoon form).

Game 2 featured the debut of Curt Schilling as a member of the Red Sox pitching staff. My wife and I actually had decided to go down to Baltimore to see this game, both to see Camden Yards for the first time and to see Schilling's debut, a real "event" in Red Sox history. As it turns out, we were not the only ones with this idea. We flew from Boston to Baltimore the morning of the game and about half the people on the plane were going to Baltimore for the game. Our pilot even came on and admitted that he was an Orioles' fan and asked why we didn't just charter a flight. My son, who met us at the airport, said that another plane had landed before ours, and many of the people from that flight came out dressed in Red Sox paraphernalia. Red Sox fans are everywhere.

The game was all that it was cracked up to be, and so was Camden Yards; it is a beautiful baseball park. The Red Sox won 4-1, with Schilling pitching 6 innings, striking out 7. He was backed up by a home run by Kevin Millar, and a bullpen of three relievers who each pitched 1 perfect inning – Alan Embree, Mike Timlin, and Keith Foulke. Foulke was outstanding in the ninth, and appeared even overpowering, laying to rest, at least temporarily, the concerns that had been raised about him during spring training.

The Red Sox went on to split the next two games in Baltimore, winning behind Derek Lowe and then losing an extra-inning game. As they went to leave Baltimore, their plane had mechanical problems and sat on the ground in Baltimore for 6 hours. The players didn't arrive in Boston until 7 AM the next day, which happened to be Opening Day at Fenway Park. As might be expected, the tired Sox lost to Toronto.

The Possible Dream

The biggest happening in April was a pair of weekend series with the Yankees, four games in Fenway on April 16-19 and then three in Yankee Stadium on April 23-25. The Red Sox pitching rotation was reshaped for the series due to two consecutive rainouts on April 13 and 14 of games scheduled with the Orioles. Originally, the rotation for Baltimore was set to be Lowe, Wakefield, and Martinez to be followed for the Yankee series opener by Schilling. Schilling had in fact been pointing to the April 16 game with the Yankees since he joined the Red Sox, having computed that that would be the first time that he was scheduled to face the New Yorkers. With the rainout, it gave Francona the chance to pitch Arroyo against the Orioles and have his top four pitchers pitch against the Yankees. Francona decided instead to pitch Martinez against Baltimore, move Wakefield into Schilling's spot in the Yankees series opener, have Lowe miss a turn completely and pitch in the third Yankee game after not pitching in 11 days, and have Arroyo start the 11:00 AM Patriots' Day game on Monday. It is inconceivable to me that Francona would not want to have his four best pitchers pitch against the team that he is trying to beat, but this seems to be the way that it is with Red Sox managers – don't go with your best against the Yankees during the season and then at the end of the year bemoan the fact that you again finished second to them.

The revamping of the rotation did not help the Red Sox against the Orioles, as the Red Sox lost to Baltimore 12-7 on the eve of the Yankee series.

The first game of the Yankee series featured Tim Wakefield pitching against new Yankee Javier Vasquez. The Red Sox got off to a good start in the bottom of the first, with Johnny Damon reaching on an error by Jason Giambi (a horrible first baseman, Giambi just bungled Damon's easy ground ball), a home run by Bill Mueller, and another home run by Manny Ramirez. Ramirez' home run was somewhat of a fluke. He hit a fly down the right field line that bounced off the top of the padding on the wall, and bounced back into the stands off the body of Yankee right-fielder Gary Sheffield. It should have been an extra base hit, but was ruled a home run. This is exactly the kind of break that always had gone the Yankees' way in the past. Could this be a harbinger of a change in the fortunes for these two teams this year? There was no dispute of the call by Joe Torre or any of the Yankees, and the Red Sox went on to a 6-2 win.

Another harbinger of potential change came at the very beginning of Game 2 on Saturday afternoon. Curt Schilling struck out the first two New York batters, Derek Jeter and Bernie Williams, the two mainstays of the Yankee team that won four World Series in five years. Was this symbolic of the torch being passed from the key Yankee duo to the new Red Sox 'gunslinger'? The Red Sox scored first on yet another set of surprises, a bases loaded walk and then a hit batsman given up by Mike Mussina, the Yankee ace who normally displays impeccable control. The Red Sox went on to win 5-2.

The third game of the series was a no-contest win for the Yankees. Derek Lowe, pitching on 11 days rest, was understandably not sharp, giving up 7 runs in less than 3 innings. On the other hand, another bad sign for New York was that even though they had handed their starting pitcher, Jose Contreras, a 7-1 lead going into the bottom of the third, he couldn't even last the inning. The Red Sox came back with 2 runs of their own before the bullpen stopped them, and wound up losing 7-3.

The Patriots' Day game pitching matchup of Bronson Arroyo and Kevin Brown started off in New York's favor, with the Yankees holding an early 4-1 lead. However, single runs in the 6th, 7th, and 8th, capped by an RBI single by Gabe Kapler, gave the Red Sox a 5-4 comeback win in the game and a 3 games to 1 win of the series. A highlight for Red Sox fans was the tough series experienced by Alex Rodriguez. In his first Yankee-Red Sox series, A-Rod was hitless in his first 16 at-bats before singling with two outs in the 9th inning of the series finale. He finished 1-for-17 for the series, made a key error in the field in that fourth game, and made a critical baserunning blunder in the first game, getting thrown out trying to steal third with 2 out and 2 on and the Yankees down by 2 runs. Red Sox fans did not expect A-Rod to go 1-for-17 in future games with Boston, but it was nice to savor the fact that he did so in this first series.

After a 3-game series with Toronto, won by the Red Sox 2 games to 1, the hostilities resumed at Yankee Stadium on Friday, April 23. Derek Lowe was back on the mound and, pitching with his normal rest, was back to his normal self. The Red Sox bombarded Yankee starter Jose Contreras with 3 early home runs, solo shots back-to-back by Kevin Millar and Mark Bellhorn, and then a 3-run shot by Bill Mueller, and built a 10-0 lead. Lowe gave up a 2-run homer to Hideki Matsui, but Manny Ramirez closed the scoring with a home run of his own, to give the Red Sox an 11-2 laugher over the Yankees.

Saturday's game was a rematch of Bronson Arroyo and Kevin Brown. The Red Sox won it in 12 innings 3-2, scoring all three runs on sacrifice flies. The Sox also were 0-for-19 batting with runners in scoring position, so the sacrifice flies were a godsend to the pitching staff.

Pedro Martinez started Sunday's game, his first appearance against the Yankees since his ill-fated eighth inning performance in game 7 of the 2003 ALCS. New York's choice for starting pitcher showed a new and unexpected sign of panic by the Yankees. Without a decent fifth starter in the rotation, Javier Vasquez was asked to pitch on three days rest. While he pitched well, Pedro pitched better. Pedro shut out the Yankees on four hits through seven innings and then gave way to Scott Williamson, who got out all six batters that he faced to preserve a 2-0 win. The two runs were provided on a titanic blast by Manny Ramirez, whose 2-run fourth inning home run by the monuments in deep left center field provided Pedro with all the runs that he would need. When Williamson struck out Gary Sheffield to end the game, the Red Sox had completed a hard-to-believe three game sweep of the Yankees in New York, and had won 6 of the 7 April games between the two teams. At the end of the series, the Red Sox were in first place with a record of 12-6; the Yankees were 8-11 and 4 ½ games behind Boston in the standings. A look at the calendar showed that this was still April, and not September or October, but this was still a very uplifting series for the Red Sox. Beating the Yankees in 6 of 7 games, playing without stars Garciaparra and Nixon, was a great accomplishment.

One note of concern in the series, however, remained the managing decisions made by Terry Francona. For game 3 of the series in New York, Francona decided to rest Bill Mueller, despite the fact that the Sox had an off-day immediately after the series, and despite the fact the Red Sox were already playing without two regulars, Garciaparra and Nixon. This left Boston with a starting infield, left to right, of Mark Bellhorn at third, Pokey Reese at shortstop, Cesar Crespo at second base, and David McCarty at first base. This is more of a lineup for an expansion team than for a World Series contender as the Red Sox were deemed to be. Luckily for the Red Sox, they did not need more hitting than these guys could provide, thanks to Pedro and Williamson combining for a shutout, but it certainly was questionable to see a good hitter like Mueller rested for the game against New York, when he could have been rested the next day (an off day), or for the next game against the Tampa Bay Devil Rays who (a) are nowhere near as much of a threat to the Red Sox as are the Yankees and (b) have not been dominating the Red Sox for the preceding 80 years. Optimists would say that all's well that ends well, but realists -- and those involved in Red Sox chronicles such as this book – see it as yet another sign that Red Sox managers … just … don't … get …it.

Following the series in New York, the Red Sox played Tampa Bay at Fenway, while the Yankees hosted the Oakland A's at Yankee Stadium. Boston fans and talk shows were buzzing with talk of the Yankees reeling and now having to face the A's three ace pitchers, Tim Hudson, Mark Mulder, and Barry Zito. When will Sox fans ever learn?

First of all, the Yankees are never reeling for very long. Secondly, the A's have shown over the years since 2000 that they are just cannon fodder for the Yankees. Predictably, the Yankees won 3 in a row over the Oakland "aces" and climbed back to a .500 won-loss record. Meanwhile the Red Sox were rained out of their opener against the Devil Rays; this was after an hour and a half rain delay (why did they wait so long, those of us at the ballpark were wondering), and the game was to be made up on Thursday afternoon. Fans had just the next day from 9:00 – 5:00 to exchange their tickets. This was not a very fan-friendly situation for a team that prides itself on having fans from all over New England. A family driving in from Maine for a Tuesday night game may not be able (a) to take off from work to come back on a Thursday afternoon or (b) to take off from work to come back on Wednesday between 9:00 and 5:00 to exchange the tickets (and since most games were already sold out or only had single seats available, exactly what could they get in exchange for these tickets?). Red Sox management really needs to rethink this policy (perhaps offering that family a refund for tickets not used, or have ticket windows open that night for exchange at least?).

On the field, the Red Sox swept the three games with the Devil Rays, winning the opener 6-0 behind Curt Schilling, and then winning a day-night double-header the next day 4-0 and 7-3. Byung-Hyun Kim made his debut in the day game, pitching brilliantly on his return from the injured-reserve list. Kim pitched 5 innings of 1-hit shutout ball, and the relief corps finished the shutout. That extended the Red Sox pitchers' streak of holding their opponents scoreless to 32 innings, dating back to the last 5 innings of the Saturday game against the Yankees, and the subsequent three games against the Yankees and Devil Rays. Tampa Bay scored in the first inning of the nightcap, ending that streak, but the Red Sox came back with 7 runs of their own in the bottom of the first, and cruised to that 7-3 victory.

With the Red Sox on a 6-game winning streak and the Yankees having started a winning streak of their own (courtesy of Oakland), the standings of these two teams at the end of April was:

	W	L	PCT	GB
Boston	15	6	.714	--
New York	11	11	.500	4 1/2

The Possible Dream

Chapter 14 – May: Storm Clouds Arise

The Red Sox were rained out of their April 30 game in Texas, but the weather was not the big story that day. Pedro Martinez, for some reason, chose that day to complain to the press about his contract situation, saying that he would no longer negotiate with the team, and calling Red Sox management liars. Why he would choose to do this when the team was playing well and he was not was a question, as was why he did not choose to follow the example of teammate Jason Varitek who was concentrating on playing on the field and not saying a word in public about his contract situation. Manny Ramirez offered to restructure his contract for less money so that the Red Sox could use some of that money to re-sign Pedro. That was a noble gesture and the sign of a good teammate, but we all know how the Major League Baseball Players' Association would react to such a move, however voluntary on the player's part (see Alex Rodriguez, winter 2003-2004, for a prime example).

The Red Sox then began the month with a five-game losing streak, losing all three games in Texas to the A-Rod-less Rangers, 4-3, 8-5, and 4-1, and then 2 more in Cleveland, 2-1 and 7-6. It was not clear whether Pedro's outburst had anything to do with the losing streak, but Pedro pitched poorly and was shelled by the Rangers in that 8-5 loss. Red Sox hitters also went into a funk, as best exemplified by the 2-1 loss to the Indians, in which they left 13 runners on base and wasted a very good pitching performance by Curt Schilling. In what is typical Schilling fashion, Curt took the blame on himself for the loss, claiming that if the team is slumping and gets only 2 runs, he should give up 1, if they get 1 he should pitch a shutout. That is a great team attitude. Too bad that others on the team don't feel the same level of teamwork (are you listening, Pedro?).

To be honest, Pedro was once the darling of Red Sox fans and could do no wrong. In fact, if he pitches well, his tirade will be forgotten by most fans. However, enough is enough. Pedro had no reason to go off on this tirade. After not winning the seventh game against the Yankees last year, he should be keeping his mouth shut and channel his energies into pitching well. That game was exactly the reason that the Red Sox had gotten Martinez in the first place – to have a pitcher like him on the mound in the seventh and deciding game of a playoff. He was there, and he failed. Not only did he fail, but it was after he was given a 5-2 lead by his teammates. Add to that the incomprehensible act of throwing at Karim Garcia in the 3rd game of that series, only apparently because he was mad at the fact that he was not pitching well (so, putting another Yankee baserunner on helps your team how?) and then getting into that abhorrent pointing at his head and at the Yankee dugout to indicate that he would throw at them more was, and still is, inexcusable. I can defend Pedro for throwing Don Zimmer to the ground when Zimmer came charging at him during a melee in game 3 of the 2003 ALCS, but I cannot, and will not, defend Pedro for throwing at another player and for implying that he would throw at the heads of others. That is, to put it bluntly, selfish, and childish. As much as I have always admired Pedro's ability, it is time for him to grow up. Perhaps it is not only the mantle of being the team's best pitcher that is passing from Pedro to Schilling, but also the position as the team leader.

While the Red Sox were in their five-game slide, the Yankees were hot, winning seven straight games and pulling into a tie with the Red Sox for first place in the AL East. The Red Sox' 4 ½ game lead had lasted 5 days. It was reminiscent of the collapse of 1978. Boston finally broke the losing streak with a 9-5 win over the Indians, thanks to two home runs by David Ortiz and one by Bill Mueller, but the Yankees again beat the A's, this time in Oakland to stay tied with the Sox for first. It seemed only a matter of time before the Sox would be behind New York by 4 ½ games (or more).

The schizophrenic Sox then rebuilt a 2 game lead by following that five-game losing streak with a four-game winning streak. The streak was highlighted by a thrilling Friday night comeback win at Fenway over Kansas City. Trailing 6-2 in the bottom of the eighth inning, the Sox pulled closer with 2 runs, but still came into the bottom of ninth trailing 6-4. With Johnny Damon on base, Mark Bellhorn belted a game-tying 2-run home run to right field, driving the crowd wild. Then, with Manny Ramirez on first, pinch-hitter Jason Varitek lined a hit down the rightfield line. The ball hugged the rightfield wall, and Royals right fielder Juan Gonzalez played the ball tentatively to keep it from going past him. Ramirez raced around the bases and came in to score – just barely – standing up, ahead of throw to give the Red Sox a 7-6 win. It was the type of win that typified the Red Sox of 2003, but it was their first such win of 2004. The win, coupled with a Yankee loss, put the Sox back up by 2 games over the second-place Yankees.

The Sox kept their AL East lead at 2 games the next day with a 9-1 victory over the Royals. It was a masterfully pitched, complete game victory by Curt Schilling, the first complete game of the year for the Red Sox. Pokey Reese was the hitting star with his first two home runs of the season. Reese's first home run was an inside-the-park homer down the same rightfield line and hugging the same wall as did Varitek's game-winning double the previous night. In this case, however, the ball did get past Juan Gonzalez, allowing Reese to steam all the way around the bases. His second home run was a blast into the seats atop the Green Monster. Reese had been becoming a fan favorite for his great defense, and this hitting performance may have solidified it.

Derek Lowe and Byung-Hyun Kim started and lost the next two games to Kansas City and Cleveland. Kim was especially bad, giving up 2 runs in each of the first 3 innings in a 10-6 loss to the Indians. After the game it was announced that he would be dropped from the rotation and replaced by Bronson Arroyo. Later in the week, Kim's demotion was made deeper as he was sent down to the minor leagues. Why Kim was acquired in the first place last year was a mystery; the Red Sox traded the same people for Kim who could have been traded for Bartolo Colon, and in getting Kim, the Red Sox got a pitcher who had already shown himself to be shaky against the Yankees (not exactly what the team needed). Why he was still viewed so positively by the team, and why he had replaced Arroyo in the rotation after Arroyo had pitched so well in the season thus far, was also a mystery to Red Sox fans. As we learned during the week of his demotion, Red Sox players were not as enamored of Kim as Red Sox Management was. Complaints were written about Kim's aloofness and insistence on doing things his way, rather than listening to veteran and knowledgeable pitchers such as Schilling, Martinez, and Wakefield. His departure was not seen as a negative by either Red Sox fans or players.

The Sox evened the series with Cleveland with another thrilling comeback win. Trailing 3-2 in the 8th inning, they tied the game on a double by Bill Mueller, and then won it on a triple by David McCarty. Unfortunately, they lost the next three nights to Cleveland (twice) and Toronto, playing atrocious defense in these games, and fell to second place behind the hard-charging Yankees. They salvaged two of the four games in Toronto, winning 9-3 on Friday night by using a 6-run 8th to overcome another bad defensive game. In the Saturday game, Bronson Arroyo, back in the rotation replacing Kim, pitched a gem. He left the game after 8 shutout innings in which he only allowed 3 hits. The Sox won 4-0.

Saturday, May 15, also saw the first in-season trade rumor involving the team. Fans who opened *The Boston Globe* that morning read about a possible 3-way trade in which the Red Sox would send CF Johnny Damon and star-crossed pitcher Byung-Hyun Kim to Seattle, Seattle would send pitcher Freddie Garcia to Kansas City, and KC would send CF Carlos Beltran to Boston. Beltran was a budding superstar who had already accumulated 10 home runs and 28 RBI on the season, and was batting .299. He was a potential free agent, however, and it was felt that the Royals would not be able to re-sign him at the end of the season. This would be a great trade for the Red Sox, who would be in position then to sign this potential superstar. The WEEI Sports Talk Radio hosts were as psyched as Red Sox fans were about the possibility of adding Beltran to the lineup. Unfortunately, as is so often the case with the Red Sox, the rumor went away almost as quickly as it came, as *The Boston Herald* that same day quoted Boston GM Theo Epstein as saying that the deal would not happen. Once again the Red Sox had failed to pull the trigger on a deal that could have greatly helped the team. Beltran ultimately wound up being traded to Houston later in June, and Trot Nixon wound up on the disabled list for a long time after a brief attempt at playing a few games. The Red Sox could have used Beltran to pick up some of the slack left by Nixon. Some things never change.

Arroyo's pitching gem shifted the attention from the aborted trade and kept the Red Sox in first place for another day. However, in the series finale with KC, the Sox wasted another good pitching performance, this time by Pedro, and lost 3-1, leaving them in second place, looking up once again at the Yankees, as they headed to Tampa Bay.

The three games in Tampa Bay featured two good pitching performances and one bad one. Tim Wakefield, who had become a father for the first time the previous weekend, won 7-3 in Tampa on a night when Randy Johnson was pitching a perfect game for Arizona. The next night Johnson's old pitching partner, Curt Schilling, raised his record to 5-3 with a 4-1 win. Schilling pitched 7 innings of 5-hit baseball. However, in the series finale, Derek Lowe continued his early season struggles, giving up 7 runs in 2 1/3 innings in a 9-6 loss to Tampa Bay, as the Red Sox fell to second place, a half game behind the red-hot Yankees.

The schizophrenia continued for the rest of the month. The Sox then went on a five-game winning streak, sweeping a three-game series with Toronto and taking the first two games of a three-game series with Oakland. David Ortiz and Manny Ramirez were hot during the stretch, and Bronson Arroyo, now back in the rotation, suddenly became shakier, losing to the A's and escaping in Toronto thanks to a 6 run eighth inning which broke a 5-5 tie. Arroyo's performance against the A's was particularly troubling, as the A's bombed the Red Sox for 12 runs in the first 4 innings of a 15-2 rout.

The Red Sox took two out of three in a weekend series with Seattle. The Sunday game was memorable in a number of ways. Schilling took a perfect game into the 6th inning, as he almost matched the perfecto that his old teammate Randy Johnson had thrown 12 days earlier. However, after Schilling left the game, the bullpen imploded, including the first blown save of the year for Keith Foulke, and the game was tied 7-7 going into extra innings. The Red Sox finally won in the 12th on a walk-off two-run home run by David McCarty on a 3-0 pitch. The Red Sox remained in first place by a half game. Little did the fans know that this would be their last day alone in first place for the season.

The month ended with another Derek Lowe disaster, a 13-4 loss on Memorial Day to Baltimore, putting the Red Sox in a virtual tie with the Yankees for first place. The month also ended with Bill Mueller and Scott Williamson joining Nomar Garciaparra, Trot Nixon, Ramiro Mendoza, and Byung-Hyun Kim on the disabled list. Garciaparra and Nixon were in rehab, however, so their season debuts seemed to be imminent. Their returns were going to become desperate, as the Sox on May 31 were now fielding a lineup that was devoid of four key starters from the 2003 season: Garciaparra, Nixon, Mueller (the defending AL batting champion), and Todd Walker (a star during the 2003 post-season). That they had weathered the storm thus far, and were even in a tie for first place was a result of some strong play by the reserves and some good pitching by the key off-season acquisitions, Curt Schilling and Keith Foulke. Nevertheless, the storm clouds were brewing as, by the end of May, the 4 ½ game lead that the Red Sox had over the Yankees a month earlier, at the end of April, had been completely dissipated. The standings of these teams at the end of May was:

	W	L	PCT	GB
New York	30	19	.612	--
Boston	31	20	.608	--

Chapter 15 – June: Prodigal Players Return – and so does the June Swoon

June started out very badly for the Red Sox. While the San Francisco Giants are a team with a reputation for "June swoons", the Red Sox are not bad in the "June swoon" department either. The loss to Baltimore on Memorial Day became a four-game losing streak as the Red Sox were swept in a two-game series with the Angels in Anaheim and lost the opener of a three-game series in Kansas City.

Bronson Arroyo continued his personal swoon in the first game of the month, blowing a 4-1 lead to the Angels, and taking the 7-6 loss to drop his record to 2-3. To be fair, he was left in the game too long by manager Terry Francona, who seemed to have more faith in Arroyo than should have been warranted given his recent performances. Still the Red Sox had a chance, until Manny Ramirez was picked off second base in the seventh inning to end a Red Sox rally (fundamental baseball, where are you?). The ominous signs continued the next night as Pedro Martinez continued his up-and-down year by blowing a 7-4 lead as the Sox lost 10-7.

In the opener in Kansas City, Red Sox bats went silent as an unknown Royals' pitcher named Jimmy Gobble retired 15 straight Sox batters after a leadoff single by Johnny Damon in a 5-2 KC win. The loss put Boston 3 ½ games behind the hard-charging Yankees, meaning that the team had lost 8 games from its once-lofty perch of being 4 ½ games ahead of the Yankees just 5 weeks earlier. The Sox bounced back the next night led by yet another strong pitching performance by Curt Schilling and a big two-run first inning home run by David Ortiz. Schilling went to 7-3 on the season with an 8-3 win. Derek Lowe won the next day, 5-3, in a game marked by one of the weirdest plays of this or any season. The Red Sox were rallying from an 0-3 deficit in the sixth inning, with a run in and the bases loaded, when Cesar Crespo hit a slow bouncer down toward Ken Harvey, the KC firstbaseman. Harvey fielded the ball and went to throw home, but Jason Grimsley, the KC pitcher coming over to cover first, got into Harvey's path. Harvey's attempted throw to the plate for a possible force out hit Grimsley in the face, as did Harvey's arm. The ball dropped to the ground, and, more importantly, so did both players. Grimsley seemed out of it for a while, but both players eventually got up and left the game under their own power. Luckily, they only sustained bruises on what was a very scary play. Though the game seemed less important after that, the Sox did rally, scoring a run on the Harvey-Grimsley play, tying the score on a Pokey Reese single, and winning it on a two-run double by Johnny Damon. Sox fans could only wonder if this sudden luck would help turn things around for Derek Lowe.

The start of inter-league play greeted the Sox on their return from Kansas City. The San Diego Padres and Los Angeles Dodgers were set to make their first appearances ever at Fenway Park. Also, fortunately for the Red Sox, one of their stars was also just about ready to make his first appearance of 2004 in the Red Sox lineup. Nomar Garciaparra had been doing his rehab stint with Boston's minor league affiliate in Pawtucket, and the feeling was that Nomar would return for the San Diego series. Nomar, however, felt that he needed more time, so he was in the Pawtucket lineup as the Red Sox and Padres squared off. Pedro Martinez and David Wells started the Boston-San Diego series with an outstanding pitchers' duel. Pedro was masterful over eight innings, allowing only two hits and striking out eight. A Johnny Damon double drove in the only run in a 1-0 Red Sox win.

Fans coming to the Wednesday game were greeted with some very positive news. Nomar was finally back! Fans cheered his every move – when he came out of the dugout to warm up, when he appeared on the Jumbotron welcoming people to Fenway Park, when he came out to his usual shortstop position, and when he came up to bat (for the first time in 2004) in the second inning. Nomar stepped out of the batter's box and tapped his heart as a way of thanking the crowd which only got them to cheer louder. The biggest cheer of the night, though, came two pitches later, when Nomar bounced a single between third and short for a base hit. It was clear that everyone was glad to see Nomar back – except maybe the American League pitchers.

Nomar's return didn't help the Sox prevent a loss, however, as a number of bad fielding plays led to an 8-1 San Diego win. With the game scoreless and two on and two out in the San Diego fifth inning, Nomar went into the hole to grab a ground ball, turned and fired a throw to first that should have ended the inning. However, for some reason, Terry Francona had put Andy Dominique (a catcher, just up from Pawtucket) at first base and Dominique couldn't handle the one-hop throw from Nomar so the runner was safe and the Padres were now ahead 1-0. Dominique compounded the mistake by then throwing the ball into the stands behind third base, allowing another run to score. An error by Mark Bellhorn at second base opened the gates to another pair of San Diego runs in the top of the sixth, and then the gates in the clouds opened and it poured. After a 2 hour 21 minute rain delay, in which most of the fans left the park, the game resumed, but it didn't get much better. Four more San Diego runs, including one more unearned run after another Bellhorn error, made the final 8-1.

Once again, Curt Schilling took the role of stopper and won the rubber game of the series, 9-3 for his eighth victory of the season. Schilling pitched seven strong innings, and Manny Ramirez hit a big home run to break a 1-1 tie and lead the Sox to the win.

The Friday night series opener with the Los Angeles Dodgers was a special one for all of us in attendance, as the storied National League franchise was making its first appearance ever at Fenway. The old Brooklyn Dodgers had been involved in the 1916 World Series with the then-defending champion Boston Red Sox (and how odd that string of words seems), but those games were moved from Fenway to Braves Field because of greater seating capacity in the Boston Braves' home park.

The Red Sox honored the long-time Dodger announcer Vin Scully by having him throw out the ceremonial first pitch. He also was throwing it to new Dodger team owner Frank McCourt, a Bostonian who had tried to purchase the Red Sox but lost on the bid by John Henry, Tom Werner, and Larry Lucchino. McCourt was going to build a stadium in South Boston, whereas the current owners have been refurbishing the existing Fenway Park, building the new Green Monster seats in 2003 over the leftfield wall, and building a new pavilion in right field with tables shaped like baseball plates and a standing room area. When McCourt lost his bid to buy the Red Sox he turned his attention to obtaining another team and was very successful, and lucky, in landing the Dodgers. As another thrill for attendees at this game, Sandy Koufax, perhaps the greatest left-handed pitcher of all time, was in attendance as well.

The game itself played up to its billing. Derek Lowe was matched up with Odalis Perez, who, coincidentally, was one of the players involved in the myriad of trade rumors during the off-season involving Nomar Garciaparra, Alex Rodriguez, the Red Sox, the Rangers, the White Sox, and the Dodgers. Lowe and Perez were locked in a 0-0 tie through 6 ½ innings. In the bottom of the seventh, David Ortiz lined a shot into the Dodger bullpen in right field to give the Red Sox a 1-0 lead. Mike Timlin protected the lead with a scoreless eighth inning, and with Keith Foulke coming in for the ninth, it looked like the game would end as a 1-0 thriller. However, with two out in the top of the ninth, Alex Cora reached first on a ground single to second that Mark Bellhorn couldn't handle cleanly. Pinch-hitter Olmedo Saenz then lofted a fly ball to left that looked like the last out of the game, but Manny Ramirez stumbled around chasing the ball in the wind and misplayed it. The ball dropped and the tying run scored. However, the Sox made up for Manny's mistake by scoring quickly in the bottom of the ninth. Johnny Damon walked and Mark Bellhorn doubled to put runners on second and third with no one out. Dodger reliever Tom Martin got two quick strikes on David Ortiz, but Ortiz lined the next pitch right down – and in fact right on – the rightfield line to bring in Damon with the winning run. With the Yankees losing to San Diego, the Sox had cut New York's AL East lead to 2 ½ games.

The lead went back up to 3 ½ the next day, as the Red Sox completely bombed out in a 14-5 loss to the Dodgers. Tom Lasorda threw out the first pitch, and the former Dodger manager must have enjoyed the show. Both Tim Wakefield and Jeff Weaver were very shaky, but a bunch of Dodger home runs and 7 LA runs in the fifth inning were enough of a margin for Weaver to leave with a win. Pedro Martinez outdueled former Sox pitcher Hideo Nomo in the Sunday night finale. The game was highlighted by a great leaping grab of a liner by Pokey Reese with two on and two out in the Dodger seventh. Reese really elevated to grab the liner and end the threat, preserving Pedro's seventh win of the season.

With inter-league play moving to the National League cities, Red Sox pitchers were preparing to bat and keep from embarrassing themselves. Bronson Arroyo was the first to face this, as the Sox moved to Denver to play the Colorado Rockies. Arroyo continued his string of shaky performances as the Sox lost to the Rockies 6-3 to break an 8-game Colorado losing streak. The Sox left 12 runners on base and squandered many bases loaded situations, including one in the ninth that ended with Jason Varitek striking out with three runners on base.

The game on June 16 featured the long-awaited return of Trot Nixon. In his 2004 debut, Nixon hit a long flyout to deep centerfield, but then connected later in the game for his first home run since he hit one in game 7 of the ALCS to give the Sox and Pedro an early 2-0 lead over Roger Clemens and the Yankees. Kevin Youkilis and Jason Varitek also homered, but the Sox still fell to the lowly Colorado Rockies 7-6. A David Ortiz home run, and the second consecutive game of 7 shutout innings by Derek Lowe allowed the Red Sox to salvage the series finale, and pull back to within 4 ½ games of the first-place Yankees.

The Possible Dream

The biggest and best news for the Red Sox in Denver came off the field, however. Curt Schilling returned to Boston after the 7-6 loss to get an MRI on his sore right ankle. Schilling had been getting injections of painkillers before his starts, and the fear was that he would have to go on the disabled list and be shut down from pitching for 2-4 weeks. That would have been disastrous for the Red Sox. The MRI results showed that there was no risk of additional damage, though, and Schilling was cleared to make his next start, at home against the Twins. Red Sox fans breathed a huge sigh of relief at hearing that news.

The next stop on the Red Sox road trip was San Francisco, and that meant only one thing – the Sox facing feared Giants' slugger Barry Bonds. Bonds has long been viewed by many fans and sportswriters as being either aloof (the polite description), surly (the less polite), or a jerk (the harshest description), and all of his bad traits became evident in this series. Before the series even opened, Bonds blasted Boston as being a racist city, and said that he would never want to play there. While Boston had a negative racial climate in the 1970's, much has improved since that time, so it was not clear how Bonds could claim this, especially since he admitted that he has never been in the city. It seems that there are enough racial issues in the country to deal with without having some identified and stereotypes perpetuated by an aloof person who has never been in the city that he is condemning and who has no idea what the city is like. The Fox Network announcers who covered the Saturday Red Sox-Giants game blasted Bonds for his attitude and comments, so this certainly seemed not to be just a local issue.

On the field, Bonds also was a disappointment. His nonchalant attempt to come in on what turned out to be a looping single by Trot Nixon in the 8th inning of the Saturday game was a horrible play. He didn't charge in for the ball, then he attempted to bare hand it, and missed, allowing three runs to score and tying the game at 4-4. In that same game, in the bottom of the 8th, Bonds hit a ground ball to the right side. The ball was bobbled by Mark Bellhorn, who had it bounce off of him and bounce a few feet in front of him. Nevertheless, he had time to throw out Bonds, since Barry did not hustle at all out of the batter's box and down the line. The San Francisco fans booed Bonds, and deservedly so, for his lack of hustle. The Giants wound up winning that game on a pinch-hit two-run home run by Edgardo Alfonso, and won the Sunday Fathers' Day game, a very impressive one-hitter pitched by Giant ace Jason Schmidt, 4-0 on a grand slam home run, also by Alfonso. Only a great comeback by the Red Sox on Friday, erasing a 7-2 Giants' lead for a 14-9 win behind home runs by Millar, Ortiz,

Ramirez, Nixon, and Mirabelli, prevented the Back Bay team from being swept in the City by the Bay.

When the Red Sox returned to Fenway for a game with Minnesota on June 22, they finally were close to fielding the lineup that they expected to have on Opening Day. With the exception of Bill Mueller, who was still on the disabled list, the return of Garciaparra and Nixon had really bolstered the lineup. The results were quickly apparent as a grand slam by Nomar, coupled with Manny's 19th home run of the season and David Ortiz' 16th, gave the Sox a 9-2 win. Curt Schilling raised his record to 9-4 with the win. His 9 wins tied him for most wins by a pitcher in the majors. The win also kept his record a perfect 6-0 at Fenway Park.

The injury bug hit the Red Sox again the next night, as Pokey Reese injured his thumb diving for a ground ball in a 4-2 loss to the Twins. An injury to this same thumb had caused Pokey to miss most of the 2003 season, so again fears were raised about the seriousness of the injury, and about how long Pokey might be sidelined. MRI results showed no major problem. Pokey was cleared to play in the weekend series with the Phillies.

The series ended with a 4-3 loss to the Twins in 10 innings. The winning run was unearned, thanks to a throwing error by Nomar in the 10th. The Red Sox defense continued to be the worst in the league, leading the league in errors (it would be even worse if it included errors generously scored as hits by friendly scorekeepers). The worst news was off the field however, as it was then learned that prize outfielder Carlos Beltran was traded by the Royals to Houston, thwarting a Red Sox bid to acquire the talented Beltran. While some writers and fans wondered where Beltran could play, others saw the possibility of playing Beltran in center, moving Damon to left, Manny to DH, and Millar to the bench, given his terrible season to date. However, as was the case with A-Rod over the winter, the Red Sox did not pull the trigger on this deal. Boston's sights were set on Seattle pitcher Freddie Garcia as a potential fifth starter, but Garcia was traded to the White Sox. The Red Sox were left with no acquisitions as June headed into its final days.

A weekend series with the Phillies at Fenway resulted in three blowouts. The opener was a rain-shortened 12-1 win highlighted by 2-hit pitching by Pedro Martinez, and a HR and 5 RBI by Manny Ramirez, his 20th HR of the season. David Ortiz hit his 18th, as the Ortiz-Ramirez combination continued to be a good one. The Phillies came back the next day with a 9-2 laugher, highlighted (highlighted?) by 4 errors by the porous Red Sox defense. The Red Sox had 14 hits and a walk and managed to score only 2 runs, which is hard to fathom. Curt

Schilling righted the ship with his 10th victory of the season, a 12-3 win in which Ortiz hit another home run, his 19th of the season.

The stage was set for a showdown in New York with the first-place Yankees. While the Red Sox went into the series with a 6-1 lead in the season series, astute fans could sense that all the factors were in place for another string of embarrassments at the hand of the Yankees. The pitching matchups were Lowe-Vasquez, Wakefield-Lieber, and Martinez-Halsey. That seemed to favor the Red Sox, as did their 6-1 record over the New Yorkers, but this is the time that the Red Sox would seem to roll over and play dead for the Yankees yet again.

The opener fulfilled the fears and demonstrated all the reasons why the Red Sox had not come out on top against the Yankees for so many years. After a leadoff home run by Johnny Damon gave the Red Sox a 1-0 lead in the first, Red Sox defense showed its ugly side immediately in the bottom of the first. Garciaparra fielded a ground ball hit by Yankee leadoff batter Kenny Lofton and promptly threw it in the dirt for an error. The Red Sox escaped without a run and took a 2-1 lead on another Damon home run, only to have the defense collapse again. An error by Kevin Millar, bobbling a grounder by Lofton, opened the door to 3 New York runs in the third and a 4-2 Yankee lead. A double steal by Jeter and Rodriguez set up a 2-run single by Hideki Matsui that broke a 2-2 tie and gave the Yankees a lead they would never relinquish. It was difficult to remember the last time an opposing base-runner was caught stealing by Jason Varitek. In the fourth, with two out, Derek Jeter hit what should have been an inning-ending grounder to Garciaparra, but Nomar booted the ball and Jeter was safe. Instead of being out of the inning, the Red Sox wound up being out of the game as Gary Sheffield followed that error with a 3-run home run to left, upping the Yankee lead to 7-2. Manager Terry Francona inexplicably kept Derek Lowe in the game despite the 7 runs in 3 innings, and that decision, and shaky defense again cost the Red Sox in the fourth inning. With one out and a runner at first, Pokey Reese bobbled a potential inning-ending grounder to second. He recovered in time to get the force out at second, so no error was charged, but that brought Tony Clark to the plate. Clark had been a Red Sox player in 2002 and was a complete bust, finishing the season with a very poor .207 batting average. Thus, cynical Red Sox watchers (including myself) were absolutely convinced that Clark would homer in this situation to further humiliate the Red Sox, and Clark wasted no time in doing so. His titanic home run to center field made the score an insurmountable 9-2, with Lowe still in the game for reasons known only to Terry Francona. The only thing missing in this loss was that abominable play that is a favorite of the Red Sox – with one out, a runner on first and a 3-2 count on the batter having the man on first run so that the inning could end on a strike out-throw out double play. On the other hand, since most Red Sox followers gave up after the Clark home run, it is possible that that play did happen, which would have made this the Red Sox equivalent of a perfect humiliation. The Yankee lead was now 6 ½ games over Boston, and the Red Sox were closer to the third-place Tampa Devil Rays than they were to the first-place Yankees. Things couldn't get worse, could they?

Of course they could get worse. The Red Sox followed this stinker with another one, this one a heartbreaking 4-2 loss to the Yankees. Once again the game started well as Johnny Damon, Mark Bellhorn, and David Ortiz led off the game with consecutive singles. The Sox had a 1-0 lead, runners on first and second, Yankee starter Jon Lieber on the ropes, and Manny and Nomar coming up. A Manny double play and a Nomar pop-up (reminiscent of the many that he had hit in last year's ALCS) took the Red Sox out of that threat with just one run. Consecutive singles to start the second by Trot Nixon and Kevin Millar posed another threat, but that threat also proved illusive as Doug Mirabelli bounced into a 5-4-3 double play that could have possibly been a triple play if A-Rod had gone to third before throwing to second. They would still have had time to get the slow-moving Mirabelli at first. An Ortiz home run gave the Red Sox a 2-0 lead, that Tim Wakefield held through 6 innings. Wakefield has pitched for the Red Sox since 1995, and has always seemed to be pitching with little run support from his teammates. They continued that trend in this game, not only with the missed opportunities in the first and second innings, but with a bigger one in the seventh. The Sox loaded the bases with nobody out, but wound up with no runs (getting no runs with the bases loaded and no one out is as much a Red Sox tradition as the Fourth of July). Damon hit a grounder to Tony Clark at first who threw home for a force out. Bellhorn popped out. Ortiz took a called third strike.

Veteran Red Sox watchers just knew that this would turn things around and it did in no time flat. The Yankees loaded the bases without a hit in the bottom of the seventh. With two out, Tony Clark (there's that name again) hit a hot grounder down to first base that should have ended the inning. However, Red Sox defense struck again. David Ortiz played the ball to the side and had the ball go through his glove for an error that brought in two unearned runs and tied the score. The Red Sox announcers pointed out that the grounder actually broke Ortiz' glove. Broke his glove ?!?!? In 43 years of watching baseball I have never seen a ground ball tear someone's glove as did Clark's ground ball that broke David Ortiz' glove. Only the Red Sox could do that.

With the score tied at 2 going into the bottom of the eighth, Red Sox defense struck again. Kenny Lofton grounded a single into the shortstop hole. Nomar gloved it but then bounced his throw into the stands to let Lofton get to second and into scoring position. Derek Jeter moved the runner to third (fundamental baseball – the Yankees play it, the Red Sox don't), and a Gary Sheffield double scored the go-ahead run. Matsui singled for an insurance run, but just about everyone could sense that another run would not be needed. Mariano Rivera, the Yankee relief ace, came in to pitch the ninth and face Gabe Kapler, Doug Mirabelli, and Pokey Reese, not exactly Murderers' Row. Kapler struck out looking for the first out. Manager Terry Francona sent out Jason Varitek to pinch hit and David McCarty was on-deck to hit for Reese. This was a curious move in and of itself, as Varitek was the only pinch hitter who could possibly hit a home run, so the better move might have been to pinch hit Kevin Youkilis, who is known for getting on base, for Mirabelli and then Varitek for Reese so that a home run could tie it, not just make it 4-3.

In any case, this being the Red Sox, it all became moot anyway. Varitek struck out swinging (which he had been doing a lot of late) for the second out. McCarty took a pitch down the middle for strike one. McCarty took another pitch down the middle for strike two. After a couple of pitches just off the plate for a 2-2 count, Rivera threw his next pitch. A very weak checked swing by McCarty resulted in strike three to him as well. Rivera struck out the side. At least 5 of the pitches were strikes right down the middle that none of the three batters swung at. All three were retired without any one of their bats touching a pitch for even a foul ball. Pathetic. Weak.

It was unbelievable. And yet it was all too believable. This game, especially coupled with the 11-3 loss the night before were humiliating. Together they helped demonstrate yet again that through this point in 2004 there was nothing more certain in the universe than the Red Sox laying down and playing dead whenever they play the Yankees and have any pressure on them. There is no other way to describe it. They can beat the Yankees in April, or after they have been eliminated from pennant or wild-card contention, but not when there is any pressure on them. To give NY its due, they are a good team that will capitalize an opportunities and do what they need to do to win. Unfortunately, the other team on the field with them when they play the Red Sox just chokes when they play them, and have been doing so for over 80 years; there is no other way to describe it. Year in, year out. If you watched the weather station for 24 hours straight and they all predicted that it would be sunny an hour from now you shouldn't be as certain as knowing the Red Sox are playing the Yankees and will do something unbelievably humiliating to lose.

At the end of June, the standings of these "rivals" who did not have anything at all resembling a real rivalry (through this point in 2004) was:

	W	L	PCT	GB
New York	49	26	.653	--
Boston	42	34	.553	7 1/2

The positions were a far cry from the end of April, as the Red Sox record was a sub-.500 27-28 since their 15-6 start in April while the Yankees had gone 41-15 since they had fallen to 8-11 after their April meetings with Boston. The Red Sox lead that had been 4 ½ games at the end of that last series between these two teams had now dropped to a deficit of 7 ½, a swing of 12 games in the standings, just a little over two months later. Since September is traditionally the worst month for the Red Sox, the only question at this point was whether the season would get even worse than this. All signs pointed to yes, as the Red Sox prepared to send Pedro Martinez out to pitch against the Yankees and Brett Halsey to begin the month of July.

Chapter 16 – July: Devastation and Departures

The month of July began with the Red Sox in disarray. The two humiliating losses to the team's nemesis, the Yankees, were extremely hard to take. Owner Larry Lucchino talked on Sports Talk radio about there being a malaise on the team, and that seemed an apt description. Manager Terry Francona was getting heat for his managerial decisions, such as leaving David Ortiz in to play first and not substituting the better fielding David McCarty to help preserve the 2-0 Boston lead in the seventh inning of the second game of the 3-game Yankee series and pinch hitting Varitek with nobody on and a two-run deficit instead of waiting until Varitek could be the potential tying run. Former All-Star Nomar Garciaparra was getting heat for his terrible fielding and not-much-better hitting, and also because the general feeling was that he looked like he wanted to get out of town.

Meanwhile the New York tabloid newspapers were having a field day with the Red Sox plight and the Yankees dominance. Headlines screamed:

"Yanks Rough Up Rotten Red Sox" (New York Post, June 30)
"Sox Built For Beer League."　　　(New York Post, June 30)
"It's Hard to Believe in Boston"　　(New York Post, June 30)
"April Fools" with a picture of Nomar fielding
　　　　　(New York Daily News, June 30 - I didn't see this one
　　　　　　myself but read about it in the Boston Globe)
"With Bridesmaids Back, Yankees Exploit Their Help."
　　　　　(New York Times, June 30 – I didn't see this one
　　　　　myself but read　about it in the Boston Globe)
"Cowboy Oops"　　　　　　(New York　Post, July 1)
　　on a back cover picture of Nomar's 8th inning throwing error
" '86 Tears"　　　　(New York Daily News,　July 1)
　　referring to Boston's 1986 World Series collapse
"BOSOX Blunders Pave the Way Once Again"
　　　(New York Post, July 1)

The Boston Globe created a web page for fans to use to vent their frustrations. There were 48 web pages of entries, including references to "Terry Fran-coma" and "Nomar Garcia-popup". At least Red Sox fans were creative.

Against this backdrop came the finale of the 3-game series in Yankee Stadium. This was the Pedro Martinez – Brett Halsey match-up that should have greatly favored the Red Sox. It didn't.

The pre-game was as interesting as the game itself turned out to be. Ailing Red Sox third baseman Bill Mueller, the defending American League batting champion, was coming off a stint on the disabled list and had been on a rehab assignment with the Red Sox Triple A minor league affiliate in Pawtucket. It was announced that he would be activated for Friday night's game in Atlanta. This begged a question: if Mueller could be activated on Friday, July 2, for a game with Atlanta, why not activate him on Thursday, July 1, for a game with New York, your biggest nemesis? Would the 24 additional hours in Pawtucket make a difference? Wouldn't you want your best possible lineup out there to face the Yankees in such a crucial game? Only the Red Sox would make a decision like that.

David McCarty was inserted into the lineup at first, which was good considering the bad defensive plays made by Kevin Millar and David Ortiz the two previous nights. However, the slumping Millar was in the lineup in right field, and Trot Nixon was on the bench – a curious move. Even more curious was that Nomar Garciaparra was not in the lineup! Was he being benched? Unclear. After the game Terry Francona announced that he had been playing Nomar too much and he needed a rest. He said that Nomar had come to him late in the game and said that he could play, but Francona didn't want to put him in. What was going on here?

The game itself was a 13-inning thriller. It was highlighted by an absolutely incredible play by Derek Jeter. With two outs and two on in the 12th inning he raced after a looping fly ball to left. He looked in fact like he kicked in the after-burners to get to that fly ball and make the out and then seemed not to heed any worry about a possible serious or career-ending injury which could have happened as he tripped into a head-first dive into the stands. Rodriguez and fans in that area immediately called for medical help but Jeter did get up and walk shakily to the bench with a giant scratch on his chin, and a growing swelling under his right eye. What an effort! That this was (a) in a game in July that (b) didn't mean that much in the standings given the Yankees' 7 ½ game lead over the Red Sox, it was even more admirable that Jeter did this. The man just wants to win. That was a fantastic play, one of THE best that I have ever seen by anyone in any game. What a play. What a player.

And what a contrast to the Red Sox "All-Star Shortstop" who didn't even play. Didn't even play? With his team about to be swept by the team that they needed to catch and against whom they had always

The Possible Dream

suffered humiliation? In a 13-inning game? How do you explain that? I have no idea.

Watching this game from start to finish was like watching a train wreck that you knew would happen but couldn't avoid watching anyway. At least it was a good game, but there were still some questionable things from the Red Sox side. In the Yankee first, with two out, Pedro hit Gary Sheffield with a pitch. What was that all about? While Sheffield is despicable (when he was an infielder with Milwaukee and wanted to be traded it was reported that he deliberately would field grounders and throw the ball into the stands to try to force the trade), there was no reason for Pedro to be throwing at him. It should be time for Pedro to grow up and pitch to win, not to show off his manhood. Winners talk, and through this point in 2004, your name was not listed in the book of World Series winners, Pedro.

The Yankees took a 2-0 lead in the second inning on a home run by ... are you ready for this? ... Tony Clark. Again Clark haunts the Red Sox. He was a dud in Boston but now he's turned into a stud in New York, at least for this series. Incredible.

A Posada home run increased the NY lead to 3-0 but a two-run home run by Manny Ramirez and another run on a double play grounder tied the game at 3-3, and set up a long series of dramatics. In the 8th inning, Ortiz led off with a blast to right that looked to be gone. Sheffield in fact went back to the wall but then the wind seemed to blow the ball back in, so he had to race in and catch it while falling. Typical Red Sox luck, or fate.

The Red Sox' ace reliever Keith Foulke worked out of a bases loaded one out jam in the ninth inning, so the game went into extra innings.

In the 11th inning, Ortiz led off with a single. It seemed an opportune time to send in a pinch runner, but they did not. Ramirez followed with a single and Ortiz lumbered to third. At this point they did send in a pinch-runner. Why then? He was now 90 feet away, not 270. He could score from 3rd on a single. The time to pinch run for him was when he was on first, not when he was on third. Jason Varitek was then walked intentionally to load the bases. Bases loaded, nobody out – would anyone take a bet on how many runs the Red Sox would score? My guess was zero, as this is still a Red Sox tradition to load the bases with no outs and score no runs. It happened. Kevin Millar was the next batter. Why? Millar had been having a horrendous season, and would seem to be overmatched against Mariano Rivera. With Trot Nixon, a lefty, on the bench, the right move would have been to have him pinch hit. They didn't, and Millar hit a grounder to third that

A-Rod turned into a double play, tagging third to force Manny and throwing home where Posada tagged out Gabe Kapler who had pinch run for Ortiz. A fly out on the next play ensured that the Red Sox would get no runs from the bases loaded no out situation. So what else is new?

Second base had been the only weak spot in the Yankee lineup all season, but Miguel Cairo led off the bottom of the 11th with a triple. It looked like the winning run would surely come in, but it did not, as the Red Sox survived another threat. The Red Sox threatened themselves in the 12th, but that threat ended on that great play by Jeter, but Jeter was forced to leave the game, forcing Joe Torre to shift A-Rod to shortstop and bring Gary Sheffield in from right field to play third base.

A Manny Ramirez home run in the top of the 13th inning gave the Red Sox a 4-3 lead, and the next batter reached on a throwing error by Sheffield. However, Cesar Crespo grounded into a double play to end the inning and also end the possibility of adding insurance runs. Should Nomar have pinch-hit then? As was described many chapters ago, it is often not the shock (1 run) but the after-shock (additional runs) that wins tight extra-inning games such as this.

Still things looked good as relief pitcher Curtis Leskanic retired the first two Yankee batters in the bottom of the 13th. One out away from a big win that could have turned around their season, Leskanic gave up a ground ball single up the middle to Ruben Sierra. Still, things looked good as Leskanic got two strikes on Miguel Cairo. One strike away from that big win, Cairo doubled to right, past Kevin Millar. Sierra scored to tie the game. The next scheduled batter was Yankee pitcher Tanyon Sturtze. The Yankee maneuvering and substitution had seen them lose their designated hitter and they were down to only one player on the bench, reserve catcher, former Red Sox, light-hitting John Flaherty. Naturally Flaherty became the hero, as he belted a double to left to score the winning run. This ironic turn of fate was yet another non-surprise to Red Sox fans – a near win turned into a crushing defeat, a game lost to heroics by Red Sox castoffs. The scene at the end of the game was eerily reminiscent of the end of game 7 of the preceding year's ALCS: Yankee players leaped for joy and surrounded their unlikely hero on the field (Aaron Boone then, John Flaherty now), the Red Sox walked catatonically back to the dugout and many of the Red Sox sat in the dugout in stunned silence, too shocked to head right into the locker room. The more things change, the more they remain the same.

In any case, it was a very good ball game, won by the team that is the better team for sure. The Yankees know how to win and play every game to win, as witnessed by Jeter's play. The Yankee lead in the AL East was now up to 8 ½ games. It seemed insurmountable.

The non-appearance by Nomar in such a crucial game was hard to fathom. It did appear to many observers that he was uninterested. This was evidenced by his sitting back on the bench while all of his teammates in the dugout were on the top step watching the action in support of the team. To be honest, while the TV shots did show this, this does not seem to be Nomar's style. He has always seemed to be interested in the game and team. If this really meant that he was distancing himself from the team, though, then it was time to trade him. Rumors of a potential trade with Florida involving Nomar for pitcher Brad Penny and/or shortstop Alex Gonzalez were heard the following weekend, but it seemed to me that a better trade might be to trade Nomar to Arizona for Randy Johnson, if the rumors of Arizona looking to trade "The Big Unit" were accurate. The trade could possibly be expanded to include a prospect being sent to Arizona, or Kevin Millar being added to a trade that would also bring the Arizona first baseman to Boston, but this seemed like a good potential move for Boston. Their only hope seemed to be to get into the playoffs and hope that pitching could be the key against the powerful Yankee lineup, and a playoff rotation of Pedro, Schilling, and Randy Johnson would be very formidable; this is especially so given the success that Schilling and Randy Johnson had had against the Yankees in the 2001 World Series. Obtaining Johnson would also be a defensive move, preventing the Yankees from getting him and thereby shifting the AL power even further toward the Bronx. In any case, getting Randy Johnson and Curt Schilling, who had already proven that they could beat the Yankees in critical games in October would be a lot better move than acquiring Byung-Hyun Kim, who had a history of blowing big games to the Yankees in that same 2001 series.

The trip to Atlanta was no more successful than the visit to Yankee Stadium. The Red Sox did salvage one win in the three game there, but it took a complete game, ten strikeout effort by Curt Schilling (his 11th win of the season). That win was sandwiched around two more disheartening defeats. A 6-3 loss in 12 innings on Friday night was low-lighted by the Sox again taking a lead in extra innings, again on a hit by Manny Ramirez (this time an RBI single in the 10th inning), only to lose it. The Braves tied it in the bottom of the tenth and then won it with a three-run home run in the bottom of the 12th inning. The Sunday loss was 10-4, with the Red Sox losing a 4-1 lead due to yet another self-implosion by the erratic Derek Lowe, leading to a 9-run 5th inning explosion by the Braves. Even good-natured, Polyanna-like manager Terry Francona could not put a positive spin on this game as he came as close to criticizing Lowe as he had all season in his post-game comments, saying that Lowe had the confidence of his pitching coach, manager, and teammates, but "at some point he just needs to do the job". Since Francona had defended Nomar's non-playing in the critical third game in New York, the question again arose as to whether Francona's style is what this team needs to succeed.

The Sox limped home to play ten games with the teams that now were their top competitors for the wild-card slot: three each with Oakland and Texas before the All-Star break and then four with Anaheim afterward. Francona did shift his rotation slightly, moving Schilling in from Friday against Texas to Thursday against Oakland (on his usual four day rest). However, even that move begged for more. The right move, it seemed, would have been to start the Oakland series with Martinez, who would be pitching on his usual four day rest, given the off-day preceding the series. In that way, Francona could use Martinez against the A's on Tuesday and also against the Rangers on the Sunday before the All-Star game. It would also set up the rotation that Francona wanted earlier in the season, Wakefield being after Martinez and before Schilling, for the crucial series with the A's. Pitching Pedro twice would seem to be the right move to try to put the team in the best possible position to win. Unfortunately that kind of forward thinking on the pitching rotation has never been a Red Sox strength, and it appeared that 2004 was no different than previous years in this regard.

Tim Wakefield started the series with a brilliant 7 shutout innings, outpitching former Cy Young Award winner Barry Zito. Wakefield finally got some run support from his teammates, as a three-run homer by Bill Mueller gave the Sox and early lead (why again was it that he wasn't activated for the final game of the Yankee series?), and a 5 for 6 performance by Johnny Damon highlighted the Red Sox offensive attack.

Damon continued his hot streak as the Red Sox continued a sweep of the A's and then took 2 of 3 from Texas before the All-Star break. Damon extended his hitting streak to 15 games, during which he hit 6 home runs and raised his batting average from .286 to .322. Damon's hot hitting helped Pedro Martinez follow Wakefield's easy win with an 11-3 win of his own over Oakland. Damon was the star in the series finale as he rescued the Sox from near-disaster. Cruising along with a 7-1 lead for Curt Schilling, the Sox suddenly found themselves tied 7-7 going into the bottom of the ninth. Damon led off with a single, and then tore around the bases to score on a double to left center by Bill Mueller. It was clear that Damon was determined to score and he did make it in, though just barely, ahead of the relay throw.

The Red Sox won the opener of the Texas series behind a great pitching performance by Bronson Arroyo who contributed 8 shutout innings in a 7-0 win. The Red Sox pounded Texas 14-6 in the second game behind two mammoth home runs by Manny Ramirez. The power onslaught allowed Boston to overcome a 6-run explosion by Texas off Derek Lowe that followed a pair of errors by Mark Bellhorn. The 6 runs were unearned, but with the final runs being on a grand slam home run by Hank Blalock to give Texas a 6-3 lead, it appeared that this was going to be another implosion by Lowe. He did right himself however, and cruised to the win behind the Red Sox hitting attack to raise his record to 7-8. The Red Sox lost the final game of the series and the final game before the All-Star break to Texas, 6-5. The Red Sox had their chances for a comeback in the 9th but couldn't get the job done. Bill Mueller led off with a walk, but pinch-hitter Manny Ramirez popped up for the first out and pinch-runner Pokey Reese was picked off first base for the second. Damon reached first to keep hopes alive when his squibber couldn't be handled by the Texas third baseman or shortstop. Damon then stole second and proceeded to third as the throw bounced into the outfield. With Damon and the tying run 90 feet away, Mark Bellhorn was called out on strikes to end the game, the home stand, and the figurative first half of the season. As the team went into the All-Star break, they were in second place, 7 games behind the front-running Yankees, but had moved back into the lead for the wild-card spot with their 5 of 6 wins against Oakland and Texas. The AL East standings at the break were as follows:

	W	L	PCT	GB
New York	55	31	.640	--
Boston	48	38	.558	7
Tampa Bay	42	45	.483	13 ½
Toronto	39	49	.443	17
Baltimore	37	48	.435	17 ½

The American League division leaders at the break were the Yankees, Chicago White Sox, and surprising Texas Rangers, with the Red Sox in the lead for the wild card. The St. Louis Cardinals had the best record in the National League and were joined in first place by the Philadelphia Phillies and Los Angeles Dodgers. The San Francisco Giants were in the lead for the NL wild-card slot, meaning that baseball's most storied matchups, Red Sox-Yankees and Dodgers-Giants, were in position to highlight the October playoff matchups if things worked out.

There were a lot of teams still in contention at the break, and rumors were rampant of potential big names available for trade. The biggest of all, both literally in stature and figuratively in reputation, was

Arizona's 6'10" pitching ace Randy Johnson. Though "The Big Unit", as he is called, who had already pitched a perfect game earlier in the season, had a no-trade clause in his contract, rumors had him going to the Yankees, Red Sox, or Angels. Peter Gammons reported that Johnson would accept a trade to the Yankees but not the Red Sox. Curt Schilling, Johnson's former teammate and friend with Arizona, fielded question after question about Johnson, and Schilling's wife Shonda had arranged with Major League Baseball to sit next to Randy Johnson's wife during the All-Star game. Meanwhile there were rumors of Roger Clemens being traded back to Boston by the slumping Houston Astros, but that seemed highly unlikely. Pittsburgh righthander Kris Benson was also available, but the Mets seemed to be the front-runners to acquire him if anyone was going to do so.

In Boston, amid the rumors, were also what seemed to be the annual flurry of All-Star-time controversy involving some of its biggest stars and key performers. Pedro Martinez had left the team early to go back to the Dominican Republic for the All-Star break, as he had in previous years. Pedro's teammates were left with just a giant bobblehead doll of Pedro in their dugout for the Texas series. It was unclear why other pitchers such as Curt Schilling or Bronson Arroyo could not also leave early, since their work was done one day and two days after Pedro, but they did not ask for anything special. It did seem that Pedro was once again getting special treatment. Interestingly, had manager Terry Francona pitched Pedro on his normal rest on Tuesday, July 6, he would have also been in position to pitch on Sunday, July 11, also on his normal rest, in the finale before the All-Star break. Pedro could then have left for the Dominican right after that game. That the Red Sox lost that game is another indication of a questionable managerial decision, as having Pedro pitch twice before the break would seem preferable than having someone else pitch twice. By moving Pedro back to Wednesday, July 7, he was not in position to pitch on the 11th, and so was in position to leave early.

Controversy #2 revolved around Manny Ramirez. For the third straight year, Manny did not play in the Sunday game before the All-Star break. The reason given was that he had a sore hamstring. However, the hamstring that bothered him on Sunday did not seem to bother him when he hit two titanic home runs on Saturday, so it was not clear what was going on. Also, interestingly, Curt Schilling, the Red Sox' unofficial team leader, was seen berating Manny before the game, perhaps about his obligations to his teammates? That, like many things involving these controversies, was not clear.

A third controversy involved Nomar Garciaparra. Nomar had sat out the 3rd game of the Yankee series a week and a half

The Possible Dream

previously. One of the weak explanations given at that time was Terry Francona announcing that he remembered that Nomar had to sit out every third game to rest his Achilles Tendon. It did not seem appropriate to rest a player who is a nominal team leader in such a crucial series, when he could have been rested the day before that series or the day after. The fact that Nomar played in every game for the next week and a half after that Yankee game - 9 straight games leading up to the All-Star break, made that explanation even harder to swallow and Nomar's not playing in that Yankee game even harder to understand.

The final controversy involved Terry Francona's announcement of what his pitching rotation would be coming back from the break. Francona announced that Derek Lowe would start the first game after the All-Star break, to be followed by Pedro Martinez, Tim Wakefield, and Curt Schilling. It was not clear why a manager would choose Lowe to start the first game after the break instead of Curt Schilling or Pedro Martinez. Lowe had a won-loss record of 7-8, whereas Schilling was 11-4 and Pedro was 9-3. Lowe had had a very shaky season thus far, unlike Schilling. It was not a matter of rest between starts, since Lowe would have 4 days rest after the break, whereas Schilling would be pitching with 6 if he pitched that day and Martinez with 7. It would seem that you would start with your best pitchers and get them in as many games as possible if you want to get into the post-season. Francona's rotation did not set that up. Most importantly, with a series with the Yankees coming up the second weekend after the break, it would seem that you would arrange your rotation to have your best pitchers, Schilling (11-4), Martinez (9-3), and Wakefield (since Wakefield has had success against the Yankees in 2003-4), set up for the Yankee series. With the rotation that Francona set up, the Red Sox pitchers for the Yankee series would be Schilling (11-4), Arroyo (3-7), and Lowe (7-8). Why? Doesn't this set up another potential Red Sox humiliation at the hands of the Yankees? Red Sox fans could only pray that a few rainouts would help set up the rotation the way that the manager did not. Unfortunately, that did not happen.

The American League won the All-Star game 9-4, with Manny Ramirez and David Ortiz hitting home runs. Roger Clemens was hit hard from the start, giving up a leadoff double to Ichiro Suzuki of Seattle, a triple to Ivan Rodriguez of Detroit, a 2-run homer to Manny and later a 3-run homer to Alfonso Soriano of Texas. All of this was in the first inning. That early 6-0 lead held up. There was some speculation that Clemens' catcher, Mike Piazza, was tipping off the batters on what was coming in retribution for Clemens having thrown at him when Clemens was a Yankee facing Piazza's Mets, for hitting him in the head with a pitch, and for throwing a piece of a broken bat at him in the 2000 World Series. It would be hard to blame Piazza if he did tell AL batters what pitches were coming and where from Clemens, but Derek Jeter said that no one was telling him what was coming. It was just a bad performance by Clemens.

The other speculation at the All-Star festivities surrounded Randy Johnson. Johnson told reporters that he would agree to waive the no-trade clause in his contract to go to a contender, and if the deal could help Arizona. Most New York writers immediately began writing about Johnson in a Yankee uniform, as if it were pre-ordained, and wanting to play for the Yankees. An interesting rumor was of a 3-way deal involving the Red Sox trading Nomar Garciaparra to the Cubs for prospects that they would then bundle in a deal with Arizona to get Randy Johnson to come to the Red Sox. It was, once again, almost too good to be true. Given the histories of these franchises, a more likely scenario would have been the Red Sox trading Nomar to the Cubs to set up the deal, but then Randy Johnson getting traded to the Yankees for far less than what the Red Sox were offering. The Yankees, Red Sox, Angels, and Mets were teams that were talked about as possible bidders for Johnson, but no deal came to fruition during the All-Star break, though discussions were going to continue through the July 31 trade deadline.

On the field, the Red Sox started the post-All-Star-game portion of the season on the West Coast, playing 4 games in Anaheim and 2 in Seattle. They alternated losses and wins in the first five games, predictably winning only when Martinez and Schilling pitched (after 90 games the team was 27-11 in games started by the two aces, 23-29 in games started by others), with Pedro picking up his 10th win of the season and Schilling his 12th. Lowe pitched and lost the opener after the All-Star game 8-1, but Pedro followed that with a 4-2 win. In that 4-2 win David Ortiz became incensed after a called third strike (the umpiring in that Anaheim series was atrocious for both teams), and was ejected from the game by the home plate umpire. Back in the dugout, still steaming over the call, the usually mild-mannered Ortiz grabbed a couple of bats and threw them onto the field, narrowly missing an umpire, and undoubtedly earning himself a fine and suspension. The win was followed by an 8-3 loss the next night, in which starter Tim Wakefield was hit in the back with a line drive. Happily, a CT Scan the next day showed no problems, and Wakefield was cleared for his next start. The Sunday finale in Anaheim saw the Red Sox down 1-0 to the Angels in the 6th, with Anaheim starter John Lackey cruising against Curt Schilling (7 strikeouts through 5 innings), and Benji Molina having homered for the game's only run. Suddenly, a three-run shot by David Ortiz put the Red Sox ahead 3-1. Lackey's next pitch hit Garciaparra and both benches were warned against further throwing at batters. The Red Sox extended the lead to 4-1 on a Gabe Kapler HR, and then 6-1 into the bottom of the 8th inning. Schilling, now cruising himself, then hit Benji Molina with a pitch with one out, but was not thrown out of the game. Angel manager Mike Scoscia was incensed and was ejected, but Schilling stayed in to complete the 8th. This whole incident showed Schilling to be both a team leader – you hit one of our guys, I'll hit one of yours – and a veteran, picking his spots and hitting (a) the batter who had homered off him earlier, (b) someone in the 8th when he had a comfortable lead, and (c) someone in the 8th which he knew was going to be his last inning anyway, so an ejection would not greatly hurt the team. The Sox hung on for a 6-2 win and series split with Anaheim.

As is often the case with the Red Sox late in the season, the soap opera off the field stole many of the headlines. Manny Ramirez had missed the last game before the break with hamstring problems, but played three innings in the field in the All-Star game. Then, in coming to Anaheim, told the manager that his hamstrings were too tight to play in the field but that he could DH. Francona did put him in the lineup as DH in the Anaheim opener, but sat him down for the next three games. Some observers felt that Manny was annoyed at having played the whole game in a 14-6 win the night before the "hamstring problem" happened, while other starters came out of the game early. The idea was that perhaps Manny was faking it to get back at the manager. This was reinforced by Manny playing in the All-Star game. If the hamstrings were bothering him, he should have skipped the All-Star game to rest and get ready to help his team in the stretch run. If they weren't bothering him, he should have been able to play in the Anaheim series. Then Francona announced that Manny volunteered to DH, but that he wanted to keep him out of the lineup until he was ready to play left field. Was this a power play by the manager? Nothing was definitive, except that the Red Sox lost 2 of 4 games in Anaheim, and lost a chance to pick up any ground on the Yankees, who were also losing 2 of 4 to Detroit. All in all, it was an all too typical week in Red Sox land. One could only wonder what August and September would bring.

Manny was back in the lineup in left field (!) in Seattle, but the Red Sox seesaw of lose-one-win-one continued. Bronson Arroyo pitched well and left with a 4-1 lead, courtesy of a 3-run homer by Jason Varitek in the 8th. Arroyo had struck out 12 Mariners, including at one point getting 11 straight Mariner outs by strikeout. Mike Timlin gave up a run in the bottom of the eighth, but the Red Sox were still in good shape with a 4-2 lead going into the 9th. However, back-to-back home runs by the Mariners in the 9th tied the game and sent it into extra innings, where it was won by a walk-off grand slam home run by Bret

Boone (brother of Aaron Boone who had ended the Red Sox 2003 season with a home run). The 8-4 loss in 11 innings kept the Red Sox 7 games behind New York, which lost again, this time to Tampa Bay. Once again the Red Sox had failed on an opportunity to gain ground on the first-place Yankees.

Fundamental baseball, or, more accurately, lack thereof, continued to hurt the Red Sox. The Sox had a great opportunity with a first inning bases loaded, one out situation set up by Mueller being hit with a pitch, and Ortiz and Ramirez walking. With the pitcher struggling to throw strikes, any knowledgeable baseball person would take a pitch or two to force the wild and struggling hurler to have to throw strikes or walk in a run (and perhaps get himself an early shower). Nomar followed the hit batsman and two walks by hitting the first pitch into an inning-ending and rally-ending double play. Red Sox fans had to be scratching their heads at that.

They also had to be scratching their heads at the continued pulling of pitchers for the bullpen. There was no reason that Schilling could not have pitched a complete game on Sunday, and there was no reason why a cruising Bronson Arroyo couldn't have pitched longer in the Monday game, instead of having Embree, Timlin, and Foulke pitch.

The controversies involving Manny and Nomar, the questionable managerial moves and possible confrontation/standoff between Francona and Ramirez, the possible Ortiz suspension, the possible Wakefield injury, the continuing ineffectiveness of Kevin Millar, the trade rumors involving Nomar and Randy Johnson, and the on-going (some might say perpetual) chase of the Yankees, certainly were making things interesting. The headline of an article on the Red Sox' own web site after the 8-4 loss to Seattle may have said it all: "Never a Dull Moment".

It was never a dull moment in the final game on the West Coast swing. Trailing 1-0 in the fourth, the Red Sox bunched a number of hits into a 4-1 lead and had two men on with David Ortiz coming up. Ortiz promptly hit a 3-run homer to give the Sox a 7-1 lead. Ortiz' home run was his 26th of the season, tying him with teammate Manny Ramirez for the league lead. That tie lasted exactly one pitch, as Manny launched the next pitch into the center field seats to reclaim the league lead. Ortiz was the first to congratulate him as he came back to the dugout. The 8 run 4th inning and an 8-1 lead should have been enough for an easy win, right? Wrong. Derek Lowe developed a blister and had to leave the game. The bullpen faltered and the Mariners kept coming back. Ahead only 9-7 going into the 9th inning, the Red Sox called on Keith Foulke to try to save the game, and to come back from the nightmare of the back-to-back homers tying the game in the 9th the

The Possible Dream

previous night. Two batters later, there were two runners on and the potential winning run coming up to bat in the person of Bret Boone, the hero of the walk-off grand slam the previous night. Foulke struck him out. Next up was Edgar Martinez, one of the best hitters in baseball for years, and the man who had tied the game the previous night with a home run off Foulke. Foulke struck him out. That brought up Bucky Jacobsen who had been a hitting star in the Mariners' minor league system over the first half. Foulke struck him out. The Red Sox had held on to the 9-7 win to conclude the six games with alternating losses and wins, and making Derek Lowe the only pitcher other than Curt Schilling or Pedro Martinez to win a game on the trip.

The Sox' return home on Wednesday led to a new experience for us. The Red Sox this year had started telecasting some of their games in a small set of theaters around the state. Tickets are only $5 each. So, for the first time ever, we went to a movie theater to watch a game, the Showcase Cinemas in Worcester, MA.

Watching the game in the theater was fun. The crowd was into it. WTAG, the Worcester radio station that covers the Red Sox, had trivia contests, raffles, or give-aways every inning for the first half of the game. Peanut vendors walked around the movie aisles; the one who kept going past us would yell "Peanuts, $3.15". Whatever happened to "Peanuts. Get your red hot roasted peanuts"? Somehow yelling the price didn't sound like a good business idea to me, but having been convinced to spend $5 to watch a baseball game in a movie theater, maybe I wasn't the best judge of good business practices. People went into rhythmic clapping for a rally and stood up when a Red Sox player hit a home run. There were beach balls being hit around as there are in the bleachers at Fenway. It was certainly unusual as a way to watch a baseball game and unusual activity for being in a movie theater. What would Ebert and Roeper think?

The game down on the field (er, uh, up on the screen) was a different matter. Pedro Martinez started for Boston and retired the first 10 Oriole batters, striking out 6. Then the Orioles struck for three runs, the first two scoring on a line drive by Miguel Tejada that Johnny Damon misjudged. The ball got by Damon and rolled to the wall, leaving Tejada at third base with a triple. He scored on a sacrifice fly to right on which Gabe Kapler made a great diving catch. Kapler came up throwing, which was very good to see. Too often these days outfielders just concede the run on a sacrifice fly. At least Kapler made an attempt to throw out the runner. Kapler then tied it with a 3-run homer, but another 3-run rally by Baltimore gave them a 6-3 lead.

Baltimore extended the lead on a bizarre play. Oriole hitter David Newhan hit a long fly to center field. Damon went back and leaped at the wall but could not catch it. The ball bounced back toward the infield. Damon retrieved it and threw toward the cutoff man, but LF Manny Ramirez had somehow gotten himself in the line of the throw. He dove to catch it. From his knees he threw to the real cutoff man, Mark Bellhorn. While all of this was happening, Newhan alertly kept circling the bases and was on his way home with a potential inside-the-park home run. Bellhorn turned to throw home and bounced the ball off the pitcher's mound. Newhan scored easily. It was another case of unbelievably bad fundamental baseball by the Red Sox. A bad play by Damon, compounded by Manny being out of position and intercepting the cutoff, further compounded by his throwing the ball to Bellhorn who was still in short leftfield, finally capped by Bellhorn not being able to get a throw home. In fact, Bellhorn was only able to get it as far as the mound. Is it any wonder that a team playing this fundamentally unsound baseball has not won a championship since 1918? If you are scoring at home, as the radio announcers like to say, that might have been the first attempted 8-7-4-2 putout in baseball history. The U.S. Olympic relay team could have gotten it home faster. Many fans left the park/theater at this point. We didn't. After all, $5 is $5. The Red Sox went on to a 10-5 loss and fell 8 games behind the first-place Yankees.

It struck me in the bottom of the 7th that there was no 7th inning stretch. It's too bad. We could have sung our own variation of the old baseball seventh inning stretch song:

> *Take me out to the ball game,*
> *Or some reasonable facsimile.*
> *Buy me some coke from the soda machine.*
> *We're watching the game on a movie screen.*
> *And it's root, root, root, but not too loud.*
> *It all depends on the crowd.*
> *For it's 1, yes Cinema 1,*
> *For the old ball game.*

The Sox split a double-header with Baltimore the next day. Rookie Abe Alvarez started and lost his major league debut in the opener 8-3. Alvarez was sent back to the minors right after the game. Tim Wakefield threw 7 shutout innings in giving the Red Sox a 4-0 win and a double-header split in the nightcap. Once again it was not clear why Wakefield was taken out after 7 innings, especially since Francona had been complaining about his overworked bullpen all week. There had been three chances within the preceding six games for starters to continue when they were pulled or to go for a complete game: Schilling against Anaheim on July 18, Arroyo against Seattle on July 19, and Wakefield against Baltimore on July 22. Instead Timlin and Embree were brought in to pitch when they didn't need to be, and the bullpen was still "running on fumes" as Francona put it during the week and going into the Yankee series.

The rotation for the Yankee series was a strong Schilling, an erratic Arroyo, and a shaky Lowe. It could have been Schilling, Wakefield, and Martinez if Francona had set up his rotation properly after the All-Star break, but instead it was Schilling, Arroyo, and Lowe set to defend Red Sox Nation against the red-hot Evil Empire from the Bronx.

The Evil Empire stayed hot and extended its first-place lead to a season-high 9 ½ games with an 8-7 win in the opener. For some reason, Manager Terry Francona decided to start Ricky Gutierrez at second base in the opener of this crucial series. This was odd in that (a) Gutierrez was a shortstop and (b) he had just joined the team the day before this series. Why Francona would not start Bellhorn, who had been playing all year, was a mystery. If Bellhorn needed a rest, why not rest him against Baltimore in the series before the New York series? As an alternative why not play Bill Mueller at second base and Kevin Youkilis at third? Such a mysterious move often seems to be the case for the Red Sox as they go into a big series against the Yankees (resting Carl Yastrzemski and starting catcher Bob Montgomery at first base for the first time in his career, or bringing in reliever Bill Campbell to get some work in a 3-2 ballgame are among the many such mysteries). If the Red Sox had been contracted to do whatever they could to help the Yankees, they could not do a better job. Predictably, playing Gutierrez at second base cost the Red Sox. Holding a 4-1 lead with Curt Schilling on the mound, the Red Sox fell behind 7-4 in the 6th inning, with a key play being a high bouncer between home and first to first baseman Kevin Millar. Millar fielded it and turned to throw to first where the second baseman should have moved over to cover. Gutierrez, however, had not covered, so a run scored, everyone was safe, and the rally continued. Interestingly, Bellhorn came into the game later, so resting him didn't seem as important AFTER the key play of the game. The Red Sox wound up tying the game 7-7 behind three home runs by Kevin Millar, the third tying the game at 7, but lost on a double by Gary Sheffield and single by Alex Rodriguez in the top of the ninth.

The second game of the series on Saturday featured a brawl between the two teams, if featured can be used in this context. Trailing 3-0, pitcher Bronson Arroyo hit Alex Rodriguez with a pitch. We were at a wedding that weekend in Millbrook, NY, so didn't get to see the game, but when I heard about the fight my immediate reaction was to think that the Red Sox can't beat the Yankees on the field where it really matters, so their pitchers will throw at them and then maybe they can try to beat them up. It was similar to Pedro acting child-like and throwing at Karim Garcia in the playoffs last season. This was totally classless on their parts.

Whereas someone like Derek Jeter would have probably gone down to first without comment, and let sleeping dogs lie, A-Rod decided to yell and scream at Arroyo. Catcher Jason Varitek accompanied A-Rod down the first base line and suddenly the two were throwing punches at each other and the benches emptied as the fight expanded. Eventually Rodriguez, Varitek, Gabe Kapler, and Kenny Lofton were ejected from the game, and Yankee starter Tanyon Sturtze had to leave due to a bruised pinky and face cut. The brawl seemed to inspire the Red Sox, as they played with much more life after this than they had before (based on published reports) and came back to win 11-10 on a 9th inning two-run home run by Bill Mueller off Yankee ace reliever Mariano Rivera. Perhaps the best folklore to come out of this altercation was the story that at one point Varitek said to Rodriguez "We don't throw at .260 hitters." Varitek would not confirm that he did say this, but if he did, good for him. The other oddity was the Yankees complaining that Varitek did not take off his mask during the scuffle. That seemed a hollow complaint. First of all, would the expectation be that Varitek say "excuse me, I'm going to take off my mask in case we fight"? The action was going on and Varitek reacted. Second of all, if anyone had a protective mask on and a fight were about to start with a guy right in front of them, would that person take the mask off? Most likely that person would not, and most likely neither would A-Rod (who, by the way, did not take off his batting helmet either).

After the Saturday fight and comeback win, the Red Sox also won the series finale 9-6 on Sunday, overcoming a shaky defensive first inning behind home runs by Johnny Damon, Mark Bellhorn (well enough to play Saturday and Sunday) and the suddenly hot-hitting Kevin Millar. Millar was 10-for-13 in the series, with 4 home runs. The lead was down to 7 ½.

Off the field, the news was bad. Trot Nixon had been put on the 15 day disabled list before the Sunday game with a recurrence of the quadriceps problem that had made him miss much of the beginning of the season. The news talked about Nixon being possibly out longer, perhaps for the season, and that this was possibly career-threatening (comparisons were made of this injury to the one suffered by Boston Bruins hockey player Cam Neely that cut short his career). The Red Sox and Nixon were clearly very worried.

Also bad were reports that Randy Johnson would only agree to be traded to the Yankees. Nothing like this kind of news to bring to mind the old cliché that "them that has gets", as the Yankees, with baseball's best record, who had already been able to acquire A-Rod, one of the best hitters in the game, could now get Randy Johnson, one of the game's best pitchers. No wonder this team always wins.

The Sox finished the month by splitting four games with Baltimore and Minnesota, once again falling into their now-familiar pattern of win-lose-win-lose. The standings at the end of July were:

	W	L	PCT	GB
New York	65	38	.631	--
Boston	56	46	.549	8 1/2

The Red Sox had played exactly half a season since starting the season out so well and going 15-6 in April. In those 81 games, the Red Sox had gone 41-40 – not exactly awe-inspiring, and certainly not a post-season-worthy record.

Hope was on the way, though, with the big news coming on the trade front. Randy Johnson did not go to the Yankees, the Red Sox, or anyone for that matter. However, just before the July 31 4:00 PM trade deadline, the Red Sox did trade shortstop Nomar Garciaparra. Nomar was sent to the Chicago Cubs in a complicated four-team deal. The Red Sox wound up with two slick-fielding infielders, shortstop Orlando Cabrera from Montreal and first baseman Doug Mientkiewicz from Minnesota. In the deal, the Expos acquired shortstop Alex Gonzalez from the Cubs, along with RHP Francis Beltran and infielder Brendan Harris. The Red Sox also sent minor league outfielder Matt Murton and cash to the Cubs. In a second, separate transaction, the Red Sox acquired OF Dave Roberts from the Dodgers for minor league outfielder Henri Stanley. The additions brought defense and (amazingly) speed to the Red Sox. Cabrera had stolen 24 bases for Montreal in 2003. Roberts had stolen 40 bases for the Dodgers in 2003 and had stolen 33 bases in 34 attempts prior to the trade in 2004. August and September would prove how effective these trades were. For the Red Sox, Nomar, the player, was gone, but Nomar, the controversy, was about to heat up.

Chapter 17 – August: The Heat is On … New York!

August is usually a cruel month for Boston and for Red Sox fans. September and October are usually worse, but August has its problems. The weather starts turning cooler by the end of the month, and so do Red Sox bats. August 24 is a date on which the Red Sox seem to traditionally start to fade, either from a lead or from contention. One most notable example of this was 1974, when a 7-game first-place lead and a 70-54 record for the Red Sox on August 24, became a 7-game third-place finish for the team thanks to 24 losses in their final 38 games. Another was 2001, when the Red Sox were 71-56 and in second place, 3 games behind New York on August 24, with Joe Kerrigan having replaced Jimy Williams at manager a few days previously, and then proceeded to lose their next 9 in a row, 13 of their next 14, and 23 of their next 29. They finished 82-79 and 13 ½ games behind New York. August in the past had been cruel to Red Sox fans.

August 2004, though, had a different feel to it. The weather became hotter at the end of August than it had all summer, reaching the 90's on August 28 and staying hazy, hot, and humid for that weekend. As the weather got hotter, so did the Red Sox. After going 8-6 over the first half of the month, the team suddenly went on a tear, winning 12 of the next 13 games, to cut the Yankee lead from 10 ½ games on August 15 to 3 ½ games on August 31. The only loss during that stretch was 3-0 to Toronto on a beautifully pitched 3-hit shutout by Ted Lilly. Lilly's performance rivaled Jason Schmidt's in being the best-pitched games against the Red Sox all season.

The trade of Nomar, the new and more positive team attitude, better defense, excellent pitching, and, to be honest, a favorable schedule, helped the Red Sox create this winning streak. It should be noted, however, that the teams that the Red Sox were beating during this stretch were the same teams that were beating them earlier in the season, so the schedule was not the only thing that was in the Red Sox favor.

The month started innocuously enough. Orlando Cabrera stepped to the plate in the top of the first inning in the first game for the

Red Sox in August and in his first game for the Red Sox. Cabrera was noted for his speed but was surprisingly batting third for the Red Sox as a replacement for David Ortiz, who was serving a five-game suspension for his bat-throwing incident in Anaheim. Cabrera began his Red Sox career in style, lining a home run into the leftfield seats in the Metrodome. Unfortunately, the Red Sox got only one other hit, a home run by Manny Ramirez, and lost 4-3 to the Twins.

This was another maddening loss that maybe did not need to be a loss at all. Pedro Martinez was cruising through 7 innings, leading 3-2, and having just ended the 7th with his 10th and 11th strikeouts of the game. Pedro left before the start of the 8th inning and the lead quickly left as well in the 8th. Once again, having Pedro continue to pitch, and giving his bullpen a continued rest seemed in order for the manager, but he pulled Pedro after 7. Pitching Pedro past the 7th in the regular season would seem to be a good idea (a) if you may want him to pitch past 7 in the post-season and (b) your bullpen is still tired. However that didn't happen, Pedro still is not ready to pitch more than 7 innings in the post-season, and the Red Sox suffered another unnecessary loss in a season full of them.

The July 31 trade of Nomar Garciaparra started making more news, and continued to make news for days to come. Nomar had been a very good player and a real fan favorite for years. In a way it was sad to see him go, but it was necessary. He had really changed this year. The Red Sox wooing of Alex Rodriguez really seemed to affect him greatly. He was very bitter about that. He seemed to take a lot of time coming back to play this year after an Achilles problem that was caused supposedly by being hit by a batted ball in the ankle during batting practice in spring training, though there were rumors of it being caused by his playing soccer, or by his off-season work regimen. The rumors were buoyed by the fact that no one could remember seeing him hit with a batted ball during spring training. Nomar had also been moping around a lot this year, and had been in and out of the lineup.

The icing on the cake in terms of showing Nomar's detachment from the team was when the Red Sox had lost the first 2 games of a 3 game series with the Yankees last month, and Nomar sat out the 3rd game. That was the game that went 13 innings, in which Derek Jeter (a winner) made an outstanding catch diving into the stands, the Yankees fell behind in the top of the 13th and then came back to win in the bottom. Nomar never got off the bench and into the game despite numerous opportunities to pinch hit. The manager seemed frustrated with him. In fact, there were shots of the dugout in late innings with every Red Sox player on the top steps and Nomar the only one sitting on the bench. Everyone seemed engaged in the game except Nomar.

He then proceeded to play the next 9 games in 9 days straight before the All-Star break. So why did he miss the last game against the Yankees? It was hard to figure. He had made a key error in the second game for which he was criticized, but still, could that have been it? Who knows.

After the trade, there were reports that he had been talking to the trainers and manager about having to take "significant time off" in August to rest the Achilles, and said that he may need to go on the disabled list. That was one thing that seemed to have prompted the Red Sox to trade him. The Cubs were informed about this but still went ahead with the trade. Apparently, also, when Larry Lucchino called to wish him well in Chicago he asked Nomar how the Achilles felt. Nomar answered "Great". The owner expressed surprise about how that could be from what Nomar had said a couple of days previously. Nomar responded something like "That was then. It is great now." Neither side disputes the contents of this conversation. Nomar says that he said that but was just being sarcastic. In any case, the story is that Nomar may have faked the severity of the injury to get himself traded. If so, it worked.

The trade played to very mixed feelings in New England. Red Sox management was heavily criticized by some, but many fans had soured on Nomar this year. Personally, I thought it was a good trade for them since (a) Nomar was bitter (b) Nomar had become fragile and injury-prone (c) he was not going to sign with them and would be a free agent at the end of the year, and (d) they got something for him, which they did not do when Mo Vaughn and Roger Clemens left the team. I did think that he would blossom in a Cubs uniform, and thought that it would be interesting to see whether or not he plays every day in Chicago or does have to take significant time off.

Meanwhile, back on the field, the erratic season continued for the first half of August. The Red Sox won the first two games in Tampa Bay behind a big win by Tim Wakefield on his 38th birthday and a complete game win for Curt Schilling. With a chance to sweep the Devil Rays, the Red Sox took a 4-1 lead into the 7th inning, but lost it on a grand slam home run.

The final stop on what would be the longest road trip of the season for the team (12 games scheduled, 11 games played) was in Detroit, and the first game of that series was also a loss, 4-3 to the Tigers, as Derek Lowe suffered his 10th loss of the season. The Red Sox were now a season-high 10 ½ games behind the Yankees and seemed to be fading fast (though as it turned out, that was not the case). Martinez and Wakefield came back to win the next two games, with Wakefield winning a wild game in which he tied a major league record by giving up six home runs to the Tigers before leaving the game. He still got his 8th win of the season, as his teammates backed him at the plate for an 11-9 win.

Back at Fenway for a 10-game home stand, the Red Sox lost to the Devil Rays 8-3, as Curt Schilling suffered his first loss of the season at Fenway Park. It was probably Schilling's worst outing of the season (his split-fingered fastball especially seemed off) and Curt took the blame for the loss on himself. He truly had become the team leader. The Red Sox then won the next three games with Tampa Bay by scores of 8-4, 14-4, and 6-0. In the 6-0 game, Pedro Martinez became the first pitcher other than Curt Schilling to pitch a complete game for the 2004 Sox. Pedro gave up only 6 hits, walking none, and striking out 10, his third straight game with double-digit strikeouts. The ace had really been acting like an ace of late.

After losing 2 of 3 to the Chicago White Sox, the Red Sox were 10 ½ games behind the Yankees at mid-month and looking as if they were about to fade out of the wild-card race as well as the pennant race. Interestingly, the reverse was about to happen, as the team went on a 6-game winning streak. The streak started inauspiciously enough with an 8-4 win over Toronto at Fenway. In what appeared to be the latest entry in the "why the Red Sox never win" department, their starting second baseman that night was Doug Mientkiewicz. Yes, recently acquired, gold-glove-winning first baseman Mientkiewicz started at second base. This was because third baseman Kevin Youkilis had gotten injured the night before, so regular third baseman Bill Mueller, who had been playing second lately, had to go back to third base. Terry Francona asked Mientkiewicz if he had ever played second base and could help there in a pinch. Mientkiewicz said that he played there an inning last year, so Francona thought and even said in an interview "if he's played there one inning, he can play there nine" and so ... starting at second, Doug Mientkiewicz. No Ricky Gutierrez, an experienced middle infielder, no Pokey Reese, still recovering from some injury of over a month ago, and no second baseman in the minor leagues that they could bring up? When they made the trade of Nomar they said that defense was really a big flaw and Theo said that he didn't want it to become a fatal flaw. Playing a first baseman at second base didn't sound like a way to improve that defense. Mientkiewicz, however, should be commended for willingly doing this for the team, even though the possibility of embarrassment was high. One had to wonder if Nomar would have done the same had he been asked to move to second so that the team could acquire A-Rod, or to help the team in a pinch.

The Possible Dream

In any case, not only did Mientkiewicz not embarrass himself, he played reasonably well and actually helped the team. He made a nice play at 2nd base in the very first inning, backhanding a grounder, stepping on 2nd and then completing a DP. He also made a nice play in 2nd inning where he grabbed a grounder and tagged out Carlos Delgado on a force play. Delgado threw his forearms into Mientkiewicz and knocked him over to break up the DP, but Doug came up yelling at Delgado. It was a clean play, but not one that he was used to. He actually did better at 2B than expected in his first and only game there this season. The Red Sox played Ricky Gutierrez at 2nd the next night, and brought up 3B Earl Snyder from Pawtucket to play 3rd so that they could move Mueller back to 2nd while Bellhorn and Pokey Reese were recuperating, so Doug's days at 2B numbered just one, but it was memorable.

The Sox won the next night 5-4, scoring the winning run on a ninth inning double by Orlando Cabrera. The double hit the top of the manual scoreboard at the base of the left field wall and took an odd bounce upward. The bounce allowed Johnny Damon to race around and score from first with the game-winner. Luck had a hand in the win, but as Branch Rickey used to say, "luck is the residue of design", and so the speed of Johnny Damon and the breakneck way he raced around the bases, combined with the luck of the scoreboard bounce, gave the Red Sox this win.

Wakefield and Schilling followed that game with well-pitched wins over Toronto at home and the White Sox in Chicago. Wakefield pitched 8 strong innings for the win over the Blue Jays, and Schilling pitched 7 shutout innings to get a six-game road trip off to a good start in the windy city. A grand slam home run by Ramirez and a three-run shot by Cabrera provided Schilling more than enough of a cushion.

My family accompanied a large group of Red Sox fans to the Saturday game at US Cellular Field, taking the El (elevated train) to the game in Chicago's South Side. There were fireworks on the field with three Red Sox home runs (1 by Ramirez and 2 by Varitek) and above the field on two White Sox home runs, but the Red Sox prevailed in a wild one 10-7, barely holding on to leads of 3-0, 5-2, 7-2 , and 10-5 behind a shaky performance from Bronson Arroyo. Arroyo's was the only shaky performance by the Red Sox starters over the second half of August, as the pitching really put the team back into contention.

It was the hitting that saved the Chicago series finale, as a 4-0 Red Sox lead for Derek Lowe turned into a 5-4 deficit on a three-run Chicago HR in the bottom of the seventh. Manny Ramirez got things even by hitting his 33rd home run of the season on the first pitch in the top of the eighth, and then David Ortiz gave the Red Sox a 6-5 lead, and ultimately the win by that same score, with a home run on the very next pitch.

While the Red Sox were sweeping Chicago the Yankees were being swept by the Anaheim Angels, so the Yankee lead over the Red Sox was down to 5 ½ games. The Yankee lead of 10 ½ games on August 15 was cut almost in half in just one week.

A 3-0 loss in an excellent pitchers' duel between Pedro and Ted Lilly in Toronto only temporary slowed down the hard charging Red Sox, as they followed that loss with another winning streak, taking two from the Jays in Toronto, and returning home to sweep the Tigers in four games at Fenway. The Tiger series featured 7 stolen bases by the Red Sox (!) and only one home run, by Mark Bellhorn late in the fourth game. The Red Sox winning games with speed, pitching, and not power, and now suddenly showing good defense as well (no longer giving up piles of unearned runs) was a new experience for most fans. For once, the Red Sox starting pitchers were carrying the team while the Yankee starters were faltering. The fourth Red Sox win over Detroit, coupled with a Yankee loss to Toronto, cut the Yankee lead a game further, to 4 ½ games. The New York Post, which had published the "Cowboy Oops" headline on July 1, now screamed "Watch Out, Here Come the Sawx" on August 30. There was finally the hint of a pennant race.

The hint became more of a reality on the final night of August. The Red Sox opened a big three-game series against their closest challenger in the wild-card race, the Anaheim Angels while the Yankees began a series with the slumping Cleveland Indians. Some (including me) considered the Angels the best team in the American League, so it looked like the 4 ½ game lead was about to grow. However, the Red Sox got off to a fast start with a 4-run first inning, keyed by a 3-run home run by Manny Ramirez, stretched the lead to 5-0 on a second home run by Manny in the second, and were cruising behind Curt Schilling. Meanwhile scoreboard watchers were incredibly seeing the Yankees-Indians scores being posted as the innings moved on: a 9-0 Indians' lead, then 12-0, then 16-0, then 22-0. 22-0! Meanwhile the Red Sox had built a 10-1 lead and a lot of excitement among the fans in attendance. Schilling left in the 8th inning with the lead 10-2 and the bullpen just barely held on for a 10-7 win. Coupled with the Yankees' 22-0 loss (the worst loss in the history of the New York Yankees), the win meant that the New Yorkers' once 10 ½ game lead had now been cut to 3 ½. The New York Daily News headline of the Yankees loss was a single word: "Stinkies". New York seemed to be the team in panic. Most Red Sox fans had never seen anything like this.

The Possible Dream

The standings at the end of August (below) were far different than they had been at mid-month:

	W	L	PCT	GB
New York	81	50	.618	--
Boston	77	53	.592	3 1/2

In addition, while the Red Sox starting pitching had been solid, if not spectacular, the Yankees had only gotten one win from any of their starting pitchers over the last seventeen games of the month. There was still a little over a month to go in the season, but it did seem like the world turned upside down.

Chapter 18 – September-October: Down the Stretch They Come

The hot weather of August disappeared as September began, but the hot play of the Red Sox continued … for a while.

The team followed Curt Schilling's and Manny Ramirez' lead in the Anaheim series that started on August 31 and completed a sweep of the Angels with 12-7 and 4-3 wins behind Arroyo and Lowe, scoring early and often in both games.

With one wild-card contender having been swept as September began, another, the Texas Rangers, came into town and also left further behind after losing 2 of 3 to the Red Sox. Martinez outdueled John Wasdin in the opener, winning 2-0 behind solo home runs by Manny Ramirez and Bill Mueller. The win pulled the Red Sox within 2 games of the faltering Yankees. After falling behind Texas 8-1 in the second game (Terry Francona having left Tim Wakefield in to give up all 8 runs), the team rallied back to 8-6 on a grand slam home run by Mark Bellhorn and a solo shot by David Ortiz. It was not enough, however. The ten-game win streak was snapped, and the Sox fell back to being 3 ½ games behind the Yankees. Curt Schilling continued his season-long excellence in the finale against Texas, pitching 8 1/3 brilliant innings before turning things over to the bullpen. A four run Texas ninth made the final score 6-5, but Schilling had his 18th win of the season.

On their final west coast trip of the season, the Sox took on another strong team in Oakland, but remained hot, sweeping the A's in three games 8-3, 7-1, and 7-3. Derek Lowe won his fifth straight decision in the 7-1 win and Pedro Martinez left after 6 shutout innings of the finale. The deficit behind the Yankees was back down to 2 games, the pitching was sharp, the hitting timely, and the fans were hooked on the pennant race as the team headed north to play Seattle.

While the Red Sox were in Oakland, there were some interesting and hard to believe things going on in New York. The Tampa Bay Devil Rays were unable to leave Florida for New York on the Sunday before Labor Day because of hurricanes, and the Yankees tried to get a forfeit of their games on Monday. This very un-magnanimous gesture on the Yankees' part to people who were in the midst of what would be 4 hurricanes in the month was a real shocker. That did not seem like the Yankee way at all. It seemed rather like a near-desperate move that you would expect from someone chasing the Yankees, and a conduct unbefitting the once proud Yankee franchise itself. Major League Baseball, to its credit, wouldn't allow it. The afternoon doubleheader scheduled for Labor Day became a night game and a double-header the next day.

Meanwhile, 3,000 miles away, somewhere between leaving Oakland and arriving in Seattle, the Red Sox team must have lost some of its sharpness. The Mariners were having a bad year, so perhaps after big series against the contending Angels, Rangers, and A's, the team had a letdown. Whatever it was, the team's previously sloppy defense was back in the series-opening 7-1 loss. Tim Wakefield was the hard-luck loser, giving up 7 runs, although only 2 were earned. Schilling and Arroyo followed that with easy 13-2 and 9-0 wins, Schilling picking up his 19th win in the process. Manny Ramirez hit three home runs in the two games, including a grand slam in the 13-2 win. Schilling's continued brilliance was followed by 7 innings of 4-hit shutout ball by Arroyo. However, the chance to restore their hot streak ended early the next day. With runners on 2nd and 3rd in the first inning on a 1-out double by Manny Ramirez, Jason Varitek hit a fly to right field that looked like a sure sacrifice fly and another early lead for the Sox, as they had been doing during the hot streak. However, Manny lost track of the number of outs (as he had been doing occasionally during the team's .500 and mildly mediocre play of May, June, and July), and he was doubled off second before the run could score. This was a key play in the team's 2-0 shutout loss to Gil Meche and Seattle that ended the road trip. The Red Sox were back to 3 ½ games behind first place New York with 20 games to go in the season, but were coming home for a series with Tampa Bay and a chance to gain on the Yankees before taking on the Yankees in two crucial weekend series on Sept 17-19 in New York and Sept 24-26 in Boston.

A seeming mismatch between Red Sox pitching ace Pedro Martinez and Tampa Bay's 20-year old rookie Scott Kazmir turned into a mismatch, all right, but in favor of the Devil Rays. Tampa Bay won 5-2 and only a pinch-hit 8th inning two-run home run by Trot Nixon kept the Sox from suffering two consecutive shutouts to two unknown pitchers. An 8-6 win in the second game set up a rubber game that looked to be another mismatch for the Red Sox, with Curt Schilling going for his 20th win of the season. This one was a mismatch, but in the expected way. An 11-4 win by Boston made Schilling the first 20-game winner in the Major Leagues.

The Possible Dream

Both on and off the field Schilling had more then met the expectations that Red Sox management and fans had when he joined the team, and it was fitting then that he was the first 20-game winner in MLB. He had been a team leader and a dominant pitcher all season long. More importantly, he was an extremely hard worker and very focused pitcher. The number of Schilling-38 tee shirts that can be seen around Fenway Park these days is a real testament to how popular Schilling has become with the team's fans. He has been a joy to watch all season.

Schilling's win was the prelude to 10 days that would decide the American League Eastern Division – six games with the Yankees spread over two weekends, with the Yankees holding only a 3 ½ game lead over their pursuers from Boston. As has become the case with these two teams in recent years, there were headlines galore to come in the series. Unfortunately, as has become the history of these two teams over 80 years, the Yankees would wind up on top.

The six-game Armageddon began in New York on Friday night, September 17. The remnants of Hurricane Ivan, one of four major hurricanes to hit the East Coast in September, were heading up toward New York, and the forecast was for heavy rain later as the game began with Bronson Arroyo facing Orlando "El Duque" Hernandez. Hernandez had been out for most of 2003 and re-signed as a free agent by the Yankees earlier in the season. He did not join the roster until late in the season, but had proceeded to win his first 8 decisions and steady a very shaky Yankee pitching staff, and came into the game with a perfect 8-0 record.

The game seemed to start well for the Red Sox as a first inning single by Mark Bellhorn was followed by a Manny Ramirez blast into the left-field seats. Manny circled the bases as the third base umpire signaled home run, and it looked like the Red Sox were off to another early lead. However, the Yankees immediately protested that the ball was foul, all four umpires got together to confer, and the call was overturned. The hit was called foul. Replays showed that the ball was foul, so doing so was right, but the sequence was very curious. As described in Chapters 2 and 10, when the roles were reversed in the 1999 playoffs and the Red Sox were the victims of a bad call – the phantom tag by Chuck Knoblauch of Jose Offerman on which the second base umpire ruled him out and later said that he didn't see it – there was no umpire conference to right the wrong, and that was in the playoffs, with much more at stake, and with 6 umpires instead of 4 watching the play. Interestingly, again, a week after this game, situations were reversed and two bad umpire calls against the Red Sox did not result in umpires conferring and the bad calls reversed.

Admittedly the ball was foul, and I have no problems with the umpires conferring to get the call right, but why would it be OK to confer when the Yankees were the aggrieved party, but not when they benefited from the bad call? It's not as if the rules were changed between October 1999 and September 17, 2004 allowing umpires to confer on a close play. It's also not as if they were then changed again between September 17 and September 24 (when, as we shall see, the reverse happened again). It's also not as if the plays were so different that they could not be overruled or that they had a dramatic effect on the continuation of the play at hand. The Offerman non-tag could have been discussed, Offerman returned to second, and everyone could be in position for the next pitch. On this play the call was overruled, the ball ruled foul, Bellhorn returned to first and Manny went back to the plate, where he proceeded to draw a base on balls. There was nothing so different about the two plays that they could not have been handled the same way to get the call right. Instead they were handled in a way in which both favored the Yankees. Curious.

The Red Sox did wind up with the bases loaded but got no runs. Jason Varitek came up with the bases loaded and was greeted with a round of boos for his role in the fight with Alex Rodriguez back on July 24. Yankee fans wanted nothing more than to see Varitek strike out in this situation. Varitek struck out. In fact, Varitek wound up going 0-for-10 in the three-game series and striking out 8 times, so Yankee fans, as they always seem to do, got their revenge.

A Johnny Damon home run gave Arroyo and the Sox a 1-0 lead in the third inning, when the game was stopped for the first time at 7:57 due to rain showers. This was also curious in that the heavy rains were due between 10:00 and 11:00 and the announcers were discussing that maybe they should play through this shower to hope to get in an official game before the heavy rains. The game resumed after a 19 minute delay, but was halted again for another rain shower after the bottom of the third. When play resumed, El Duque was no longer pitching, but Arroyo was. The game stayed tight with the Yankees taking a 2-1 lead on a home run by John Olerud (just added to the team in July and now rejuvenated), and holding it thanks to 3 2/3 innings of 1-hit shutout ball by Tanyon Sturtze.

The lead held into the 9th and with Yankee ace reliever and legend Mariano Rivera coming into the game, it appeared that the Red Sox were on the verge of falling 4 ½ games behind. However, Trot Nixon worked Rivera for a walk, and pinch-runner Dave Roberts stole second (a remarkable move by a Red Sox player in the 9th inning of a key game with New York). Kevin Millar was hit with a pitch and Gabe Kapler ran for him. Orlando Cabrera then punched a single past

The Possible Dream

Miguel Cairo and John Olerud into right to score Roberts and tie the game. That Cabrera went with the pitch, to the right side, in that situation, was also fundamental baseball not usually seen from the Red Sox. Johnny Damon then blooped a single to right-center for the go-ahead run. Yankee center fielder Kenny Lofton could maybe have caught the ball with more hustle and perhaps diving for it, but he did not, and the Sox had a surprising lead off Rivera. Rivera could be seen on replays looking to center and yelling "Catch the ball" at Lofton – a chink, perhaps, in the usually unflappable Yankee demeanor?

Keith Foulke got the save in the bottom of the ninth and the Red Sox had an improbable win, a deficit in the East that was now down to 2 ½ games, and perhaps had the Yankees on the run.

That feeling lasted until the first inning of the game the next afternoon. Derek Lowe started and was abysmal, giving up 5 first inning runs in what turned out to be a 14-4 laugher for the Yankees, as they regained momentum in the pennant race. By the time the afternoon was over, Lowe had made a bad play at first and also had thrown incorrectly to third after fielding a grounder and looking a runner back there instead of looking him back and then getting the out at first. Another Red Sox pitcher failed to cover first on a grounder to the right side, and Yankee pitcher Jon Lieber took a no-hitter into the 7th inning before David Ortiz' home run broke it up. All in all, it was a lost day for Boston and the lead was back to 3 ½.

The Sunday game also turned into another lost day, an 11-1 defeat, and a 4 ½ game deficit. Pedro gave up a first inning 2-run homer to Gary Sheffield and a solo blast to Derek Jeter, and this one was also over early. The team was back to its bad play and mediocre fundamentals and was in danger of falling out of the race completely as they headed back to Boston to face Baltimore, which had been giving them fits all year (having won 7 of the 11 games played between the two teams).

The two-game losing streak became three with a 9-6 loss to the Orioles. A 5-run 4th inning spurred the Birds, with a Red Sox lowlight being a weird rundown play between third and home. After a single by Brian Roberts and walks to Melvin Mora and Miguel Tejada, a passed ball brought in one run. Red Sox starter Trim Wakefield then walked Rafael Palmeiro to load the bases, but Mora, at third, thought that the bases were already loaded and started to walk in. The Red Sox got him in a rundown but made many throws back and forth without getting him. Finally as Mora was going back to third, a throw to third, with catcher Doug Mirabelli covering, was dropped by Mirabelli. Mora started running home, but Mirabelli picked up the ball and threw home, where first baseman Kevin Millar was now covering. Millar dropped the ball, and Mora scored. In the broadcast booth, Jerry Remy said "that's about the ugliest play you'll ever see on a baseball field". He was absolutely correct. The poor fundamental play helped the Red Sox to another loss.

The next game was the last game of the season for which we had tickets, and we were lucky enough to get Curt Schilling again as he went for his 21st victory. It was a beauty of a ballgame. The teams were scoreless through 7 innings in a real pitchers' duel between Schilling and Rodrigo Lopez. In the top of the 8th, with two runners on and one out, Schilling struck out the last two Oriole batters to keep the game scoreless. Schilling left with 14 strikeouts, and having given up just 3 hits and 0 runs. He had thrown 114 pitches, 90 of which (an amazing 79%) were strikes. He also left pounding his fist into his glove in satisfaction at having stopped the Oriole threat, and also left to a standing ovation from the capacity crowd. He was truly the team leader.

The Red Sox scratched in a run in the bottom of the 8th on a sacrifice fly by Kevin Millar. Keith Foulke came in for the 9th to save the game and Schilling's 21st win (this was the right move, as Schilling had thrown those 114 pitches). The move did not work out, however, as Foulke gave up a 2-out, 2-run home run on a 3-2 count to Javy Lopez. The Orioles took an excruciatingly painful 2-1 lead into the bottom of the ninth.

The Sox rallied, though, as pinch-hitter Kevin Youkilis walked (Dave Roberts then pinch ran for him), and Bill Mueller doubled off the wall in left. The rally seemed to die as pinch-hitter David McCarty popped out to first, Johnny Damon took a called third strike, and Mark Bellhorn came up after having hit into a double play in the first and striking out in his next two at-bats. Oriole closer Jorge Julio came in and blew a 96 MPH fastball past Bellhorn. However, Bellhorn connected on another fastball and drove it into right center for a game-winning double, scoring Roberts and Mueller. Fenway Park was delirious.

It was a great night all around with fans on the edge of their seats for much of the game and then standing and sitting often in the last few innings as Schilling and Foulke would get two strikes on batters. We were up and down as much as Congress is during a State of the Union Address. A number of fans (including us) stayed for many minutes after the game. It was difficult to leave after such a great pitching performance and such an emotion-numbing and then exhilarating series of events in the 8th and 9th. What a game.

The Possible Dream

Those fans who came the next night saw another thriller. Again Foulke gave up a home run in the 9th, this time to tie, and again the Red Sox won it in dramatic fashion. This time a 12th inning home run by Orlando Cabrera was the game winner. The lead was now down to 3 ½.

The lead was back up to 4 ½ after Thursday night's game, another poor performance by Derek Lowe (5 runs in 5 innings). Down 7-5 in the ninth, Francona brought in Byung-Hyun Kim for his first appearance for the team in months. Francona wanted to "save the bullpen" ostensibly for the upcoming Yankee series and since they had been overworked and made weary by his previous moves. The move backfired as Kim gave up 2 runs, so a 2-run rally by Boston in the 9th fell for naught. The loss took a little of the luster off the Yankee series as now it appeared that the Sox would not catch them unless they could sweep the three-game series.

The opener on Friday was another nail-biter. The Yankees took a 2-0 lead, but a Manny Ramirez 2-run homer tied it. The Red Sox took a 3-2 lead on a solo home run by Johnny Damon, but the Yankees tied it. The Red Sox then took a 4-3 lead in the bottom of the seventh on another solo home run, this one by Johnny Damon. With Pedro having thrown 101 pitches at this point, it seemed clear that Francona would bring in his now-rested bullpen to save the lead. He did not. In a scenario eerily reminiscent of Grady Little's meltdown in the 8th inning of game 7 of the 2003 ALCS, Francona left Pedro in to absorb a crushing defeat. Hideki Matsui homered on Pedro's second pitch of the 8th inning to tie the game again (for the last time). The look on Pedro's face as he saw the ball leave the field was on of deep frustration and pain. Francona STILL did not take Pedro out at this point, and Bernie Williams doubled. Francona STILL did not take Pedro out at this point, and Reuben Sierra singled him home. The Yankees now led 5-4 and Pedro was finally taken out. The final was 6-4 New York, but deep damage had been done to the Red Sox pennant chances and to the psyche of (a) Red Sox fans and, more importantly, (b) Pedro.

At the post-game press conference, the usually confident Martinez was completely subdued. He talked about being frustrated at not being able to beat the Yankees; the loss made his Red Sox record against them 10-10, and the Yankees have won 19 of the 30 games that they have played with him pitching for the Red Sox. Pedro also said that he would just have to say that the Yankees were his daddy (in the current vernacular of saying "who's your daddy" to someone that you dominate). He talked about how frustrated he was by losing to them again and again, and how he wished that "they would f***ing disappear". It is hard to remember any professional athlete saying things like that. It's understandable, since the Yankees have pretty much owned him the last few years.

Of course this all would have been avoidable if Francona had only lifted him before the eighth. It was hard to believe that he sent Pedro back out for the 8th inning after Damon's HR had put Boston up 4-3. Was Francona watching game 7 last year? If not, didn't he read about it? Hasn't he been watching Pedro pitch this year and hasn't he seen how Pedro's game deteriorates after he has thrown 100 pitches? He had brought Kim in the night before to save his bullpen (Embree, Timlin), so it is not clear why he didn't use that bullpen in the 8th. As has been said many, many times previously, when will they ever learn?

The game also had some very memorable plays. In the third inning, an Alex Rodriguez single scored Miguel Cairo with the first run of the game, and Rodriguez moved to second on an error by Trot Nixon on the throw in. Rodriguez then tried to steal third, and was called safe even though replays showed that Bill Mueller had clearly tagged him out before he touched the base. Tim McClelland, the third base umpire called him out, even though he was behind the play and could not see the tag being made because the bodies of Mueller and Rodriguez blocked his vision. The Red Sox argued, but unlike the previous Friday when the Yankees complained about a bad call and the umpires conferred and reversed it, there was no umpire conference and no reversal of the call to get a wrong call right. Why not? Don't the rules of baseball apply to all teams? Apparently not, and the Yankees benefited on the scoreboard as Rodriguez scored on a grounder to second by Gary Sheffield.

In the eighth inning, after Pedro's departure, there was another play at third and again McClelland got it wrong. With Sierra on 2nd base, Mueller fielded a grounder, tagged Sierra and threw to first for the out. Sierra was called safe (incorrectly) and after throwing to first the usually quiet and unflappable Mueller immediately whirled around and protested the call. Again the runner had blocked McClelland's view, so he could not see the tag. Yet again McClelland did not see fit to confer with any other umpire, particularly the home plate umpire who had a much better view of when the tag was made.

In any case, the Yankee lead was now 5 ½ games and seemed insurmountable again. The Red Sox did come back to win the final two games of the weekend series, winning 12-5 on Saturday night thanks to a 7-run 8th inning. On Sunday, Curt Schilling got the 21st win that he had been denied in his brilliant performance earlier in the week against Baltimore. This was also a great performance by Schilling, 7 innings of 1-hit baseball. The only hit was a single up the middle just under

The Possible Dream

Schilling's glove that scored two runs (Schilling, normally with great control had uncharacteristically walked three straight batters to load the bases before the hit). The final out of the inning was a grounder on which Schilling covered the bag and took the throw for the out, and he spiked the ball to the ground in frustration, though he had a 7-2 lead at the time. Competitor that he is, he did not want the Yankees to get themselves back in the game at all, and especially because of bases on balls. He cruised after that to an 11-4 win.

The Red Sox then headed down to Tampa Bay, just after yet another hurricane had hit the Sunshine State. Their Sunday night flight was canceled (there was no record of the Devil Rays asking for a forfeit as the Yankees had earlier in the month when the Devil Rays had problems traveling to New York after a previous hurricane), and so they flew down on Monday, the day of the first game. Bronson Arroyo, who had become at worst the third most reliable starter on the team by this point, won his tenth game of the season, 7-3. With the win, the Red Sox had clinched a spot in the playoffs as at least a wild-card team. They were the fifth team to clinch a post-season spot, joining the Cardinals, Yankees, Twins, and Braves in that circle. That win, and a 10-8 eleventh inning win the next night (thanks to a 2-run homer in the 11th by Kevin Millar), pulled the Red Sox once again to within 2 ½ games of first place with 5 games to go in the season.

With the Yankees forced to play a double-header against Minnesota and face Twin ace Johan Santana (the only other 20-game winner besides Curt Schilling in the majors), there was a good possibility for gaining further ground, but it was not to be. The Twins took an early 3-1 lead over New York, but then lifted Santana, a dominating pitcher, after 5 innings. Against lesser pitching, the Yankees rallied for 4 runs in the seventh inning and won 5-3. A second Yankee win in the nightcap, coupled with a 9-4 loss by Pedro to Tampa Bay, clinched the Yankees at least a tie for the AL East, and they clinched the title with a win over the Twins on September 30 while the Red Sox were idle. It was frustrating to see the Twins lift Santana, who gave them their best chance to win. This was particularly questionable since the Twins were still in the running for the second best record among division winners (which would keep them from having to play the Yankees in the playoffs) and since the Yankees were still in a battle for the division title. Tampa Bay Manager Lou Piniella, in contrast, was playing his regulars in the Red Sox series even though the Devil Rays were well out of contention. The Twins, who still had a lot riding on the outcome of the games, should have at least done the same.

The Pedro loss also meant that he had lost four games in a row for the first time in his career. Though the Red Sox had clinched a wild-card spot, their pitching other than Curt Schilling, had suddenly become very suspect.

Weekend series with the Orioles for the Red Sox and Blue Jays for the Yankees had now just become playoff tune-ups. The Red Sox won three of four and the Yankees lost two of three, so the final AL East standings for the season were:

	W	L	PCT	GB
New York	101	61	.623	--
Boston	98	64	.605	3
Baltimore	78	84	.481	23
Tampa Bay	70	91	.435	30 ½
Toronto	67	94	.416	33 ½

The Anaheim Angels won the AL West by 1 game over the Oakland A's, after taking two of three in a weekend series with the A's. The Red Sox had to wait until the final day of the season to see what team they would be facing in the first round of the playoffs. A loss by the Twins in their last game of the season sent the Twins to New York to face the Yankees and the Red Sox to Anaheim to face the Angels (92-70 for the season). Over in the National League, the division winners were the Cardinals, Braves, and Dodgers, and the Astros wound up winning the wild-card on the last day of the season. Only the Cardinals (105 wins) and Yankees (101) had better records than the Red Sox over the course of the season.

It was time for the playoffs.

The Possible Dream

Chapter 19 – The American League Playoffs – They Beat the Yankees!

The first order of business for the playoffs was to determine the pitching rotation. Curt Schilling deserved to be the starter in Game 1 based on his outstanding season, and he was so named. Pedro Martinez was named the starter for Game 2, and Bronson Arroyo and Tim Wakefield were identified as the starters for Games 3 and 4. Derek Lowe, who had been shaky over his last few starts, was moved to the bullpen for the ALDS.

The second order of business was to set the 25-man playoff roster. After much deliberation, Terry Francona settled on the following:

Catchers (2)	Jason Varitek, Doug Mirabelli
Infielders (8)	David Ortiz, Kevin Millar, Mark Bellhorn, Orlando Cabrera, Bill Mueller, Pokey Reese, Doug Mientkiewicz, Kevin Youkilis
Outfielders (5)	Manny Ramirez, Johnny Damon, Trot Nixon, Gabe Kapler, Dave Roberts
Starting Pitchers (4)	Curt Schilling, Pedro Martinez, Bronson Arroyo, Tim Wakefield
Relief Pitchers (6)	Keith Foulke, Mike Timlin, Alan Embree, Mike Myers, Derek Lowe, Curtis Leskanic

Left off the roster were Scott Williamson, David McCarty, Ricky Gutierrez, Byung-Hyun Kim, Terry Adams, Ramiro Mendoza, Adam Hyzdu, and Ellis Burks.

With rosters, rotation, and opponent now set, it was time to play the games.

ALDS Game 1, Oct 5, 2004 – Boston 9 Anaheim 3

The Red Sox started off their playoff run in grand fashion, beating the Angels 9-3 behind Curt Schilling. The Sox started the scoring with two out in the first. On a 3-2 count, a hit down the third base line by Manny Ramirez banged off the glove of third baseman Chone Figgins and into left field. The play was generously ruled a double though it should have been an error. On the next pitch David Ortiz hit a grounder to right that should have been knocked down by Angel second baseman Alfredo Amezaga but was not; Ramirez scored on the play. This was a good omen starting the playoffs - the plays and bounces that for years had gone against the Red Sox now seemed to be going in their favor.

Nothing in baseball favors winning more than good pitching, and for once, the Red Sox seemed to have that. New ace Curt Schilling started off the bottom of the first with a strikeout of Figgins, the Angel lead-off hitter, on three pitches. He was ready.

The 1-0 lead held until the 4th, when the Red Sox drove Angel starter Jarrod Washburn from the game with a seven-run rally. The seven runs was the biggest one-inning total in Red Sox post-season history. David Ortiz led off by walking on four pitches, and Kevin Millar followed with a home run to left field to make it 3-0. With the bases loaded and one out, Johnny Damon hit a grounder to third. Chone Figgins double clutched and then threw home wildly, allowing two runners to score, and increasing the lead to 5-0. Two batters later, Manny Ramirez blasted a drive over the centerfield fence for a three-run homer and an 8-0 lead. With Schilling on the mound, the Red Sox looked golden, and they were, cruising to a 9-3 victory in the ALDS opener.

The ninth Red Sox run was scored on a bunt single (with two outs!) in the 8th inning by Doug Mientkiewicz, scoring Johnny Damon from third (a bunt single - are these really the Red Sox?). Terry Francona gets the credit for this strategy. Great defense by Orlando Cabrera also helped the Sox hold the lead. Schilling lasted 6 2/3 innings, and was followed by Alan Embree, who got out the only batter that he faced, and Mike Timlin who closed the game by getting the Angels out 1-2-3 in both the 8th and 9th innings, striking out the side in the 9th.

Later that night in the Bronx, the Yankees were shut out by the Twins 2-0. A Ruben Sierra drive into the leftfield seats which was originally called a home run was later overturned and correctly ruled a foul ball after an umpire conference. Maybe the tide had turned after all? It remained to be seen with a lot of baseball still to be played, but the first day of the Division Series went almost exactly as the Red Sox might have planned.

ALDS Game 2, Oct 6, 2004 – Boston 8 Anaheim 3

The big question going into game 2 of the ALDS centered on Pedro Martinez – would he be the dominating Martinez of old, or the Martinez coming off four straight losses at the end of the season? It may not have been vintage Pedro, but it was much like the Pedro of old in a strong 7-inning performance that helped the Red Sox go off to a 2-0 ALDS series lead.

The Red Sox had their chances early, loading the bases in the first and second but only getting 1 run, and that on a bases loaded walk to Manny Ramirez. With two out in the second and David Ortiz up after Ramirez' walk forced in a run, Mark Bellhorn inexplicably was picked off second by Angel catcher Jose Molina. Bellhorn slipped trying to get back to the base as Molina threw but he seemed to have much too big a lead for the situation, since there was a runner on third ahead of him and since he could have scored from second with two outs on almost any hit. The play took the bat out of Ortiz' hands and took the Red Sox out of a potentially big inning.

The Angels took a 3-1 lead with two runs in the fifth inning, their first (and as it turned out, only) lead in the series. However, that lead lasted only a half inning as the Red Sox tied it in the sixth on a two-run home run by Jason Varitek. A sacrifice fly by Manny Ramirez gave Boston and Pedro a 4-3 lead in the seventh, and then the Sox put it away with four runs in the 9th inning, behind an RBI single by Trot Nixon and a three-run double by Orlando Cabrera.

The Red Sox' two pitching aces had come through and the team was heading back home to Boston on the brink of sweeping the series.

ALDS Game 3, Oct 8, 2004 – Boston 8 Anaheim 6 (10 innings)

Game 3 of the ALDS was a thriller, though it should not have been. It should have been a much easier win for Boston.

Bronson Arroyo turned in the third consecutive outstanding effort by a Boston starter, pitching 6+ innings of 3-hit ball and leaving the game with a 6-1 lead in the 7th. Boston had built up that lead behind some solid hitting by Johnny Damon and David Ortiz, but left two runners on base in each of the first, second, third, fourth, and fifth innings. The squandered opportunities were bothersome but it looked like the team had enough runs to win the game and series.

Arroyo started the seventh inning by walking Jeff DaVanon. It did not appear that Arroyo was tired, and he later said that he was not tired, but Terry Francona took him from the game at that point. I thought at the time that it was a bad move. Arroyo had been pitching excellently, having the Angels off-balance all night (except for a long home run in the fourth by Troy Glaus, he had pitched brilliantly). It was also the bottom of the Angels' order coming up with DaVanon on. I thought Arroyo should have at least pitched to the next batter. If that batter had gotten on, then maybe it would have been time to go the bullpen. If not, it seemed that Arroyo had enough to get through the bottom of the order in the seventh and then turn it over to the bullpen in the eighth. Instead, by going to the bullpen then, I thought it set up the bullpen for disaster.

Mike Myers was first in and walked the only batter that he faced. Myers' availability was thus wasted in the seventh inning when he could have been saved to be available later. This move to Myers then necessitated brining in another pitcher, Mike Timlin. Timlin, who had been a post-season star for the team in 2003 and again in the first two games of this series, just wasn't his usual sharp self. David Eckstein singled and Darrin Erstad walked (forcing in a run) and then Vladimir Guerrerro hit a game-tying and Fenway-quieting grand slam home run. Another reliever, Alan Embree had to be brought in to get the final out. By pulling Arroyo early, Francona had lost the lead and had three relief pitchers used when maybe none would have been required.

Another reliever, stopper Keith Foulke, then had to come in to get the last two outs of the eighth, and then got in trouble in the ninth. A Darrin Erstad double off the wall put Angel runners on second and third with one out. The dangerous Vladimir Guerrerro was walked intentionally to load the bases. That brought up cleanup hitter Garrett Anderson, who was to be followed by slugger Troy Glaus. The tension level at Fenway was enormously high. Foulke toughed it out, striking out both Anderson and Glaus, and keeping the game tied.

After two tough innings, it was clear that Foulke's night was finished. Because of the earlier bullpen moves, Derek Lowe and Curtis Leskanic were the only pitchers left for the Red Sox, and it was Lowe who came in for the tenth inning. The first batter hit a long drive to center field that Johnny Damon chased down in front of the wall. A walk and a sacrifice put the potential go-ahead run on second with two out. David Eckstein hit a high hopper toward short (for what used to be called "a Baltimore chop"). Shortstop Orlando Cabrera made a good play and strong throw to first, but the ball had bounced so high and took so long to get to Cabrera that Eckstein got safely to first ahead of the throw, sending the runner to third. Chone Figgins was next up and he set up to bunt on the first pitch but pulled it back. He then hit another high bouncer to short. Cabrera again made a great play taking it on the short hop. He fired to first and got Figgins out, preventing the run from scoring. It was a great play by Cabrera, one that his predecessor, Nomar, would not likely have made.

That brought the Sox up in the bottom of the tenth. Johnny Damon started things off with a shot up the middle for his third hit of the game. Mark Bellhorn laid down a good bunt to attempt to sacrifice Damon to second, but Figgins got to it quickly and threw to second. David Eckstein made a great play to get the out, stretching out on the ground, fielding the ball on a hop, while keeping his foot on the bag. Manny Ramirez then took a called third strike for the second out of the inning, and Angel Manager Mike Scioscia brought lefty Jarrod Washburn in to face David Ortiz. Ortiz blasted Washburn's first pitch into the Green Monster seats to win the game and complete the series sweep. The Fenway crowd went wild. All the Red Sox players raced out of the dugout to greet Ortiz at home. There was a lot of bouncing at home plate and a lot of hugging with Ortiz at the center of it all, as he deserved to be. It was one of the most dramatic post-season wins in Red Sox history.

- - -

While the Red Sox were winning their series with Anaheim, the Yankees were doing the same with the Twins, though it took four games and some terrible decisions on the part of Twins' manager Ron Gardenhire to do so. After winning game 1, the Twins had a lead in extra innings in Game 2, but Gardenhire left closer Joe Nathan in for three innings and the Twins blew the lead. A New York win in Game 3 in Minnesota gave the Yankees a 2-1 series lead. Gardenhire then correctly started ace Johan Santana for the pivotal Game 4, but inexplicably took him out after 5 innings, so once again the Yankees rallied, this time from a 5-1 deficit, and won the game and series. The Twins could have and should have won the series in 4 games and possibly would have done so with better managing. If Minnesota had wanted to give the series to the Yankees, they could not have done a better job.

In any case, the scene was set for another Armageddon series between the Red Sox and Yankees.

ALCS Game 1, Oct 12, 2004 – New York 10 Boston 7

The only roster change for Boston going into this series was replacing backup third baseman Kevin Youkilis with relief pitcher Ramiro Mendoza. Mike Mussina and Curt Schilling were the starting pitchers and the key stories in Game 1 of the ALCS with New York.

In a pre-game press conference Schilling talked about how nice it is to be the pitcher and in control and pitching well and being able to make 55,000 New Yorkers shut up. The words were great, and a healthy Schilling could have backed them up, but Schilling was pitching on a bad ankle; he had torn the tendons in the ankle as a result of a play in Game 1 of the Anaheim series. He started Game 1 but did not seem to be able to push off on his right foot. The Yankees got 2 runs in the first and 4 in the third, and Schilling's night was done. At this point it seemed like the right move would have been to bring Tim Wakefield to pitch, but Terry Francona instead brought in Curtis Leskanic. Interestingly, Leskanic was the only pitcher on the Red Sox roster during the ALDS who did not see action, yet he was the first person out of the bullpen against the Yankees? Ramiro Mendoza, who was not even on the Red Sox roster for the ALDS, followed him. The Yankee lead swelled to 8-0.

Meanwhile, maddeningly, Mike Mussina was pitching a perfect game for the Yankees, retiring the first 19 Red Sox batters that he faced. The worst inning for the Sox was the fourth, as Johnny Damon, Mark Bellhorn, and Manny Ramirez all were called out on strikes. How three consecutive batters could each take strike three in this situation when Mussina had been throwing strikes all night was difficult to understand, but they did and the perfect game stayed intact. With one out in the seventh Mark Bellhorn finally got a hit to break up the perfect game. The Red Sox then actually launched a comeback, cutting the lead to 8-7 in the eighth inning, with momentum on their side. However, Mike Timlin gave up hits to A-Rod and Gary Sheffield to start another Yankee rally in the eighth. Hideki Matsui was due up next and the expectation was that Francona would bring in lefty specialist Mike Myers to face both lefty-batting Matsui, who already had 5 RBI in the game, and switch-hitter Bernie Williams. He did not, making one wonder then why Myers was even on the roster. Timlin did get Matsui out, but Williams doubled in two runs, and made it to third thanks to a very weak relay throw by the usually reliable Orlando Cabrera. The lead was 10-7 and it held up for a 1-0 series lead for New York.

The news between games 1 and 2 was even worse, as it appeared that Schilling's injury was severe enough that his season would be over. The man who had been the heart and soul of the team, and a team leader, was now sidelined. Things did not look good for Boston.

ALCS Game 2, Oct 13, 2004 – New York 3 Boston 1

Things looked even worse during and after Game 2. It was Pedro Martinez on the mound for Boston and Jon Lieber for New York. Red Sox batters were again helpless in the first six innings, mustering only a single by Orlando Cabrera. The Yankees meanwhile struck right away against Martinez. Derek Jeter starting things with a leadoff first

The Possible Dream

inning walk on four pitches, not a good sign. He immediately attempted to steal second, and although Varitek's throw beat him, Bellhorn dropped the throw, so Jeter was safe. A-Rod was hit by a pitch, and Gary Sheffield singled to make it 1-0 New York. The lead held up until the sixth, when a two-run homer by John Olerud increased the lead to 3-0. Mike Timlin relieved Martinez in the seventh, but with two out and Matsui coming up, Francona brought in a lefty to face him (Alan Embree). It was a similar situation to the night before, but this time the move was made to bring in a lefty. It was hard to understand the inconsistency.

Johnny Damon, who suddenly was slumping badly, took a called third strike from Mariano Rivera to end the eighth inning with one run in and Jason Varitek on third. Rivera finished off the save in the ninth, and the teams left for Boston with the Yankees up in the series two games to none.

ALCS Game 3, Oct 16, 2004 – New York 19 Boston 8

Disgusting, Disgraceful, Despicable.

There is no better way to describe the Red Sox performance in Game 3 of the ALCS than with a "3D" summary such as that.

The final score was New York 19 Boston 8, and it was one of those games for which you can say that the score was not indicative of how much the Yankees dominated.

Bronson Arroyo started and just didn't have it in this game after pitching very well down the stretch. He lasted only 2+ innings as the Yankees got 3 in the first and 3 more in the third off of him. Jeter walked to lead off the first and raced home hard to score on a double by Rodriguez. With one out, Matsui homered, and the Yankees were immediately up 3-0.

In the bottom of the first, Manny Ramirez had an infield single with two outs, and David Ortiz followed with a single to right. Hope flickered for Red Sox fans for an instant but were immediately dashed as Ramirez was thrown out trying to go to third on the single by Ortiz to end the inning. Replays showed that Manny had actually beaten the tag, but most fans, and the Fox TV announcers, wondered why Manny had even tried for third, since he had to stop to let Ortiz' hit go by him, his team was already down 3-0, and he is not a good baserunner. This was another 'Tale of Two Cities' situation, as the contrast between Jeter scoring on a double in the top of the inning was offset by Manny getting thrown out trying to go from first to third in the bottom of the inning.

The Red Sox actually took a lead of 4-3 with 4 runs in the second inning, helped by a 2-run home run by Trot Nixon, but the lead lasted only 7 minutes, as Alex Rodriguez hit a leadoff home run in the third to tie it, and the Yanks were on their way to a big victory. It was clear that Arroyo did not have it and perhaps should have been taken out at this point, but he was left in to give up a walk and a double after the A-Rod home run before he was lifted for a reliever.

Before the top of the third completed, there was an absolutely embarrassing play that led to another Yankee run. With runners on first and third and trailing 5-4, reliever Ramiro Mendoza stepped back off the rubber, but still threw a pitch to the batter. It was clearly a balk, and an incredibly egregious error. I have never seen a major league pitcher step off the rubber and throw a pitch, but Mendoza did this at this point. A run scored to make it 6-4 New York. It was a terrible play, a gift run given by the Red Sox and former Yankee Mendoza to New York, and Mendoza should have been immediately pulled for such a bonehead play (at least Francona replaced him on the roster after the series; it was not clear how anyone could have confidence in Mendoza after this).

The Red Sox tied it 6-6 in the bottom of third, but that is as far as the drama lasted, as the Yankees bombed the Sox for 5 in the fourth and 2 more in the sixth to go up 13-6. Another 4 runs in the seventh made the score 17-6 and sent many discouraged and disheartened (two more negative 'D' words) fans home early.

Alex Rodriguez finished the day 3 for 5, with 5 runs scored and 3 RBI. Gary Sheffield was even better, finishing 4 for 5, with 3 runs scored, and 4 RBI. The best day of all, though, was Hideki Matsui's. He was 5 for 6, with 5 runs scored, and 5 RBI. Matsui was positioned to win the ALCS MVP, and the Yankees were poised for a series sweep, their 40th pennant, and continued and everlasting humiliation of the Red Sox.

Other than taking a brief lead (very brief), the only shining light for the Red Sox in this game was Tim Wakefield volunteering to pitch to help save the bullpen for the rest of the series. Wakefield had been scheduled to be the starting pitcher in Game 4 the next day, but put his team ahead of himself and went to Francona to volunteer to pitch. He did pitch 3 1/3 innings, giving up 5 runs himself to the hot-hitting Yankees, and did wind up giving up that Game 4 start as a result, but did also save the bullpen to some extent. This was yet another example of how great a team player Tim Wakefield has always been. He certainly deserved to be a winner.

The Possible Dream

No team in baseball history had ever come back from an 0-3 deficit. In fact, no team in the NBA had ever done so either, and only 2 NHL teams had done so – the 1942 Toronto Maple Leafs and the 1975 New York Islanders. A 3-0 series lead was always described in the press as "insurmountable". Given that it was the Yankees who now had that lead over the Red Sox, and given that the Yankees had just blasted the Red Sox 19-8 in Game 3, "insurmountable" did not seem strong enough a description.

In the pre-game reports and festivities before Game 4, reporter Jackie McMullan said "I'm not hearing any of these players say 'this is my chance'" (to step up and be a leader). She was right. It looked like the 2004 Red Sox season was about to end.

- - -

Who knew that sports history was about to be made – the other way!?!?

ALCS Game 4, Oct 17 (-18), 2004 – Boston 6 New York 4 (12 innings)

Down 3 games to 0 in the ALCS, down 4-3 in the ninth inning, and facing Yankee super-closer Mariano Rivera, the seemingly moribund Red Sox mounted a surprising comeback, and began an historic march to a championship. Kevin Millar opened the ninth inning with a walk, and Francona sent in pinch-runner Dave Roberts to replace the slow Millar. Roberts stole second base. That in itself was shocking – when was the last time that a Red Sox player stole a base in any kind of key situation, let alone with the team facing elimination? The stolen base would later be looked upon as a real turning point in the series and for the whole season. Bill Mueller singled up the middle to drive home the tying run. A sacrifice by pinch-hitter Doug Mientkiewicz, and an error by first baseman Tony Clark who bobbled a grounder by Johnny Damon put runners at the corners. At this point, with Orlando Cabrera up and only one out, my thought was to go for a suicide squeeze. Cabrera is a good bunter, and Rivera is a pitcher who throws strikes, and even if it didn't work, the Sox would have runners at first and second with Manny Ramirez up. That may have been too much to ask, and, in any case, that's not what Terry Francona called, and the Red Sox did not score again in the ninth. The game went on into extra innings and through many more dramatics before David Ortiz finally ended it at a little before 1:30 AM with a walk-off two-run home run in the bottom of the 12th inning off of Paul Quantrill.

Besides Ortiz, Roberts, and Mueller, there were two other big Red Sox heroes in this game: Derek Lowe and Keith Foulke. Lowe was the unexpected starting pitcher for the game (given Curt Schilling's injury in game 1 and Tim Wakefield's having to make a relief appearance in game 3). Lowe responded with 5 1/3 innings of solid pitching, giving up only 2 runs while he was in there, both coming on a two-run home run by Alex Rodriguez in the third inning. A third run was charged to him for a runner that he left on base for Mike Timlin. Lowe was the first Red Sox starter to do well, however, and the first, in fact, not to give the Yankees any first-inning runs. Keith Foulke made his earliest appearance of the season, coming to the mound in the 7th inning to relieve a shaky Timlin. Foulke responded with 2 2/3 innings of no-hit baseball to get the Red Sox into the ninth inning trailing only 4-3 and setting the stage for the dramatic comeback.

There were memorable plays galore in this one. A-Rod's home run was sent way over the Green Monster seats in left field. As Lowe prepared to pitch to Gary Sheffield, play was stopped when the ball came back over the Green Monster seats, having been thrown back by a Red Sox fan who did not want this particular souvenir. Johnny Damon retrieved the ball and threw it back over the seats and onto Lansdowne Street. However, once again the ball came back onto the field, having been thrown back by the street fans. This time the second base umpire Joe West picked up the ball and pocketed it, and play was able to resume.

Manny Ramirez had an unusual night at the plate, not taking the bat off his shoulders once during his first three at-bats (two walks and a strikeout). It was somewhat maddening to see Ramirez, the team's best hitter, not swing at all on strikes on these three at-bats with the season on the line. This is when leaders lead and that did not happen here.

There was the brilliant defense of Orlando Cabrera, who made a good play to nab a runner, Hideki Matsui, at the plate and cut off a potential Yankee run in the second inning. Terry Francona had pulled his infield in (a good move early in the game under these circumstances) and Cabrera made a nice backhanded grab of the ball that was hit to his right side and threw home to Varitek for the out tag on Matsui.

There was the shaky defensive play of Mark Bellhorn, who knocked down a grounder by Tony Clark in the sixth, but then bobbled it trying to pick it up and throw out the slow-moving Clark. The bobble allowed the Yankees to score their fourth run and take that 4-3 lead that almost held up for the series sweep.

The Possible Dream

There was a nicely placed bunt by pinch-hitter Doug Mientkiewicz that moved Bill Mueller into scoring position in the ninth. Even though this did not lead to a run, it was very good fundamental baseball.

For David Ortiz, the walk-off home run was his second in the 2004 post-season, and according to Boston radio station WEEI made him the first player in baseball history to have two walk-off post-season home runs in the same season.

Most importantly, the 6-4 win put the Red Sox back in the series. The best quote of the day came from Doug Mientkiewicz: "we have one breath left and we're going to use it." One was definitely better than none.

ALCS Game 5, Oct 18, 2004 – Boston 5 New York 4 (14 innings)

Breathing of any kind was hard to come by in the 5th game, which started at 5 PM, just 16 hours after Game 4 had finished. It would last 14 innings and almost 6 hours, and was filled with not only breath-taking, but also nail-biting, heart-stopping drama.

Pedro Martinez was the Red Sox starter and pitched well, until he hit the 100-pitch barrier that had seemed to plague him all season. A bases-loaded double by Derek Jeter on that 100th pitch in the sixth inning erased a 2-1 Pedro lead, and put the Yankees again on the brink of victory, leading 4-2.

David Ortiz blasted another big-time home run in the 8th, this time over the leftfield wall, to cut the lead to 4-3 and give Red Sox fans a little bit of hope. Then the Red Sox tied it again 4-4 with another run scratched out in very un-Boston-like style in the 8th. Kevin Millar walked, and Dave Roberts pinch-ran again for him. Yankee relief pitcher Tom Gordon seem to be unnerved by having the speedy Roberts at first, throwing over a number of times, and seemingly being more worried about Roberts at first than Trot Nixon at the plate. Nixon singled to center and the speedy Roberts raced to third with the potential tying run.

Ace reliever Mariano Rivera again came in to try to nail things down, and amazingly, for the second consecutive game, did not hold the lead and blew the potential series-winning save. Jason Varitek hit a sacrifice fly to score Roberts, and tie the game. Fenway Park was rocking, and the drama was just beginning.

Keith Foulke, who had pitched 2+ innings in Game 4, was on the mound again for the Red Sox in the eighth and ninth, and again came up big, holding New York scoreless. The ninth was especially tense. With Ruben Sierra on at first after a walk, former Boston player

Tony Clark blasted a shot to right field. Fortunately for the Red Sox, the ball bounced up into the stands for a ground rule double, and Sierra had to stop at third. He certainly would have scored easily had the ball stayed in play. Once again, this was the type of play that always had seemed to go against the Red Sox in the past. Was luck moving from the Yankee dugout to the Red Sox dugout for the first time in Boston's collective memory? With runners on second and third and with the season on the line, Foulke got Miguel Cairo to pop up to first to end the inning. The threat had been averted.

Tim Wakefield came on in the 12th, and Esteban Loaiza was pitching for the Yankees. This set up what seemed like the nightmare scenario for Red Sox fans: the valiant Wakefield being on the mound again this year as the Yankees score the series-winning run, probably on a home run by Red Sox bust Tony Clark, making a winner of Esteban Loaiza, who had been a bust himself for the Yankees since coming over in mid-season from the White Sox. But it didn't happen. Wakefield pitched 3 innings of 1-hit, shutout baseball, including one harried inning where he struck out the lead off man, only to have the third strike get past Varitek, putting the runner on. Varitek wound up with three passed balls in the inning, putting runners on second and third with two out. Wakefield, a true leader and team player as is Schilling, gave Varitek a palms down and patting "it's all right" signal after one of the passed balls, and then proceeded to make it all right himself by striking out Sierra to end the threat.

In the bottom of the 14th, Loaiza walked Johnny Damon with one out and Manny Ramirez with two out, bringing up David Ortiz, the hero from earlier in the morning. Ortiz responded and became the hero again, looping a single to center to score Damon and giving the Red Sox another improbable last-inning win.

- - -

The Red Sox had risen from the dead with two dramatic extra inning wins, and were now on their way back to New York, the scene of many disappointing defeats. However, this one had a different feel to it. Just as in 1978 the first-place Red Sox had seemed to be chasing the second-place Yankees, it now seemed that the Yankees, even still with a 3-2 lead in the series, were gasping for air and were the team in the desperate situation. This reversal of feeling was uncanny.

ALCS Game 6, Oct 19, 2004 – Boston 4 New York 2

In all of Boston Red Sox history, there is nothing to compare to Curt Schilling in Game 6 of the 2004 ALCS. Suffering from the tendon problems that had seemed to end his season, Schilling allowed surgeons to suture his tendon to his skin to keep the tendon from sliding back and forth over his ankle bone. This was a procedure that had never been done before, anywhere. The doctors doing this reportedly experimented with doing this on a couple of cadavers, and then went ahead with the procedure on Schilling. What makes this even more amazing is that the cadavers (a) clearly didn't try to put any weight on it or walk on it after the surgery and (b) certainly didn't have to try pushing off a pitching rubber on it to throw a 90 MPH fastball. The whole idea seemed pretty risky. It didn't stop Schilling though, and it did work out as he pitched the Red Sox to a victory, getting them even in the series.

After the game doctors took the sutures out of Schilling's ankle so that it wouldn't get infected. The whole procedure and experience were incredible from beginning to end. What a warrior Schilling proved himself to be yet again.

Schilling pitched 7 gutty innings, allowing only 4 hits, and 1 run, a 7th inning home run to Bernie Williams. Shots of Schilling on the mound focused on his ankle and viewers around the country could see blood seeping through the white sanitary stocking on Schilling's foot. It was clear that this was no ordinary injury. It was even more clear that this was no ordinary man.

The Red Sox backed him with four big runs in the fourth inning. Kevin Millar doubled and scored on an RBI single by Jason Varitek to break the ice and give the Red Sox and Schilling a 1-0 lead. Orlando Cabrera also singled, and then Mark Bellhorn homered to left to score three runs and make it a 4-0 game.

The home run was initially called a double by the leftfield umpire, but replays showed clearly that the ball had hit a fan in the stomach area and then bounced back into the field. Matsui, playing left field, stopped and did not go after the ball, again an indication that he knew it was gone. For some reason, however, the leftfield umpire did not call it a home run. Baseball officials had to be wondering what he was doing, since MLB adds umpires in the post-season specifically to man the leftfield and rightfield lines in the outfield and ensure that calls like this are made correctly. Their job is two-fold: (1) make sure that calls are correct on fair or foul, and (2) make sure that calls are correct on home run or not. This umpire had clearly failed his second responsibility. Fortunately, all the umpires convened (something that would not have been done in previous years) and reversed the call, correctly giving Bellhorn the home run and the Red Sox a 4-0 lead. A key call was reversed and the reversal favored Boston. It was hard to believe. Did the Yankees know then that history was about to be reversed?

More drama and tension were waiting for Boston fans in the eighth and ninth innings. Bronson Arroyo replaced Schilling at the start of the eighth inning and gave up a double to the pesky Miguel Cairo and an RBI single to Derek Jeter. That brought up Alex Rodriguez, who was representing the potential tying run. Rodriguez hit a roller down the first base line. Arroyo came over from the mound to field it, but so did Mientkiewicz coming down from first, so there was no one covering first for Arroyo to throw it to. He had to make a tag. The next thing that fans saw was the ball flying down the rightfield line having been knocked from Arroyo's glove, Jeter scoring to make it 4-3, and A-Rod standing at second base in position to score the tying run. It looked like bad things were about to happen to the Red Sox again.

Replays showed, however, that A-Rod had knocked the ball out of Arroyo's glove by slapping his arm, clearly an illegal play. Once again the umpires converged and once again they reversed the call in Boston's favor. After a few minutes of discussion, they called A-Rod out for interference, and returned Jeter to first base. Arroyo got Sheffield to foul out to Varitek, and the lead stayed at 4-2.

The interference call was the correct one (did the Yankees know then that history was about to be reversed?), though it did not stop fans from throwing debris on the field in protest. Riot police had to be brought in to man positions on the foul lines. The police stayed there through the top of the ninth, but then, with the Red Sox coming out to the field, inexplicably left the field. A rational thinker might think that more protection or police presence would be necessary with the Red Sox in the field and that the fans would be more likely then to throw things, but that was apparently not what Yankee Stadium Security personnel believed.

Keith Foulke came on in the ninth for his third consecutive high-pressure outing. He walked Matsui to open the ninth, increasing the level of nervousness among Sox fans. He also walked Ruben Sierra with two out, bringing up Tony Clark in the continuing nightmare scenario that Clark could win the pennant with one swing of the bat and a home run. The count ran to 3-2, but then Foulke struck Clark out swinging on a nasty pitch to end the game.

It was unbelievable! The Red Sox had become the first team in baseball history to force a seventh game after falling behind three games to none in a series. They had done it by beating the Yankees in Yankee Stadium in Game 6. It was now on to Game 7, and with all of the pitching changes that had been made in Games 3-6, neither manager was sure as Tuesday night ended who would be their starting pitcher in Game 7 on Wednesday night.

One way or another, history was about to be made.

ALCS Game 7, Oct 20, 2004 – Boston 10 New York 3 !!!!!

While in all of Boston Red Sox history there was nothing to compare to Curt Schilling in Game 6 of the 2004 ALCS, it is even more so that in all of Boston sports history of any kind, there is nothing to compare with what happened in Game 7. The Red Sox reversed eight decades of history and frustration at the hands of the New York Yankees.

It was Derek Lowe against Kevin Brown, and Derek Lowe was absolutely brilliant. He pitched 6 innings of 1-hit, 1-run baseball. Meanwhile, the Red Sox hitters exploded for a thrilling 10-3 win that sent the Red Sox off to their first World Series since 1986.

- - -

The game got off to a nervous start for Boston. Johnny Damon, mired in a series-long slump, singled and stole second. With one out, Manny Ramirez singled to left. Damon had to slow down before seeing the ball go through into left field. Matsui fielded the ball as Damon got to third, but, surprisingly, Damon was waved home by oft-criticized third base coach Dale Sveum. Matsui threw in to Jeter who relayed to the plate well in time for Posada to tag Damon out. For many fans, the thought was probably "here we go again" with the Red Sox running into outs, accumulating missed opportunities, and falling short when they seemed so close to winning. Those thoughts settled down immediately though, as David Ortiz rocketed a home run into the rightfield seats on the very next pitch for a 2-0 Boston lead.

Kevin Millar got things started with a one-out single in the second inning. After Kevin Brown walked Bill Mueller and Orlando Cabrera, Yankee Manager Joe Torre replaced him with Javier Vasquez. That move backfired as Vasquez' first-pitch fast ball was hit high and deep and into the rightfield seats by Johnny Damon for a grand slam home run. In the biggest game of their lives, the Red Sox suddenly were ahead 6-0.

Derek Jeter singled in the third to drive in Miguel Cairo, who had been hit by a pitch and had stolen second (amazingly, that turned out to be the only hit in the game for New York off Derek Lowe). The score was now 6-1, but that run started Red Sox fans worrying again. However, the now red-hot Johnny Damon blasted another home run off Vasquez in the fourth, a two-run shot. This one was a blast into the upper deck in right, and the Sox were now amazingly up 8-1. Could this really be happening?

The lead held up through the sixth inning. After the Red Sox went out in the top of the seventh, everyone sat through another of those interminable seventh inning stretches at Yankee Stadium. Like many fans, I have no problems with the singing of "God Bless America" in the seventh inning stretch, but other parks just get it done; at Yankee Stadium it takes forever. I timed it in one playoff game at 5 minutes and 40 seconds between the last pitch of the top of the seventh and first of the bottom of the eighth. There is a long, slow introduction. Then the singer – in this case Ronan Tynan – slowly walks out to the field, then sings a preamble to the song that no one is familiar with. Then he sings the song, v-e-r-y s-l-o-w-l-y. Then players come back onto the field. It is just too long (as long as reading about it just now may have felt).

At this point, the Red Sox surprisingly brought Pedro Martinez in to relieve Lowe. This was a maddening move for a number of reasons:

- Lowe was pitching a 1-hitter when he was taken out.

- Lowe had only thrown 69 pitches (admittedly he was working on just two days rest, but he had not been used a lot before his start in Game 4, so he was not exactly suffering from overwork).

- Lowe is a sinkerball pitcher, so even if he was tired, a tired sinkerball pitcher will still generally throw low, inducing ground balls, not home runs.

- Lowe had just retired the top three hitters in the Yankee lineup in order in the sixth, getting Jeter to ground to short, A-Rod to ground to short, and Sheffield to strike out.

- The Yankee Stadium crowd was quiet with their team behind 8-1, and bringing Pedro in would get them up and chanting, "Who's Your Daddy", so bringing Pedro in would get the crowd back into the game.

- The first Yankee batter was Hideki Matsui who had been red-hot earlier in the series and who had been hitting Pedro well for the last two seasons.

- Bringing Pedro in would mean that if the Red Sox actually won and went to the World Series, he would now be unable to start Game 1 of the World Series (as he could have done had he not been used).

The Possible Dream

I thought that the right move would have been to have Lowe start the seventh and bring in relief only if the Yankees got a couple of runners on. I thought that bringing Pedro in at that point was playing into the Yankees' hands and setting them up for a potential rally.

As expected, Yankee fans started chanting, "Who's Your Daddy" and were now back in the game. Also predictably Matsui started with a double, and the Yankees rallied for 2 runs, cutting the lead to 8-3. How they scored is something that won't be recorded here, since I left the room yelling and not wanting to watch, and went to log on to get some work done. Unfortunately, I couldn't stay away, and so returned with the Red Sox batting in the eighth.

Not predictably, in that eighth inning, Mark Bellhorn got a run back on a solo home run off the rightfield foul pole. The ball made an audible clang as it hit the pole, amidst the cloud of silence that now engulfed Yankee Stadium. The Yankee fans now seemed to know that it was over. Did the Yankee players also?

Interestingly, all nine Red Sox runs up to this point were scored on home runs off the Bronx Bombers and all four home runs were hit to right field, the field patrolled by Babe Ruth and the seats into which he hit most of his 714 career home runs. History was indeed in the process of being reversed.

Orlando Cabrera knocked in another run in the top of the ninth to make it 10-3. Still, Red Sox fans were not sure. Could this really be happening?

Mike Timlin was the pitcher as the ninth inning started (he had come on in the eighth and had gotten Jeter, A-Rod, and Sheffield 1-2-3). The ever-troublesome Matsui reached, but Timlin got the next two batters, Bernie Williams on a ground out, and Jorge Posada on a pop up. Kenny Lofton walked, and Terry Francona came out to replace Timlin with Alan Embree. Ruben Sierra came up to pinch hit for John Olerud.

The first pitch to Sierra was ball one. The second was hit weakly toward second base. When the camera shifted from the batter to the field, it was clear that it should be an easy play for Pokey Reese, in as a defensive replacement for Bellhorn. It was indeed an easy play. Reese scooped it up and tossed it to defensive replacement Doug Mientkiewicz at first base for the out that ended 86 years of Red Sox frustration at the hands of the Yankees.

- - -

The series was over! The Red Sox had become the first team in the history of baseball to come back from an 0-3 deficit to win a post-season series. They had done it against the Yankees. They had done it in Yankee Stadium. They had avenged in three days the bitter losses to the Yankees in 1978, 2003, 1949, and numerous other years. They had finally turned this Yankee-Red Sox match-up into a real rivalry.

The shoe was now on the other foot, as it were, and the Yankees would now be facing an off-season of criticism, second-guessing, and fan scrutiny such as they had never experienced previously.

Never again would the Red Sox have to endure all of the comments about 1978, about the Yankee superiority over the Red Sox. Never again would any lead over the Yankees be as much a cause for consternation as it has for oh so many years.

For Red Sox fans or Boston sports fans, there is no way to describe this. Absolutely no way. It was great when the Celtics won championships, especially in 1984, 1974, 1968, 1966, 1969, but always. It is still amazing that the long-dreadful New England Patriots have won two Super Bowls and are generally regarded as being the best team in the NFL and maybe all of sports (the Patriots?). The 1967 Red Sox were and always will be the favorite sports team of all time for many fans. But nothing in sports will ever -- ever -- bring a bigger smile to the face of Boston fans today, tomorrow, and in years to come than the 2004 Red Sox coming back from 0-3 down to beat the Yankees. Finally! Unbelievably! The Red Sox had beaten the Yankees.

The Possible Dream

Chapter 20 – The World Series: Winning it All

It was a glorious few days for Red Sox fans everywhere after the ALCS. The team had finally exorcised one demon -- one major demon -- that had haunted them for many years, the New York Yankees. Now there was one left: capturing the World Series title that had eluded them for over eight decades.

To their credit, headlines in New York's newspapers were as clever in New York defeat as they had been when New York was lording it over the Red Sox in years' past, and even within this season, as described previously in the 2004 season summary. The front and back page of the New York Post had headlines that read "Damned Yankees" and "What a Choke". The Daily News front page headline was "The Choke's on Us", with a subtitle on the front page of "Worst Postseason collapse in Baseball History". The Daily News back page was the best of the bunch as it showed a picture of a celebrating Red Sox player with arms raised skyward, underneath the headline "Hell Freezes Over".

As the Sox fans basked in the glow of this victory, they also watched the St. Louis Cardinals advance to the World Series with two dramatic Game 6 and Game 7 wins of their own. Jim Edmonds hit a walkoff home run to win Game 6, and the Cardinals came back from being behind 2-1 in Game 7 to defeat Roger Clemens and the Houston Astros 4-2. The big hits were a tying double by Albert Pujols and a two-run home run by Scott Rolen.

The Cardinals had a very tough lineup, with a powerful 2-3-4-5 combination of Larry Walker, Pujols, Rolen, and Edmonds. Pujols was generally considered to be one of the best hitters in baseball, and he, Edmonds, and Rolen were all considered NL MVP candidates. The Cardinals had led the major leagues by winning 105 games, and were undefeated at home in the National League Playoffs. They played in a great baseball town and had terrific fan support. History was also on their side, as they had defeated the Red Sox in seven games in both the 1946 and 1967 World Series. The Red Sox had many more demons to exorcise.

The final roster move of the 2004 season was to replace pitcher Ramiro Mendoza with third baseman Kevin Youkilis. The move was made to get another bat on the roster, since three of the games were scheduled for St. Louis where no Designated Hitter could be used, and more pinch-hitters were needed. The move may also have been made as a result of Mendoza's horrendous performance in the ALCS, including a step-off-the-rubber and throw-a-pitch-anyway balk that had plated a run for the Yankees in Game 1. It was good to see Mendoza gone, but I would have been more tempted to replace him with another pitcher, precisely because baseball in National League parks also often require more pitchers. I would have also replaced him with a pitcher given Curt Schilling's fragile ankle situation, which may have required all the other starters to start games and left just a 5-man bullpen. If he had been healthy, Scott Williamson would have been my choice for the 11th pitcher. If Williamson was not healthy, Terry Adams would have been the choice.

In any case, the roster was set, and Terry Francona set his pitching rotation. Tim Wakefield was to start Game 1. Curt Schilling was to get his ankle re-sutured and start Game 2. For the games in St. Louis, it would be Pedro Martinez and Derek Lowe. Lowe was now back in the rotation after his great performances against the Yankees. Bronson Arroyo was shifted to the bullpen, but the thought was that he might have to be moved back into the rotation if Schilling's ankle could not hold up.

2004 World Series Game 1, Oct 23, 2004 – Boston 11 St. Louis 9

ALCS hero David Ortiz got the Red Sox off and running quickly in the first inning, belting a three-run home run in his first World Series at-bat. The only other Red Sox player to accomplish that feat was pitcher Jose Santiago, who hit an improbable home run off Cardinal ace Bob Gibson in Game 1 of the 1967 World Series. Kevin Millar followed Ortiz' home run by blasting a double off the leftfield wall. He scored on a single by Bill Mueller, and the Red Sox had a quick 4-0 first inning lead. An early lead was the perfect antidote for what could have been a letdown after the win over New York.

The Cardinals battled back to 4-2 after 2 ½ innings, with one run scoring on a big solo home run by Larry Walker. The Red Sox came back and chased Cardinals' starter Woody Williams from the game with a 3-run fourth, with Damon, Cabrera, and Ramirez each getting an RBI. However, Wakefield's control escaped him in the fourth, as he walked the first three batters of the inning. Mike Matheny hit a sacrifice fly to score one run, and another scored on a throwing error by Kevin Millar (into the Cardinals' dugout) on the relay from the

The Possible Dream

outfield. Another run scored on a fielder's choice cut what had been a 7-2 Red Sox lead to 7-5.

The Cardinals pulled even in the sixth, and again Red Sox fielding failed them. Cardinal left fielder So Taguchi hit a bouncer to the infield that Bronson Arroyo threw away, and Edgar Renteria and Larry Walker each doubled home a run. It was 7-7 and all of the worries of Red Sox fans had returned.

The roller-coaster ride that watching the Red Sox has always been continued. In the seventh, Mark Bellhorn and Orlando Cabrera walked, and Manny singled up the middle for a run. With Ortiz due up, St. Louis Manager Tony LaRussa signaled to the bullpen for his only left-hander, Ray King. Ortiz hit a shot to second that bounced up into second baseman Tony Womack and bounced hard into his left collarbone. The ball bounced into short right field and another run scored for a 9-7 Boston lead. Womack was in obvious pain, and had to leave the game. He had lost feeling in his arm and hand (though he would recover and start again the next night).

The Cardinals came back and tied it again in the eighth. Mike Matheny started the rally with a single off Mike Timlin. With switch-hitter Roger Cedeno up to pinch-hit, Francona brought in Alan Embree to replace Timlin. It was not clear why, since now Cedeno turned around to bat righty in a park built for right-handed hitters. Cedeno singled to put runners on first and second (pitcher Jason Marquis was the pinch-runner for Matheny at second base and stumbled rounding second, so he was not able to go to third on the hit). At this point Embree was taken out even though the dangerous lefty Larry Walker (already a perfect 4-for-4 at the plate at this point) was now on deck. Edgar Renteria then grounded a single into left field. Marquis initially stopped at third, but Manny misplayed the hit for the third Red Sox error of the night, and Marquis, seeing the misplay, raced home to make it 9-8. Larry Walker then lofted a fly ball to left. Manny came in, started to slide, slid awkwardly, and had the ball hit the back of his glove and bounce toward the leftfield stands. Another run scored on yet another Red Sox error, and it was suddenly tied 9-9.

This was the Red Sox fourth error of the game, and every error had led to Cardinal runs. The game had the makings of a disaster.

Julian Tavarez came in to pitch for St. Louis in the bottom of the eighth. An error by shortstop Edgar Renteria, the only St. Louis error of the game, put Jason Varitek on first base. Mark Bellhorn then hit his third home run in as many games, a shot off "Pesky's Pole", the right field foul pole (his second consecutive game hitting a home run off of the rightfield foul pole), and the Red Sox hung on for an 11-9 victory.

The Red Sox won despite committing four errors, four very costly errors, and despite having their starter last only 3 2/3 innings. Maybe it was the Red Sox year after all?

2004 World Series Game 2, Oct 24, 2004 – Boston 6 St. Louis 2

Curt Schilling forever etched himself into Red Sox lore with an absolutely courageous pitching performance in Game 2.

The Red Sox scored six runs on 3 two-out hits: a first inning two-out triple by Varitek to the triangle in right following walks to Ramirez and Ortiz, a fourth inning double to the base of the centerfield wall by Mark Bellhorn, and a sixth inning single off the leftfield wall by Orlando Cabrera. The Red Sox once again overcame four errors, including three by third baseman Bill Mueller and one by second baseman Mark Bellhorn, to win a game. Embree, Timlin, and Foulke rounded out the win.

However, THE story, before, during, and after the game, was Curt Schilling.

He had once again on Saturday had the procedure to suture his skin to the tendon in his ankle. However, this time, he woke up at 7:00 on Sunday morning; he was in great pain and had difficulty even walking, as he described in the post-game press conference. He called the trainers and after examining him, they wound up removing one of the sutures, which had irritated a nerve and caused the problem. He did wind up pitching, which he was not sure that he could do when he woke up, and he once again pitched brilliantly. He lasted six innings, and only gave up 4 hits and 1 walk. The only run scored off him was unearned, having been scored on a two-out error by Bill Mueller in the fourth inning, as Mueller could not handle a ground ball bouncing to his right with a runner on third.

It was also obvious that Schilling was not as strong as he had been on the mound in New York. He seemed to limp more than he had that night, and there was at least one instance where he squatted down and looked like he was trying to relieve some pressure or pain from the ankle. Once again there was blood on his sock, and since Schilling knew that the camera would focus on that, he had written a message on his shoe for the cameras to pick up. The message was simply "K ALS", a message to strike out ALS (Lou Gehrig's disease), a cause for which Curt and Shonda Schilling contribute greatly.

In the post-game press conference, Schilling showed just how much of a man he is. He started by saying that he would never use the words "unbelievable" and "Lord" in the same sentence. He responded with modesty to questions about whether what he did was

The Possible Dream

"courageous" or "brave". He responded to a question about whether he would be able to pitch again in Game 6 if need be by saying that he wasn't thinking about that yet, that he just wanted to enjoy what was happening. The first time that he smiled was when one of the questioners asked him about a teammate, Jason Varitek. Schilling took the opportunity to compliment Varitek's play, play-calling, etc. Lastly, when asked about how he felt in the sixth inning when two-out errors on grounders to Mueller and Bellhorn put runners on first and second and brought up the potential tying run, he responded that it isn't often that a pitcher gets to pick up the guys in the field who do it for him all the time, and he was glad to be able to do it. What a teammate.

It isn't often that a man overshadows an event as much as Schilling overshadowed the World Series on this night. Despite what he may have said, Schilling was a real hero, to fans, to his teammates, and maybe most importantly, to anyone stricken with ALS who could take some inspiration from him. Quite simply, he deserves every accolade that he will get.

2004 World Series Game 3, Oct 26, 2004 – Boston 4 St. Louis 1

What more could a Red Sox fan ask for than a 2-0 series lead and Pedro about to take the mound for Game 3? Of course, this being the Red Sox, anything is possible in that situation, but what should have happened actually DID happen. Pedro was superb. He overcame a shaky start to pitch 7 innings of 3-hit shutout baseball. He retired the last 14 batters that he faced, and only one of those got the ball out of the infield. The Red Sox 4-1 win put them one win away from that extremely elusive World Series title.

- - -

As they had in the first three games of the World Series and in the 7th game of the ALCS, the Red Sox jumped out to a first inning lead. It was Manny Ramirez supplying the power this time with a huge home run to left field in Busch Stadium.

The lead almost fell quickly in the first inning. The Cardinals loaded the bases on a one out walk to Larry Walker followed by an infield hit by Albert Pujols and a walk to Scott Rolen. The Pujols hit was actually a generous gift of official scoring, as it should have been another error charged to Bill Mueller. Jim Edmonds then lifted a fly to shallow left for the second out. Walker tagged at third and tried to score on the play but was thrown out at the plate to end the inning. Jason Varitek acted as if the throw was not coming in and then grabbed the one-hop throw from Ramirez to easily tag Walker out. Albert Pujols also seemed to be running on the fly ball and could have been doubled off second, as the Cardinals suddenly seemed to be developing the type of baserunning problems that had always seemed to plague the Red Sox in the past.

The 1-0 lead was threatened again in the third inning. Pitcher Jeff Suppan led off with a slow roller down the third base line for a hit. Edgar Renteria than blasted a shot to right field that bounced off the warning track and wall. Trot Nixon slipped on the turf, which was still wet from heavy pre-game rains and fell, but Suppan was only able to make it to third, with Renteria pulling up at second with a double. With runners now on second and third, Larry Walker hit an easy bouncer to second. The Red Sox were conceding the run, as Mark Bellhorn didn't even look to third but threw to first for the out. Fortunately for Boston, Jeff Suppan did not come home on the grounder. He was hung up between third and home. First Baseman David Ortiz, playing in the field since there was no DH in the National League park fired a bullet to Bill Mueller who tagged out Suppan for a big double play. Replays showed both the Cardinal third base coach and manager disgusted with the play.

In his post-game press conference, Tony LaRussa said that Jose Oquendo, the third base coach, had yelled "Go, go" to Suppan, but Suppan heard "No, no". This was similar to a key play that had worked against the Red Sox in the 1975 World Series, when Denny Doyle heard "Go, Go" instead of the "No, no" that third base coach Don Zimmer said that he was yelling. Doyle was thrown out at the plate in a tie game in the ninth inning. Could the world have really turned upside down? What used to work against the Red Sox was now working for them. Odd plays such as that one from 1975 were now being negated by plays like this from the other side. Sometimes it is true that what goes around comes around and this seemed -- finally -- to be the case for the Red Sox in 2004.

A Bill Mueller double and Trot Nixon single in the fourth made it 2-0. A Johnny Damon double in the fifth followed by singles by Cabrera, Ramirez, and Mueller plated two and ended the Red Sox scoring for the night.

Pedro continued his magnificent pitching through the seventh. Mike Timlin pitched a perfect eighth. Keith Foulke retired the side in the ninth, although he did give up a home run to Larry Walker to make the final 4-1.

The Red Sox were now up in the series 3 games to none. They were on the brink of what would be an incredible championship.

The Possible Dream

2004 World Series (the anxious hours between Games 3 and 4)

With a 3-0 series lead, there was excitement all around Boston and with Red Sox fans everywhere. There was some nervous confidence that the team would finally win that championship. However, Red Sox fans were still very worried. There was a Derek Lowe, coming off a shaky 2004 season, set to pitch Game 4. There was a knuckleballer (always risky) ready to go in Game 5 in Tim Wakefield. There was an uncertain injury situation involving Curt Schilling for Game 6 (including talk that another suturing would not be possible). There was fear that the Cardinals were primed to start hitting as they did all season. Nothing is ever easy for the Red Sox or their fans.

The feeling was eerily different, however. Fans and writers began talking about a potential championship, and for once it did not seem to be completely out of line. This was not akin to painting a World Series logo at Fenway in 2003 when there was still a Game 7 to be played at the Yankee Stadium house of horrors. This was a feeling of the quiet confidence that comes from watching a winner, not the trepidation that comes from watching a team trying to overcome a pile of negative history on top of their sagging shoulders.

My son, Mike, a Red Sox fan since he was a year old in 1975, and now the author of an interesting web site with commentary on politics, sports, and entertainment (www.bunkosquad.com), was inspired by columns that he had seen elsewhere, including the "Sons of Sam Horn" web site to write this column describing people for whom he was hoping that the Red Sox would win it:

Win It For

Win it for Ted and Yaz and Bobby and Johnny Pesky and Pudge and Dewey and Jim Ed. A part of every single one of them will be holding that trophy soon.

Win it for Ellis Burks, whose career has taken him some interesting places. And when they hand out the rings in April, let Greenie come running onto the field and crash into him one last time.

Win it for Jay, and Mark, and Dave and Peter and John and Fred and Pat, and Eric and Brian, and Jimmy, and Hillary, and Kentucky Jim, and Mark, and Cheryl, and Travis, and Kathy and Kerry, and John and Liz, and Alex, and Chris, and Steve and Churchill and Amy and Hilary and Cathy, and Mark and Carole and Mike, and Dana and Terri, and Amanda and Tony, and Vicki and Jeanne and Molly and Justin. This is a rough chrononological list of every friend who's shared my Red Sox mania (mostly at Fenway) for at least three hours. Amazing how many people will be going through my mind this month, thinking, "I wonder how they feel".

Win it for Dan Shaughnessy, who can finally move on and write something else soon. For Joe and Jerry, who've grown on me exponentially over the last couple years. Digress away, fellas; no one wears their hearts on their sleeves more. For Sean and Don and Jerry, all a million times more worthy of being in the booth tonight than these Fox guys. Why can't the World Series be simulcast on NESN?

Win it for Sooz, and show her I wasn't kidding when I said this would happen someday. With any luck there'll be a critical balk tonight.

Win it for Yves, a born-and-bred New Yorker who made the risky decision to voluntarily become a Red Sox fan. Justify his love.

Win it for my sister Christine. I don't know exactly when the switch went on that turned her into a lifelong fan (probably about the time Tim Wakefield arrived in town, heh heh) but she's there. And for everyone sitting in the bleachers with me and her on 4/15/1997, still the most fun evening I've ever spent at a ballpark.

Win it for my three grandparents who aren't here to watch this team. For Grandpa Frank; I don't think "they stink" anymore! For Grandpa Walter and Grandma Helen: wherever they're watching this Series from, I hope they're not sitting behind a pole.

Win it for my Grandma Ann. She had a triple bypass two weeks ago; at one point while she was recuperating, my Aunt Carol told her how the Red Sox came from behind and beat the Yankees. Grandma nodded and drifted off to sleep. A few minutes later, she woke up out of the blue and yelled, "The Red Sox won!" She was two years old in that far-off, mythical land we know so well as 1918. There's literally no one who's been alive and waiting for this moment longer.

Win it for my Dad. He claimed for a long time that he'd given up on the Red Sox. Yeah, right. But during some down time last summer, he wrote a book about how the team could turn itself around. Then when they announced that Schilling would be starting the second game of the 2004 season, he bought plane and game tickets to Baltimore. If this season has been about one thing, it's been about new beginnings. I think he's enjoyed *his* new beginning with this team.

Win it for my Mom. That book my Dad wrote? She got to hear every bit of raw material that went into it...and a million more besides. Sometimes a little louder than she *wanted* to hear it. But who else talked about (literally) dancing in the street every time Greenwell

The Possible Dream

homered in the '95 Pennant Race? Who else got such a kick out of every defensive indifference call, and every manufactured run? This one's for you, Mom. After all these years, they've finally played to their level.

One more.

That feeling seemed to be pervasive. As a potential championship drew ever closer, many Red Sox fans thought about lost loved ones and current family and friends, and what a Red Sox win would mean, or would have meant, to them. There are very few other teams, fans, or experiences, like this in sports anywhere. Everyone was now set for Game 4 ...

2004 World Series Game 4, Oct 27, 2004 – Boston 3 St. Louis 0

UNBELIEVABLE !!!

All of the accumulated worries and concerns of Red Sox fans faded away forever at 11:40 PM Eastern time on October 27, 2004 as Keith Foulke fielded a bouncer hit back to the mound by Edgar Renteria with two outs in the ninth. Foulke took a few steps over to first, took a few more steps over toward first, and then made a nice, easy, underhanded toss to Doug Mientkiewicz for the out that ended the inning, the World Series, and 86 years of frustration for the Red Sox and their fans.

All over New England, at least, and in many other places around the country, the scene was probably one of family and friends hugging or high-fiving. Many fans thought of loved ones who had passed away after watching and waiting for years for this moment.

The Red Sox were champions of the world!

- - -

The World Series was easier than expected. The Red Sox never trailed. They were only tied twice, at 7-7 and 9-9 in game 1. At all other times, they were in the lead. There was never an inning in the series in which they did not have a lead for at least part of that inning. They scored in the first inning in every game.

Their sweep made them the first team in baseball history to win eight straight games in a post-season, breaking the old mark of seven. Their three top starters did not give up an earned run. Curt Schilling pitched six innings and allowed no earned runs in his courageous Game 2 (the only run was unearned, scoring on a Bill Mueller two-out

The Possible Dream

error). Pedro Martinez pitched seven shutout innings in a masterful Game 3 performance. Derek Lowe pitched seven shutout innings in a dominating performance in Game 4. The only run that the Cardinals scored in the two games in St. Louis was on a meaningless ninth inning home run by Larry Walker in Game 3. The Red Sox simply dominated the World Series.

Game 4 got off on exactly the right foot in the top of the first with a leadoff home run by Johnny Damon on the fourth pitch of the game. The Sox and Lowe were quickly up 1-0.

The lead was extended to 3-0 in the third on a two-out bases loaded double by Trot Nixon. Nixon's hit came as he was given a green light to swing by Terry Francona on a 3-0 count. Nixon blasted the ball of the wall in right center, narrowly missing a grand slam home run. Francona's move was a good one, as he expected a fastball by Cardinals' starter Jason Marquis, and Marquis obliged.

Meanwhile, Derek Lowe was continuing his outstanding streak of post-season pitching, retiring 13 Cardinals in a row between the first and fourth innings. He finished his seven-inning stint giving up only three hits and 1 walk. Bronson Arroyo and Alan Embree got the Cardinals in the eighth, and Keith Foulke came in to end it all in the ninth.

In the ninth, after an Albert Pujols lead off single, Foulke retired cleanup hitter Scott Rolen (who would wind up hitless for the entire series) and struck out power-hitting Jim Edmonds. It was the third time in four at-bats in the series that Foulke had struck out Edmonds, whose only hit in the series was a bunt single against a shifted infield in Game 1. The # 3-4-5 hitters in the Cardinals lineup were only 6-for-45 in the series, a great tribute to Red Sox pitching.

That brought Edgar Renteria to the plate, and that led to the bouncer back to the pitcher that ended the series.

All of the demons were now exorcised, and all of the bad things and turns of fate that had seemed to go against the Red Sox for many years, now had gone in their favor. This included one final piece of irony. Renteria's uniform number was 3, the same as the number worn by Babe Ruth. Retiring the Cardinals #3 to finish off a long-awaited championship also symbolically retired the too-often mentioned Curse of the Bambino.

In so many ways, history had definitely been reversed. The feeling was amazing.

The Possible Dream

SECTION 3 – THE POSSIBLE DREAM

Chapter 21 – To Wake as Champions

A lot of Red Sox fans probably woke up on Thursday, October 28, 2004 (those that went to sleep anyway) and immediately checked newspapers, television, or radio, to make sure that it actually happened, or to relive how it did. For almost all Red Sox fans, this was the first time ever that they had woken up with their team as champions. It was still hard to believe that the Red Sox won it. The positive feeling was simply great.

- - -

The evening before, after the third out was made, the streets of Boston were filled with people celebrating. People walked around Boston, Cambridge, and other cities, and many congregated around Fenway Park. Horns were honking and people were congratulating each other or slapping high-fives. Strangers walking the streets were slapping hands with people driving past them in cars. Boston was euphoric.

- - -

A lot of writers and commentators speculated that it would be disappointing and a major letdown for Red Sox fans and followers that the team actually won. They were wrong. That has not been the case at all. Everyone was reveling in the win, and it seemed as if it would continue for some time to come.

Part of this may be due to the fact that they have not won for so so long that it would be hard to have a letdown when they did.

Part of this also may be due to how they won, and whom they had to beat to do so: the powerful Yankees who had always haunted them (one might say "who had always been their daddy"). At last, this so-called rivalry had become a real rivalry.

Also, the Red Sox, more than the Patriots, Braves, Pistons, Knicks, Marlins, or most other teams, seemed to link generations together. The columns asking the Red Sox to "Win it For" all those people was an example of that. In all of professional sports, this is true for perhaps only the Red Sox and Cubs. The positive cross-generational feelings of Red Sox or Cubs fans were not the types of feelings that would fade away quickly, if at all.

Another claim was that, by winning, the Red Sox would now become just another team, like the Marlins, or Phillies, or Indians, or Tigers; the idea was that by having lost and lost so dramatically over the years, the Red Sox had built a unique tradition, and that this tradition would now be lost. However, it seemed extremely unlikely that the Red Sox would become "just another team", especially after a wait of so many years, culminated in the way that they beat the Yankees. At least they wouldn't be just another team during the 2004-2005 off-season and 2005 season. After that remains to be seen, but it still seems unlikely.

- - -

There was one interesting obituary in the Worcester paper the day after the World Series. An elderly woman died on the night of Game 4. The obituary said that she was a life-long Red Sox fan, who died peacefully shortly after the Red Sox scored the winning run in Wednesday night's game. The assumption is that this happened after Damon's home run, but that was poignant and sad. At least she got to live to see the team get to the precipice of the great victory. May she rest in peace.

- - -

The Red Sox victory parade was held on Saturday, October 30. Boston did it in classy fashion. There was a ceremony in Fenway before the parade in which team officials and many players spoke (along with Boston Mayor Tom Menino and Massachusetts Governor Mitt Romney). After the ceremonies, players boarded Boston's amphibious duck-tour vehicles, rode a parade route through the streets, and then had the duck boats go into the Charles River so that fans could see them from the Boston and Cambridge shores. It was a great idea. The estimates were that a crowd of over 3 million people attended the parade, and it was orderly (thankfully).

- - -

The Red Sox also did well to include lots of people in the celebration. They even flew up the man who is their clubhouse attendant at the spring training site in Fort Myers to attend a World Series game and take part in the celebration. These new owners at least are doing things the right way.

- - -

The Possible Dream

It also must be said that the Yankees also did things the right way after losing to Boston. There were stories about the Yankee Stadium people keeping the lights on after Game 7 and letting Boston fans go onto the field and take pictures. That is classy. Tim Wakefield especially appreciated them keeping the lights on. He talked about going out after a lot of people had left the field to stand on the mound at Yankee Stadium which he walked off as a loser on the Aaron Boone home run last year. He said he was thinking about all that has happened in the year since. It was a nice touch all around.

- - -

Curt Schilling had surgery in November to repair his injured ankle, and he and his wife Shonda appeared shortly thereafter at a reception held by the ALS Association for people who had participated in the "Curt's Pitch for ALS" fund-raiser.

It isn't often that reality meets expectation, especially when you are talking about an athlete or celebrity of any kind, but it was absolutely the case with Schilling. He came across as an outstanding human being who understands that what he does isn't important in the long run (though he IS proud of what he does) and who is doing what he is doing for charity because he really wants to help.

There were some presentations and awards to groups that had raised a good deal of money for the Association. One of them was a group of kids who brought up a giant replica of a check that showed that they raised so much money. After they shook hands and had pictures taken they were leaving the area where Curt was and he called them back. He said that he wanted to get their autograph on the check so that he could remember them (and he told them to "write legibly" so that he could read their signatures). Another young boy wearing a Red Sox jersey also did a presentation, and Curt called him back and had the boy turn around so that he could autograph the jersey. In the long-term scheme of things these are not big deals, but I'll bet those kids will remember it forever. And so will a lot of the people who were there.

In the question-and-answer session that followed, Schilling was simply terrific.

When someone asked him "Why ALS?" as his primary charity, he replied something to the effect that "No one has ever asked me, when I was standing next to a patient, why do you work with ALS? When you see someone with ALS, it becomes blatantly obvious why." He talked about meeting people with the disease and wanting to do something for them. He said that at first it's in part for you cause you feel good doing it, but as you see what can be done, it becomes more and more about other people and you want to do more. He said something like "if what we do here is to help one person have one day better than they otherwise would have, then it's all worth it."

When asked who his favorite player was when he was growing up, he replied "Roberto Clemente". He added Nolan Ryan and Dave Parker, and indicated that the first baseball player that he ever met was Dwight Evans. But he indicated that Clemente was his father's favorite and his. That again says something positive about Schilling, since Clemente was not only a great baseball player, but also a great human being, who died in a plane crash on New Year's Eve, 1972, while trying to deliver food to the needy in Central America. Schilling mentioned telling Shonda that one award that he wanted to win some day was the Roberto Clemente Humanitarian Award, which is given annually to a player who best exemplifies Clemente's commitment to helping others. He added that winning such an award tells people more about who you are than the Cy Young Award or MVP. If, no *when*, Schilling wins that award, it will be well deserved.

There were a number of questions asked about the Red Sox and the 2004 season. Larry Lucchino was there representing the Red Sox. He talked about the meetings with Schilling last year in Arizona at Thanksgiving time to discuss the possible trade of Schilling to the Red Sox. Schilling was asked later how he thinks Lucchino and Theo Epstein should spend their Thanksgiving this year. He said that he hoped that this Thanksgiving they're spending time at Jason Varitek's. It was clear that Schilling wanted his teammate and battery mate signed to play again with the Red Sox.

He also indicated no regrets about finishing second to Johan Santana in the balloting for the Cy Young Award. He said that he didn't feel that he had lost it; he felt that Santana had won it. He said Santana was someone who had elevated his game this year, and that he was one of the players that Schilling liked to watch pitch whenever he could.

He said that his ankle felt good after surgery, "but it's not important how I feel now." He added that he believes that he will report to spring training in great shape, "although maybe a week or two late." For all Red Sox fans it was certainly good to hear that news about his recovery.

There are many other stories from the Q&A session that day, but these help illustrate again what a good teammate and human being Curt Schilling is. In talking with people at the ALS Association the week before the event, they told me that a lot of money was contributed for ALS the day after Game 2 of the World Series. That was when Schilling

The Possible Dream

pitched and had scratched "K ALS" on his shoe because he knew the TV camera would show shots of his bloody ankle. He didn't have to do that, but he did, and it was effective. And he made no big deal out of it himself. I think that says again that he's sincere and is a guy who "gets it". Mr. Schilling is a winner in more ways than one.

- - -

The Red Sox continued celebrations at various stops around New England, bringing the World Series trophy with them to each of the stops. A crowd of about 3,000 greeted Larry Lucchino, Mike Timlin, and Trot Nixon in Worcester on November 22. Some fans began arriving 4-5 hours before the event to make sure that they would be there and have a good location to watch the festivities. As was the case in most of the places that such events were held, fans chanted, "Thank you, Red Sox" in appreciation for what they had done. This showed again that the good feeling for fans that came out of this win is not something that will diminish over time. There would be no letdown. This was a great feel-good win for too many people for that to happen.

- - -

After the World Series and parade celebration, a little bit of reality started creeping in amidst the euphoria. The team decided not to renew the contract of Curtis Leskanic, so he was released. Gabe Kapler signed as a free agent to play in Japan with the Yomiuri Giants. A number of other players also had filed for free agency, most notably Pedro Martinez, Derek Lowe, Jason Varitek, and Orlando Cabrera. However, all players indicated a desire to stay with Boston. Cabrera said that the team could now dominate in the American League. Varitek talked about Boston fans finally being able to hold their heads high when they walk into Yankee Stadium. Lowe talked about no longer having to hear the chants of "1918" in Yankee Stadium. Martinez talked about wanting to stay with Boston and saying that he would not sign with the Yankees.

It is sad that the team will have to change, since it would be very interesting to see the Red Sox try to come back and defend their newly-won title with pretty much the same team that won it. The other fabled team in recent Red Sox history, the almost mystical 1967 team, came back nearly intact (adding pitchers like Ray Culp and Dick Ellsworth) and it would have been good to see this 2004 team shore up some weaknesses, such as long relief, and go after a second championship.

- - -

The Red Sox made the cover of *Time Magazine* as well as *Sports Illustrated* after winning the World Series. *Time* put them on the cover the week of the Presidential Election, which was quite a surprise. Johnny Damon appeared on the David Letterman show and a group of players appeared on the Tonight Show with Jay Leno. The Red Sox suddenly seemed to be the darlings of the media.

- - -

The Red Sox as a team were chosen as the Sportsmen of the Year by *Sports Illustrated*. The article accompanying the selection was less about the players and the team, however, than it was about the fans and what this victory meant to a number of people across many generations. It was great to read the summaries of how the Red Sox win affected so many people in so many positive ways.

- - -

When this book was originally drafted in 2003, the final chapter was a set of recommended changes that needed to be made to get the team to the top of the baseball world. They included building as strong a pitching staff as possible, being as aggressive as possible in trades and player acquisitions, adding speed to the roster, and hiring a good manager who had been a winner previously and who could really lead the team.

Adding Curt Schilling and Keith Foulke were masterstrokes. I was hoping in the fall of 2003 that the Red Sox would enter the bidding for Schilling, who had been a proven winner (and a personal favorite of mine) for many years. That they were able to sign him was a great step. One of the first commercials featuring Schilling showed him hitchhiking from Arizona to Boston and telling the driver of the Ford Pickup that picked him up that he was off to Boston "to break an 86-year-old curse". He did just that. With Schilling and Foulke added to Martinez, Lowe, Wakefield, Arroyo, Embree, and Timlin, the Red Sox pitching was the best in baseball, the first time that could ever be said. The fact that it resulted in the first championship in 86 years is not coincidence.

The trade of the very popular Nomar Garciaparra was not only aggressive, but a very bold move by Theo Epstein. It helped to turn the season around.

Speed was still not plentiful on the team, but there might not have been a bigger play all season than the stolen base by Dave Roberts in the ninth inning of Game 4 of the Yankee series. As Terry Francona put it, without that stolen base, he would have been watching the World Series. All of us would have been watching also, but we would have been watching the Yankees playing in it, not the Red Sox.

Francona himself, the new manager, was a key reason that the Red Sox won. My first choice as the man to succeed Grady Little as manager had been Frank Robinson. Robinson has been tough, but fair, not afraid to make decisions (as his stint in the Major League Baseball front office had shown), and he was a proven winner, who turned the Orioles into champions through his style and leadership as a player. My feeling was that he could do the same as a manager with the right team. He has been a good decision-maker, strong on fundamentals and could perhaps have been the equivalent of Dick Williams in stressing fundamentals for the team. He knows what it takes to win the World Series, having played in 5 and won 2.

Francona may have had an up-and-down regular season, as chronicled in Section 2, but he rose to the challenge in the post-season. There were a number of questionable decisions, most notably pitching Pedro in relief in Game 7 against the Yankees, but he also made a number of bold moves, including sticking with Mark Bellhorn and Johnny Damon when they were slumping (and they rewarded him in that same Game 7), and resurrecting Derek Lowe, not being afraid to change a decision. It is hoped that Francona will be even better in years to come thanks to the experience that he gained in 2004 when he emerged as a champion.

The 2004 experience in general, and finally exorcising the demons that have plagued the team for so many years, can now serve as a starting point for how the team can move from being a perennial also-ran and heart-breaking team to being a multiple-year champion.

Having won once was fantastic, and something that no one will ever forget. Now let's hope that the team will do everything it can to have it happen again.

86 years was too long a wait.

APPENDICES

Appendix A – 2004 Season Summary

Day-by-Day Summary

G	Date	H/A	Versus	Game Result	Record	Standings	GB (GA)	Starter	POR	Home Runs	Comment
1	4/4/04	A	Baltimore	L 2 - 7	0-1	5	1/2	P.Martinez (0-1)	-	-	Javy Lopez HR in 2nd leads to 3 runs
2	4/6/04	A	Baltimore	W 4 - 1	1-1	3	1/2	C.Schilling (1-0)	-	K.Millar (1)	Schilling 7K's in 6; Embree, Timlin, Foulke, each 1 perfect inning
3	4/7/04	A	Baltimore	W 10 - 3	2-1	1	(+ 1/2)	D.Lowe (1-0)	-	D.Ortiz (1)	7 run 2nd inning
4	4/8/04	A	Baltimore	L 2 - 3 (13)	2-2	2	1/2	T.Wakefield	B.Jones (0-1)	E.Burks (1)	Jones walks 4 in 13th
5	4/9/04	H	Toronto	L 5 - 10	2-3	3	1	B.Arroyo	M.Timlin (0-1)	J.Varitek (1)	3 in 8th, 3 in 9th wins for Jays
6	4/10/04	H	Toronto	W 4 - 1	3-3	1 T	-	P.Martinez (1-1)	-	D.Ortiz (2), M.Bellhorn (1), M.Ramirez (1)	0-0 into 6th Pedro-R.Halladay duel, then Ortiz HR
7	4/11/04	H	Toronto	W 6 - 4	(12) 4-3	1 T	-	C.Schilling	M.Malaska (1-0)	D.Ortiz (3)	Ortiz 2-run HR to deep left in 12th wins it
8	4/15/04	H	Baltimore	L 7 - 12	(11) 4-4	2 T	1/2	P.Martinez	B.Arroyo (0-1)	B. Mueller (1)	Sox blow 5-2, 7-4 leads
9	4/16/04	H	New York	W 6 - 2	5-4	1 T	-	T.Wakefield (1-0)	-	B.Mueller (2), M.Ramirez (2), D.Mirabelli (1)	Wakefield 7 inn., 4 runs in 1st for Sox, 2 NY errors in 1st, A-Rod out at 3rd on attempted steal late in game
10	4/17/04	H	New York	W 5 - 2	6-4	1 T	-	C.Schilling (2-0)	-	M.Ramirez (3)	Schilling strikes out 1st two Yanks, A-Rod 0-4
11	4/18/04	H	New York	L 3 - 7	6-5	2	1	D.Lowe (1-1)	-	-	6 run 3rd off Lowe, who was pitching for 1st time in 10 days
12	4/19/04	H	New York	W 5 - 4	7-5	2	1/2	B.Arroyo	M.Timlin (1-1)	J.Varitek(2)	Patriots' Day, comeback from 1-4, A-Rod 1-17 in series

#	Date	H/A	Opponent	W/L	Score	Record	GB	Pitcher		HR	Notes
13	4/20/04	A	Toronto	W	4 - 2	8-5	2 1/2	P.Martinez (2-1)	-	-	Pedro 7 strong inn. Over Halladay
14	4/21/04	A	Toronto	W	4 - 2	9-5	1 (+ 1/2)	T.Wakefield (2-0)	-	D.Mirabelli 2 (2,3)	Mirabelli 2 HR, 3 RBI
15	4/22/04	A	Toronto	L	3 - 7	9-6	2 1/2	C.Schilling (2-1)	-	D.Ortiz (4)	3-1 lead in 6th->3-3 in 7th->3-7 in 8th
16	4/23/04	A	New York	W	11 - 2	10-6	2 1/2	D.Lowe (2-1)	-	K.Millar (2), M.Bellhorn (2), B.Mueller (3), M.Ramirez (4)	5 run 2nd, back-to-back HRs by Millar, Bellhorn
17	4/24/04	A	New York	W	3 - 2	(12) 11-6	1 (+ 1/2)	B.Arroyo	K.Foulke (1-0)	-	3 sac flies overcomes 0-19 Sox w runners in scoring position
18	4/25/04	A	New York	W	2 - 0	12-6	1 (+ 1 1/2)	P.Martinez (3-1)	-	M.Ramirez (5)	Ramirez titanic HR to left center
19	4/28/04	H	Tampa Bay	W	6 - 0	13-6	1 (+ 2)	C.Schilling (3-1)	-	J.Varitek (3)	Schilling brilliant in 7 1/3
20	**4/29/04**	H	**Tampa Bay**	**W**	**4 - 0**	**14-6**	**1 (+ 2 1/2)**	**B.Kim (1-0)**	**-**	**D.Ortiz (5)**	**Kim 5 inn 1 H in 1st start after IR, 32 straight shutout innings by Sox pitchers**
21	4/29/04	H	Tampa Bay	W	7 - 3	15-6	1 (+ 2 1/2)	D.Lowe (3-1)	-	J.Varitek (4)	7 run 1st
22	5/1/04	A	Texas	L	3 - 4	15-7	1 (+ 3)	B.Arroyo	M.Malaska (1-1)	-	6 game win streak ends
23	5/1/04	A	Texas	L	5 - 8	15-8	1 (+ 2 1/2)	P.Martinez (3-2)	-	-	Martinez shelled 1 day after blasting Sox about his contract
24	5/2/04	A	Texas	L	1 - 4	15-9	1 (+ 1 1/2)	T.Wakefield (2-1)	-	-	Wakefield only gives up 2 R
25	5/3/04	A	Cleveland	L	1 - 2	15-10	1 (+ 1)	C.Schilling (3-2)	-	-	2 run HR in 1st by V.Martinez, Sox 13 LOB & terrible hitting w men on base
26	5/4/04	A	Cleveland	L	6 - 7	15-11	1 T -	D.Lowe (3-2)	-	M.Ramirez (6), J.Damon (1)	4 run 9th not enough … Yankees who were once 5 games behind now tied
27	5/5/04	A	Cleveland	W	9 - 5	16-11	1 T -	B.Kim	B.Arroyo (1-1)	D.Ortiz 2 (6,7), B.Mueller (4)	Ortiz HR in 1st and 3 run HR in 3rd help build lead, Mueller's 3 run blast breaks 5-5 tie

The Possible Dream

#	Date		Opp	W/L	Score			Record	Pitcher		HRs / Notes
28	5/6/04	A	Cleveland	W	5 - 2	1	(+ 1)	17-11	P.Martinez (4-2)	-	M.Ramirez (7) Pedro settles down after 1st pitch HR and hits by 1st three batters
29	5/7/04	H	Kansas City	W	7 - 6	1	(+ 2)	18-11	T.Wakefield	M.Timlin (2-1)	J.Damon (2), M.Bellhorn (3) great comeback - 2 in 8th and Bellhorn 2-run HR in 9th to tie, Varitek double down RF line to win in 9th
30	5/8/04	H	Kansas City	W	9 - 1	1	(+ 2)	19-11	C.Schilling (4-2) **	-	P.Reese 2 (1,2), D.McCarty (1) Complete Game for Schilling, 2 HRs (1 inside the park) for Pokey Reese
31	5/9/04	H	Kansas City	L	4 - 8	1	(+ 1)	19-12	D.Lowe (3-3)	-	B.Mueller (5), M.Ramirez (8) Early 2-0 lead wiped out
32	5/10/04	H	Cleveland	L	6 - 10	1	(+ 1/2)	19-13	B.Kim (1-1)	-	J.Varitek (5), B.Daubach (1) Kim gives up 6 runs in 3 1/3 innings and is removed from rotation
33	5/11/04	H	Cleveland	W	5 - 3	1	(+ 1/2)	20-13	P.Martinez	A.Embree (1-0)	G.Kaplar (1), D.Ortiz (8) Trailing 3-2 in 8th, Mueller 2b ties it, D.McCarty 3B wins it
34	5/12/04	H	Cleveland	L	4 - 6	1	(+ 1/2)	20-14	T.Wakefield (2-2)	-	1 run for Cleve in 1st 2nd 3rd 5th
35	5/13/04	A	Toronto	L	6 - 12	2	1/2	20-15	C.Schilling (4-3)	-	D.Ortiz (9) Schilling leaves down 2-3 after 5, bullpen collapses, defense collapses, Sox fall to 2nd place behind Yankees (ho hum)
36	5/14/04	A	Toronto	W	9 - 3	1	(+ 1/2)	21-15	D.Lowe	A.Embree (2-0)	6 run 8th overcomes bad defense
37	5/15/04	A	Toronto	W	4 - 0	1	(+ 1/2)	22-15	B.Arroyo (2-1)	-	M.Bellhorn (4), K.Youkilis (1), D.Ortiz (10) Arroyo brilliant in 8 inning, 3 hit innings of shutout pitching; Youkilis HR in 1st Major League game
38	5/16/04	A	Toronto	L	1 - 3	2	1/2	22-16	P.Martinez (4-3)	-	Sox scoreless in last 8 innings
39	5/18/04	A	Tampa Bay	W	7 - 3	1	(+ 1/2)	23-16	T.Wakefield (3-2)	-	M.Bellhorn (5) Wakefield, new daddy, wins on night when Randy Johnson pitches prefect game vs. Atlanta
40	5/19/04	A	Tampa Bay	W	4 - 1	1	(+ 1/2)	24-16	C.Schilling (5-3)	-	J.Damon (3), M.Ramirez (9) Schilling 7i, 5h, 1 ER, 5 K
41	5/20/04	A	Tampa Bay	L	6 - 9	2	1/2	24-17	D.Lowe (3-4)	-	J.Varitek (7) Lowe 7 r in 2 1/3 innings

The Possible Dream

#	Date	H/A	Opponent	W/L	Score	Record			Win Pitcher	Loss Pitcher	HR	Notes
42	5/21/04	H	Toronto	W	11 - 5	25-17	1	(+ 1/2)	B.Arroyo	M.Timlin (3-1)	M.Ramirez (10)	6 run 8th breaks 5-5 tie
43	5/22/04	H	Toronto	W	5 - 2	26-17	1	(+ 1 1/2)	P.Martinez	A.Martinez (1-0)	M.Ramirez (11)	Trailing 0-2, Bellhorn hits shot off Ted Lilly's leg, and Manny follows with monster blast to tie game
44	5/23/04	H	Toronto	W	7 - 2	27-17	1	(+ 1 1/2)	T.Wakefield (4-2)	-	-	Ortiz 3-5 with 3 RBI, Wakefield's 50th career win at Fenway Park
45	5/25/04	H	Oakland	W	12 - 2	28-17	1	(+ 1 1/2)	C.Schilling (6-3)	-	M.Ramirez (12), M.Bellhorn (6)	Tim Hudson: 5 runs, 9 hits, 4 walks and season-high 15 baserunners in 4 innings
46	5/26/04	H	Oakland	W	9 - 6	29-17	1	(+ 1 1/2)	D.Lowe (4-4)	-	J.Varitek (8)	Bobby Crosby error allows 3 runs to score to break open 2-2 game
47	5/27/04	H	Oakland	L	2 - 15	29-18	1	(+ 1/2)	B.Arroyo (2-2)	-	-	A's bomb Sox for 12 runs in 1st 4 innings
48	5/28/04	H	Seattle	W	8 - 4	30-18	1	(+ 1/2)	P.Martinez (5-3)	-	M.Ramirez (13), D.Ortiz (11)	Ortiz grand slam gives Pedro win
49	5/29/04	H	Seattle	L	4 - 5	30-19	2	1/2	T.Wakefield (4-3)	-	M.Ramirez (14)	Ortiz ground rule 2B could have tied score if it hadn't bounced into stands
50	5/30/04	H	Seattle	W	9 - 7	(12) 31-19	1	(+ 1/2)	C.Schilling	A.Martinez (2-0)	D.McCarty (2)	McCarty walk off HR in 12th on 3-0 count
51	5/31/04	H	Baltimore	L	4 - 13	31-20	1 T	-	D.Lowe (4-5)	-	K.Millar (3)	Lowe finishes difficult May
52	6/1/04	A	Anaheim	L	6 - 7	31-21	2	1	B.Arroyo (2-3)	-	K.Millar (4), B.Daubach (2)	Arroyo left in too long; 4-1 lead blown; Manny picked off 2nd in 7th to end rally
53	6/2/04	A	Anaheim	L	7 - 10	31-22	2	2	P.Martinez	M.Timlin (3-2)	M.Ramirez (15)	Pedro blows 7-4 lead and doesn't make it out of 6th inning
54	6/4/04	A	Kansas City	L	2 - 5	31-23	2	3 1/2	T.Wakefield (4-4)	-	D.Mirabelli (4)	Jimmy Gobble retires 15 straight after Damon leadoff single
55	6/5/04	A	Kansas City	W	8 - 3	32-23	2	3 1/2	C.Schilling (7-3)	-	D.Ortiz (12), K.Youkilis (2), M.Bellhorn (7)	Ortiz 2-run HR in 1st starts Sox off on ending losing streak

The Possible Dream

#	Date		Opp	W/L	Score	Record		GB	Pitcher	Save	HR	Notes
56	6/6/04	A	Kansas City	W	5 - 3	33-23	2	2 1/2	D.Lowe (5-5)	-		Bizarre play in which KC 1B Harvey throws ball into face of KC pitcher Grimsley while trying to throw home is key in 5 run 6th for Boston
57	6/8/04	H	San Diego	W	1 - 0	34-23	2	2 1/2	P.Martinez (6-3)	-		Pedro masterful (8 I, 2 h, 8 K) in real pitchers' duel w David Wells
58	6/9/04	H	San Diego	L	1 - 8	34-24	2	3 1/2	B.Arroyo (2-4)	-	J.Damon (4)	Nomar returns (1st game of 2004); 4 unearned runs incl. 2 to break scoreless tie on error by 1B Andy Dominique (why was he playing there?)
59	6/10/04	H	San Diego	W	9 - 3	35-24	2	3 1/2	C.Schilling (8-3)	-	M.Ramirez (16), P.Reese (3)	Schilling strong again in 7 innings, Ramirez HR breaks 1-1 tie
60	6/11/04	H	Los Angeles	W	2 - 1	36-24	2	2 1/2	D.Lowe	K.Foulke (2-0)	D.Ortiz (13)	Ortiz HR in 7th breaks 0-0 tie; Manny error with 2 out in 9th ties it; Ortiz 1B in bottom 9th wins it
61	6/12/04	H	Los Angeles	L	5 - 14	36-25	2	3 1/2	T.Wakefield (4-5)	-	M.Ramirez (17)	7 run 5th as LA bombs Wakefield
62	6/13/04	H	Los Angeles	W	4 - 1	37-25	2	3 1/2	P.Martinez (7-3)	-		Pedro strong again in 7 innings; great defensive play by Reese saves Sox (line drive with 2 on 2 out (in 7th?)
63	6/15/04	A	Colorado	L	3 - 6	37-26	2	4 1/2	B.Arroyo (2-5)	-		Colorado breaks 8 game losing streak as Sox have 12 LOB
64	6/16/04	A	Colorado	L	6 - 7	37-27	2	5 1/2	C.Schilling (8-4)	-	K.Youkilis (3), T.Nixon (1), J.Varitek (9)	Nixon returns, and hits a homer, but Sox fall to lowly Rockies again
65	6/17/04	A	Colorado	W	11 - 0	38-27	2	4 1/2	D.Lowe (6-5)	-	D.Ortiz (14)	2nd striaght game of 7 shutout innings for Derek Lowe

211

The Possible Dream

#	Date		Opponent		Score	Record		GB	Starter	Decision	HR	Notes
66	6/18/04	A	San Francisco	W	14 - 9	39-27	2	3 1/2	T.Wakefield	M.Timlin (4-2)	D.Ortiz (15), M.Ramirez (18), K.Millar (5), T.Nixon (2), D.Mirabelli (5)	7 run 5th overcomes 2-7 deficit
67	6/19/04	A	San Francisco	L	4 - 6	39-28	2	4 1/2	P.Martinez	A.Embree (2-1)	-	Sox tie with 3 in 8th but Edgardo Alfonso pinch-hit 2 run HR in 8th wins it
68	6/20/04	A	San Francisco	L	0 - 4	39-29	2	4 1/2	B. Arroyo (2-6)	-	-	Jason Schmidt masterful 1-hitter (6th inning 2b by Youkilis), Edgardo Alfonso grand slam
69	6/22/04	H	Minnesota	W	9 - 2	40-29	2	4 1/2	C.Schilling (9-4)	-	N.Garciaparra (1), M.Ramirez (19), D.Ortiz (16)	Nomar grand slam in 6 run inning caps Sox power barrage
70	6/23/04	H	Minnesota	L	2 - 4	40-30	2	4 1/2	D.Lowe (6-6)	-	T.Nixon (3), M.Bellhorn (8)	Pokey Reese hurt
71	6/24/04	H	Minnesota	L	3 - 4	(10) 40-31	2	5 1/2	T.Wakefield	K.Foulke (2-1)	D.Ortiz (17)	Nomar error leads to winning run
72	6/25/04	H	Philadelphia	W	12 - 1	(8) 41-31	2	5	P.Martinez (8-3)	-	M.Ramirez (20), D.Ortiz (18)	Manny 5 RBI, Pedro 2-hitter in rain-shortened game
73	6/26/04	H	Philadelphia	L	2 - 9	41-32	2	5	B.Arroyo (2-7)	-	-	14 hits and only 2 runs? 4 errors didn't help either
74	6/27/04	H	Philadelphia	W	12 - 3	42-32	2	5 1/2	C.Schilling (10-4)	-	M.Bellhorn (9), D.Ortiz (19)	early 0-3 deficit overcome behind Schilling reverting to fastballs
75	6/29/04	A	New York	L	3 - 11	42-33	2	6 1/2	D.Lowe (6-7)	-	J.Damon 2 (5,6), D.Ortiz (20)	Pathetic defense: 2 Nomar errors, 1 by Millar, botched DP by Pokey; 3 SBs off Lowe-Varitek
76	6/30/04	A	New York	L	2 - 4	42-34	2	7 1/2	T.Wakefield	M.Timlin (4-3)	D.Ortiz (21)	with 2-0 lead in 7th David Ortiz error allow Yanks to tie; Nomar error in 8th sets up winning run for NY

The Possible Dream

#	Date			W/L			Record		GB	Starter	Decision	HR	Notes
77	7/1/04	A	New York	L	4 - 5	(13)	42-35	2	8 1/2	P.Martinez	C.Leskanic (0-1)	M.Ramirez 2 (21,22)	Thriller of a game highlighted by amazing catch by Derek Jeter diving into stands in 12th inning; Manny HR in 13th, 2 Yankee runs after 2 out in 13th
78	7/2/04	A	Atlanta	L	3 - 6	(12)	42-36	2	8 1/2	B.Arroyo	A.Martinez (2-1)	-	Again Manny drives in run in extra innings (10th) but Sox blow it; HR by Green in 12th wins it
79	7/3/04	A	Atlanta	W	6 - 1		43-36	2	7 1/2	C.Schilling (11-4) **	-	J.Damon (7), N.Garciaparra (2), D.Mirabelli (6) **	Complete Game for Schilling, grand slam for Mirabelli
80	7/4/04	A	Atlanta	L	4 - 10		43-37	2	7 1/2	D.Lowe (6-8)	-	-	Lowe implodes again as 9 run 5th overcomes 4-1 Sox lead
81	7/6/04	H	Oakland	W	11 - 0		44-37	2	7	T.Wakefield (5-5)	-	B.Mueller (6)	7 shutout innings for Wakefield, 3-run HR by Mueller, 5-for-6 night for Damon
82	7/7/04	H	Oakland	W	11 - 3		45-37	2	6	P.Martinez (9-3)	-	M.Bellhorn (10), N.Garciaparra (3), M.Ramirez (23)	Oakland starter shelled again, Sox win 2 straight for 1st time since 6/17-18
83	7/8/04	H	Oakland	W	8 - 7	(10)	46-37	2	6	C.Schilling	C.Leskanic (1-1)	M.Ramirez (24), D.Ortiz (23)	Sox blow 7-1 lead, win in 10th as Damon races home from 1st on 2b to left center by Mueller
84	7/9/04	H	Texas	W	7 - 0		47-37	2	6	B.Arroyo (3-7)	-	J.Damon 2 (8,9)	Arroyo 8 shutout innings

The Possible Dream

#	Date	H/A	Opponent	W/L	Score			Record	Pitcher	Save	HRs	Notes
85	7/10/04	H	Texas	W	14 - 6	2	6	48-37	D.Lowe (7-8)	-	M.Ramirez 2 (25, 26), N.Garciaparra (4), J.Varitek (10), M.Bellhorn (11)	Two titanic Hrs by Manny overcomes 6 unearned runs after 2 Bellhorn errors
86	7/11/04	H	Texas	L	5 - 6	2	7	48-38	T.Wakefield	K.Foulke (2-2)	D.Mirabelli (7), J.Damon (10)	Sox in 9th get 1b by Mueller, but Reese (PR) is picked off, Damon reaches on error, gets to 3rd on SB/error, stranded as Bellhorn takes called strike 3
	7/13/04		Houston	-		-	-		-	-	M.Ramirez, D.Ortiz	All-Star Game: AL 9-4
87	7/15/04	A	Anaheim	L	1 - 8	2	8	48-39	D.Lowe (7-9)	-	-	5 run 5th
88	7/16/04	A	Anaheim	W	4 - 2	2	7	49-39	P.Martinez (10-3)	-	N.Garciaparra (5), G.Kapler (2)	Ortiz tossed from game afert protesting called 3rd strike, throws bats on field
89	7/17/04	A	Anaheim	L	3 - 8	2	8	49-40	T.Wakefield (5-6)	-	J.Damon 2 (11,12)	Wakefield hit in back by line drive (OK afetr CT Scan)
90	7/18/04	A	Anaheim	W	6 - 2	2	7	50-40	C.Schilling (12-4)	-	D.Ortiz (25), G.Kapler (3)	Schilling 8 IP; Ortiz 3-run HR in 6th overcomes 0-1 deficit
91	7/19/04	A	Seattle	L	4 - 8	2	7	(11) 50-41	B.Arroyo	C.Leskanic (1-2)	J.Varitek (11)	2 Seattle HRs in 9th tie it; walkoff grand slam by Bret Boone in 11th wins it
92	7/20/04	A	Seattle	W	9 - 7	2	7	51-41	D.Lowe (8-9)	-	D.Ortiz (26), M.Ramirez (27)	8 run fourth with back-to-back HRs is barely enough for win
93	7/21/04	H	Baltimore	L	5 - 10	2	8	51-42	P.Martinez (10-4)	-	G.Kapler (4), K.Millar (6)	Saw game in movie theater; ugly OF play/fundamentals
94	7/22/04	H	Baltimore	L	3 - 8	2	9	51-43	A.Alvarez (0-1)	-	K.Millar (7)	Abe Alvarez loses ML debut
95	7/22/04	H	Baltimore	W	4 - 0	2	8 1/2	52-43	T.Wakefield (6-6)	-	K.Youkilis (4)	Wakefield 7 strong shutout innings

The Possible Dream

#	Date		Opp	W/L	Score	Record	Pos	GB	Pitcher	Decision	HRs/Players	Notes
96	7/23/04	H	New York	L	7 - 8	52-44	2	9 1/2	C.Schilling	K.Foulke (2-3)	K.Millar 3 (8,9,10); B.Mueller (7)	3 Millar HRs are not enough
97	7/24/04	H	New York	W	11 - 10	53-44	2	8 1/2	B.Arroyo	R.Mendoza (1-0)		Mueller 2 run HR off Rivera in 9th
98	7/25/04	H	New York	W	9 - 6	54-44	2	7 1/2	D.Lowe (9-9)	-	J.Damon (13); M.Bellhorn (12); K.Millar (11)	Sloppy start for Sox in field overcome by 3 run HR by Damon and solo shots by Bellhorn, Millar
99	7/26/04	A	Baltimore	W	12 - 5	55-44	2	7 1/2	P.Martinez (11-4)	-	-	3 hits by Gabe Kapler
100	7/28/04	A	Baltimore	L	1 - 4	55-45	2	8	C.Schilling (12-5)	-	D.Ortiz (27)	only 4 hits for Red Sox
101	7/30/04	A	Minnesota	W	8 - 2	56-45	2	7 1/2	B.Arroyo (4-7)	-	J.Varitek (12)	3 hits for Kapler, Ortiz, Varitek
102	7/31/04	A	Minnesota	L	4 - 5	56-46	2	8 1/2	D.Lowe	A.Embree (2-2)	M.Bellhorn (13)	Twins tie in 7th, win in 8th
103	8/1/04	A	Minnesota	L	3 - 4	56-47	2	9 1/2	P.Martinez	M.Timlin (4-4)	O.Cabrera (1), M.Ramirez (28)	Pedro departed after 7 innings, lead departed after 1 out in 8th.
104	8/2/04	A	Tampa Bay	W	6 - 3	57-47	2	9	T.Wakefield (7-6)	-	D.McCarty (3)	Wakefield wins on 38th birthday
105	8/3/04	A	Tampa Bay	W	5 - 2	58-47	2	8	C.Schilling (13-5) **	-	J.Varitek (13)	3rd CG for Schilling (only 3 the team has)
106	8/4/04	A	Tampa Bay	L	4 - 5	58-48	2	9	B.Arroyo (4-8)	-	B.Mueller (9)	Arroyo left in to give up grand slam in 7th to turn 4-1 lead to 4-5 loss
107	8/6/04	A	Detroit	L	3 - 4	58-49	2	10 1/2	D.Lowe (9-10)	-	J.Varitek (14)	Sox tie in top of 6th; lead is gone by 4 pitches in bottom of 6th
108	8/7/04	A	Detroit	W	7 - 4	59-49	2	10 1/2	P.Martinez (12-4)	-	-	4 run 7th clinches win
109	8/8/04	A	Detroit	W	11 - 9	60-49	2	10 1/2	T.Wakefield (8-6)	-	D.Ortiz (28). K.Youkilis 2 (5,6)	Wakefield wins despite tying a record by giving up 6 home runs
110	8/9/04	H	Tampa Bay	L	3 - 8	60-50	2	10 1/2	C.Schilling (13-6)	-	G.Kapler (5)	Schilling's 1st loss at Fenway
111	8/10/04	H	Tampa Bay	W	8 - 4	61-50	2	9 1/2	B.Arroyo (5-8)	-	-	3 runs in 5th 5 in 6th

The Possible Dream

#	Date		Opponent	W/L	Score	Record		GB	Save	Pitcher	HR/Batters	Notes
112	8/11/04	H	Tampa Bay	W	14 - 4	62-50	2	9 1/2	-	D.Lowe (10-10)	K.Millar (12)	3 runs in 1st 5 in 2nd
113	8/12/04	H	Tampa Bay	W	6 - 0	63-50	2	9 1/2	-	P.Martinez (13-4) **	K.Youkilis (7)	CG, 6 hitter for Pedro, with 0 walks, and 10 strikeouts
114	8/13/04	H	Chicago	L	7 - 8	63-51	2	10 1/2	-	T.Wakefield (8-7)	M.Ramirez (29), K.Millar (13)	2 runs in 9th falls short
115	8/14/04	H	Chicago	W	4 - 3	64-51	2	10 1/2	-	C.Schilling (14-6)	D.Ortiz 2 (29, 30), M.Ramirez (30)	Ortiz HR in 8th breaks tie wins game
116	8/15/04	H	Chicago	L	4 - 5	64-52	2	10 1/2	-	B.Arroyo (5-9)	-	Quality start by Arroyo wasted
117	8/16/04	H	Toronto	W	8 - 4	65-52	2	10	-	D.Lowe (11-10)	-	Doug Mientkiewicz starts at 2B
118	8/17/04	H	Toronto	W	5 - 4	66-52	2	9	K.Foulke (3-3)	P.Martinez	J.Damon (14), J.Varitek (15)	Cabrera 2b in 9th off scoreboard in left drives in Damon w winning run
119	8/18/04	H	Toronto	W	6 - 4	67-52	2		-	T.Wakefield (9-7)	-	8 innings 2 R for Wakefield; 4 runs in 1st for Boston
120	8/20/04	A	Chicago	W	10 - 1	68-52	2	7 1/2	-	C.Schilling (15-6)	M.Ramirez (31) **, O.Cabrera (2)	7 shutout innings for Schilling; grand slam Manny; 3-run HR Cabrero
121	**8/21/04**	**A**	**Chicago**	**W**	**10 - 7**	**69-52**	**2**	**6 1/2**	**-**	**B.Arroyo (6-9)**	**M.Ramirez (32), J.Varitek 2 (16,17)**	**Sox leads of 3-0, 5-2, 7-2, 10-5 are just barely held on to for win**
122	8/22/04	A	Chicago	W	6 - 5	70-52	2	5 1/2	C.Leskanic (2-2)	D.Lowe	M.Ramirez (33), D.Ortiz (31), D.Mientkiewicz (1)	After White Sox come back from 0-4 to take 5-4 lead Ramirez and Ortiz hit back-to-back 1st pitch HRs in 8th
123	8/23/04	A	Toronto	L	0 - 3	70-53	2	6 1/2	-	P.Martinez (13-5)	-	Ted Lilly CG 3 hitter
124	8/24/04	A	Toronto	W	5 - 4	71-53	2	6 1/2	-	T.Wakefield (10-7)	-	D.Mirabelli (8) Mirabelli 3-run shot proves winner

The Possible Dream

#	Date		Opp	W/L	Score		GB	Pitcher		HR	Notes
125	8/25/04	A	Toronto	W	11 - 5	72-53	2	5 1/2	C.Schilling (16-6)	-	M.Ramirez (34), D.Ortiz 2 (32, 33), O.Cabrera (3)	Manny, Ortiz, Cabrera HRs in 5th turn 0-1 deficit to 5-1 lead
126	**8/26/04**	**H**	**Detroit**	**W**	**4 - 1**	**73-53**	**2**	**5 1/2**	**B.Arroyo (7-9)**	-		**Arroyo 7 1/3 innings 1 unearned run, Timlin K, F7, Foulke FO, F6, K for 5 straight outs to end game**
127	8/27/04	H	Detroit	W	5 - 3	74-53	2	5 1/2	D.Lowe (12-10)	-		-
128	8/28/04	H	Detroit	W	5 - 1	75-53	2	5 1/2	P.Martinez (14-5)	-		-
129	8/29/04	H	Detroit	W	6 - 1	76-53	2	4 1/2	T.Wakefield (11-7)	-	M.Bellhorn (14)	
130	**8/31/04**	**H**	**Anaheim**	**W**	**10 - 7**	**77-53**	**2**	**3 1/2**	**C.Schilling (17-6)**	-	**M.Ramirez 2 (35,36), D.Roberts (1)**	**10-1 lead after 7 after Manny 3 run HR in 1st, solo in 2nd; Yanees lose to Cleveland 22-0**
131	9/1/04	H	Anaheim	W	12 - 7	78-53	2	3 1/2	B.Arroyo	T.Adams (1-0)	K.Millar (14)	Another 4 run first, though Arroyo can't hold lead (Sox have to break 5-5 tie)
132	9/2/04	H	Anaheim	W	4 - 3	79-53	2	3 1/2	D.Lowe (13-10)	-	B.Mueller (10)	All runs scored in 1st 3 innings
133	9/3/04	H	Texas	W	2 - 0	80-53	2	2 1/2	P.Martinez (15-5)	-	M.Ramirez (37), B.Mueller (11)	Two solo home runs off John Wasdin win it
134	9/4/04	H	Texas	L	6 - 8	80-54	2	2 1/2	T.Wakefield (11-8)	-	M.Bellhorn (15) *, D.Ortiz (34)	Bellhorn grand slam and Ortiz HR not enough to overcome 1-8 deficit
135	9/5/04	H	Texas	W	6 - 5	81-54	2	2 1/2	C.Schilling (18-6)	-	D.Ortiz (35)	Schilling 8 1/3 brilliant innings; Rangers rally for 4 in 9th not enough
136	9/6/04	A	Oakland	W	8 - 3	82-54	2	2 1/2	B.Arroyo (8-9)	-	M.Ramirez (38), D.Ortiz (36)	4 run 9th clinches it after two good outfield plays kill A's in 8th

The Possible Dream

#	Date		Opponent	W/L	Score	Record		GB	Pitcher	Relief	HRs	Notes
137	9/7/04	A	Oakland	W	7 - 1	83-54	2	2 1/2	D.Lowe (14-10)	-	J.Damon (15), G.Kapler (6), K.Millar (15)	Damon homers in 1st after missing 4 games due to finger injury; Lowe wins 5th straight decision
138	9/8/04	A	Oakland	W	7 - 3	84-54	2	2	P.Martinez (16-5)	-	-	3 in first after 3 walks; Pedro leaves after 6 shutout innings
139	9/9/04	A	Seattle	L	1 - 7	84-55	2	3 1/2	T.Wakefield (11-9)	-	O.Cabrera (4)	Sloppy defense returns
140	9/10/04	A	Seattle	W	13 - 2	85-55	2	2 1/2	C.Schilling (19-6)	-	M.Ramirez 2 (39, 40*), D.Ortiz (37)	5 runs in 6th 6 runs in 7th
141	9/11/04	A	Seattle	W	9 - 0	86-55	2	2 1/2	B.Arroyo (9-9)	-	M.Ramirez (41), M.Bellhorn (16)	7 shutout innings on 4h by Arroyo
142	9/12/04	A	Seattle	L	0 - 2	86-56	2	3 1/2	D.Lowe (14-11)	-	-	Gil Meche shutout
143	9/14/04	H	Tampa Bay	L	2 - 5	86-57	2	4	P.Martinez (16-6)	-	T.Nixon (4)	Great pitching by 20 year old Scott Kazmir
144	9/15/04	H	Tampa Bay	W	8 - 6	87-57	2	4	T.Wakefield	M.Myers (1-0)	M.Bellhorn (17), K.Millar (16)	Sox come back from 6-6 tie in 5th
145	9/16/04	H	Tampa Bay	W	11 - 4	88-57	2	3 1/2	C.Schilling (20-6)	-	K.Millar (17), J.Damon (16)	Schilling is first 20 game winner in MLB 2004; Millar HR give RS 200 for year
146	9/17/04	A	New York	W	3 - 2	89-57	2	2 1/2	B.Arroyo	M.Timlin (5-4)	J.Damon (17)	2 runs in 9th off Rivera on singles by Cabrera and Damon for comeback win
147	9/18/04	A	New York	L	4 - 14	89-58	2	3 1/2	D.Lowe (14-12)	-	D.Ortiz (38), D.Roberts (2)	Abysmal game. Lowe off, mental mistakes on covering first and throwing to 3rd, 6 2/3 no-hit innings by Jon Lieber
148	9/19/04	A	New York	L	1 - 11	89-59	2	4 1/2	P.Martinez (16-7)	-	-	Another abysmal game. Pedro again gives up first inning runs. Sox offense not productive against Mussina
149	9/20/04	H	Baltimore	L	6 - 9	89-60	2	4 1/2	T.Wakefield (11-10)	-	D.Ortiz (39)	5 run 4th lowlighted by botched rundown (2 dropped throws)

The Possible Dream

150	9/21/04	H	Baltimore	W	3 - 2	90-60	2	4 1/2	C.Schilling	K.Foulke (4-3)	-	Schilling 8 innings, 0 runs, 3 hits, 14 K's; 0-0 game until bottom 8; Millar hits SF 1-0; with 2 out in 9th Foulke gives up 2 run HR to J.Lopez. W 2 out in 9th, Bellhorn singles in 2 runs for win
151	9/22/04	H	Baltimore	W	7 - 6	(12) 91-61	2	3 1/2	B.Arroyo	C.Leskanic (3-2)	D.Ortiz (40); O.Cabrera (5)	Cabrera HR in 12th wins it after Foulke gives up another 9th inning HR, to tie
152	9/23/04	H	Baltimore	L	7 - 9	91-61	2	4 1/2	D.Lowe	R.Mendoza (1-1)		Lowe (5 R in 5 innings) and Kim (2 runs in 9th) put Sox in hole that 2-run 9th rally can't save
153	9/24/04	H	New York	L	4 - 6	91-62	2	5 1/2	P.Martinez (16-8)	-	M.Ramirez (42); T.Nixon (5), J.Damon (18)	Pedro can't hold 3-2 lead or 4-3 lead; Damon 7th inning HR makes it 4-3; Matsui homers on 2nd pitch of 8th
154	9/25/04	H	New York	W	12 - 5	92-62	2	4 1/2	T.Wakefield	K.Foulke (5-3)	D.Mirabelli (9)	7 run 8th inning breaks 5-5 tie
155	9/26/04	H	New York	W	11 - 4	93-62	2	3 1/2	C.Schilling (21-6)	-	B.Mueller (12)	Sox bomb Brown, Loaiza for 7 in first 2 innings; Schilling: 7 IP, 1 hit
156	9/27/04	A	Tampa Bay	W	7 - 3	94-62	2	3	B.Arroyo (10-9)	-	J.Damon (19); M.Ramirez (43), J.Varitek (18), D.McCarty (4)	Sox clinch wild card; Scott Kazmir ejected after 3 1/3 no-hit innings after hitting Ramirez and Millar (Millar after being warned)
157	9/28/04	A	Tampa Bay	W	10 - 8	(11) 95-62	2	2 1/2	D.Lowe	R.Mendoza (2-1)	K.Millar (18)	Millar 2-run HR in 11th wins it; Lowe again ineffective in 2 1/3 innings
158	9/29/04	A	Tampa Bay	L	4 - 9	95-63	2	4	P.Martinez (16-9)	-	T.Nixon (6), A.Hyzdu (1)	4th straight loss for Martinez
159	10/1/04	A	Baltimore	W	8 - 3	96-63	2	3 1/2	T.Wakefield (12-10)	-	D.Ortiz (41); J.Damon (20)	Wakefield 6 IP 2 ER, pitched himself into post-season rotation
160	10/2/04	A	Baltimore	W	7 - 5	97-63	2	3	B.Arroyo	T.Adams (2-0)	-	6 run 2nd inning; Arroyo limited to 4 innings and 45 pitches in post-season tune-up

The Possible Dream

#	Date		Opponent	W/L	Score	Record			Win/Loss Pitcher	Losing Pitcher	Save/HR	Notes
161	10/2/04	A	Baltimore	W	7 - 5	98-63	2	2	P.Anastacio	B.Kim (2-1)	O.Cabrera (6)	Mientkiewicz 2 run triple in 7th
162	10/3/04	A	Baltimore	L	2 - 3	98-64	2	3	D.Lowe	S.Williamson (0-1)	-	Sox finish with most wins since 99 in '78

PLAYOFFS - ALDS

#	Date		Opponent	W/L	Score	Record		Win/Loss Pitcher	Losing Pitcher	Save	HR	Notes
1	10/5/04	A	Anaheim	W	9 - 3	1-0	-	C.Schilling (1-0)	-		K.Millar, M.Ramirez	7 run 4th inning including 2-run HR by Millar and 3-run HR by Ramirez
2	10/6/04	A	Anaheim	W	8 - 3	2-0	-	P.Martinez (1-0)	-		J.Varitek	Varitek 2 run HR ties it at 3, Manny SF makes it 4-3; 4 in 9th clinches it
3	10/8/04	H	Anaheim	W	8 - 6	3-0	-	B.Arroyo	D.Lowe (1-0)		D.Ortiz	

PLAYOFFS - ALCS

#	Date		Opponent	W/L	Score	Record		Win/Loss Pitcher	Losing Pitcher	Save	HR	Notes
1	10/12/04	A	New York	L	7 - 10	0-1	-	C.Schilling (1-1)	-		J.Varitek	6 1/3 perfect innings by Mussina; 8-0 NY lead becomes 8-7 but rally falls short
2	10/13/04	A	New York	L	1 - 3	0-2	-	P.Martinez (1-1)	-		-	6 innings of 1 hit ball by Leiber
3	10/16/04	H	New York	L	8 - 19	0-3	-	B.Arroyo	R.Mendoza (0-1)		T.Nixon, J.Varitek	Horrible performance by Red Sox
4	10/17/04	H	New York	W	6 - 4 (12)	1-3	-	D.Lowe	C.Leskanic (1-0)		D.Ortiz	Ortiz walk-off 2 run HR in 12th keeps Sox alive
5	10/18/04	H	New York	W	5 - 4 (14)	2-3	-	P.Martinez	T.Wakefield (1-0)		D.Ortiz	Ortiz walk-off single scores Damon with game-winner in 14th
6	10/19/04	A	New York	W	4 - 2	3-3	-	C.Schilling (2-1)	-		M.Bellhorn	Schilling pitches 7 strong, gutsy innings on ankle with separated tendon that was sutured the day before
7	10/20/04	A	New York	W	10 - 3	4-3	-	D.Lowe (2-0)	-		D.Ortiz, J.Damon (2), M.Bellhorn	Red Sox 1st team in history to come back from 0-3 deficit and win series; Lowe 6 innings, 1 hit; Damon grand slam; incredible win for Red Sox

2004 World Series

The Possible Dream

#	Date		Opp		Score	Series		Pitcher	Save	HR	Notes
1	10/23/04	H	St.Louis	W	11 - 9	1-0	-	T.Wakefield	K.Foulke (1-0)	D.Ortiz, M.Bellhorn	Ortiz 3 run HR in 4 run 1st, but Bellhorn 2 run HR in 8th wins it
2	10/24/04	H	St.Louis	W	6 - 2	2-0	-	C.Schilling (3-1)	-		Schilling 6 innings, 4 hits, 0 earned runs on re-sutured ankle
3	10/26/04	A	St.Louis	W	4 - 1	3-0	-	P.Martinez (2-1)	-	M.Ramirez	Pedro 7 innings, 3 hits, 0 runs; two Cardinal baserunning errors help Sox
4	10/27/04	A	St.Louis	W	3 - 0	4-0	-	D.Lowe (3-0)	-	J.Damon	Leadoff HR by Damon, 7 shutout innings by Lowe ......WORLD CHAMPIONS!!!!!!!

Red Sox are 2004 WORLD CHAMPIONS!!!!!!

The Possible Dream

Team Batting Leaders – 2004 Season

Home Runs			RBI	
Manny Ramirez	43 (Led League)		David Ortiz	139
David Ortiz	41		Manny Ramirez	130
Johnny Damon	20		Johnny Damon	94
Kevin Millar	18		Mark Bellhorn	82
Jason Varitek	18		Kevin Millar	74

Hits			Stolen Bases	
Johnny Damon	189		Johnny Damon	19
Manny Ramirez	175		Jason Varitek	10
David Ortiz	175		Mark Bellhorn	6
Kevin Millar	151		Pokey Reese	6
Mark Bellhorn	138			

Batting Average			Runs	
Trot Nixon	.315 (48 games)		Johnny Damon	123
Manny Ramirez	.308		Manny Ramirez	108
Johnny Damon	.304		David Ortiz	94
David Ortiz	.301		Mark Bellhorn	93
Kevin Millar	.297		Bill Mueller	75

Team Pitching Leaders - 2004 Season

Wins			Strikeouts	
Curt Schilling	21- 6 (Led League)		Pedro Martinez	227
Pedro Martinez	16- 9		Curt Schilling	203
Derek Lowe	14-12		Bronson Arroyo	142
Tim Wakefield	12-10		Tim Wakefield	116
Bronson Arroyo	10- 9		Derek Lowe	105

ERA			Complete Games	
Scott Williamson	1.26		Curt Schilling	3
Kevin Foulke	2.17		Pedro Martinez	1
Curt Schilling	3.26			
Ramiro Mendoza	3.52		Saves	
Pedro Martinez	3.90		Keith Foulke	32

Manny Ramirez and David Ortiz are the first Red Sox teammates to hit 40+ home runs in the same season since Carl Yastrzemski and Rico Petrocelli both hit 40 in 1969. Their 84 home runs is the most by any two players combined in one season for the team.

Pedro Martinez and Curt Schilling are the first Red Sox teammates to strike out 200+ opposing batters in the same season.

The Possible Dream

Appendix B –
Miscellaneous Lists

Many a Red Sox fan has spent time recovering from Red Sox disappointments by making lists. This book would be remiss without a compilation of lists of its own, to provide food for thought for Red Sox fans.

Since most of this book has been focused on the last 43 seasons, the most obvious list to start with is the Red Sox best players by position over that time period. Here is one man's opinion of the best of the Red Sox since 1961:

Best Players by Position since 1961

P	Curt Schilling
RP	Dick Radatz
C	Carlton Fisk
1B	David Ortiz
2B	Jerry Remy
SS	Rico Petrocelli
3B	Carney Lansford
LF	Carl Yastrzemski
CF	Fred Lynn
RF	Tony Conigliaro
DH	Tommy Harper
LR	Tim Wakefield

The reasons for these picks over other possibilities are as follows:

Curt Schilling, Starting Pitcher – Until 2004, the choice for starting pitcher would have been Luis Tiant. However, in 2004, Curt Schilling won over an entire region and generation of fans. He came to the Red Sox to win. One of the first commercials with him was a truck commercial of him hitchhiking from Arizona to Boston where he was going, as he told the driver, "to break an 86-year-old curse". Then he did everything he could to do just that. He won 21 games. He saluted his teammates. He showed extraordinary courage in having his ankle sutured to be able to pitch against the Yankees in the ALCS and the

Cardinals in the World Series. He was everything that Red Sox fans wanted him to be, and more.

Luis Tiant had been, quite simply, one of the best money pitchers that the Red Sox have ever had. There are few pitchers that Red Sox fans would rather see on the mound in the big game, or with a lead to protect. His comment that the only way that the Blue Jays would beat the Red Sox in the important final regular season game of 1978 would be "over my dead body" says it all.

Lonborg was great in 1967, Clemens and Martinez have been very good in their Red Sox careers, Tiant was special, but Schilling's leadership and courage make him the choice.

Dick Radatz, Relief Pitcher – Radatz was the first real closer in baseball. His seasons of 1962-64 were among the best, if not the best, for any relief pitcher in history. He was nicknamed "The Monster" by Mickey Mantle after Radatz befuddled Mantle in a big Red Sox win, one of many times that Mickey was struck out by Radatz. His 15-9 record in 1963 is amazing. He also was more than a one-inning relief pitcher as most pitchers are today, once pitching 9 innings in relief in a 16-inning win for the Red Sox.

Carlton Fisk, Catcher – Fisk is the best catcher in all of Red Sox history. He was a great clutch player, as exemplified by his game-winning home run in game 6 of the 1975 World Series. He was unafraid to dive into the stands to catch foul balls, or block the plate to save a run. Early in his career he would also race down the first base line on ground balls, and wound up saving an errant throw on more than one occasion. Fisk did not deserve the treatment that he got from Haywood Sullivan and Buddy Leroux. What he did deserve was a championship. Too bad he never got one.

David Ortiz, First Base – This would have been a difficult choice until the 2004 post-season, when David Ortiz proved himself in the clutch over and over again. Although he was primarily a Designated Hitter, he played some first base. It was his bat and clutch hitting that make him the choice at this position. He won Game 3 of the ALDS with a walk-off home run in the tenth inning. He won the pivotal Game 4 of the ALCS with the Yankees with a walk-off twelfth inning home run. He won Game 5 of the ALCS with a fourteenth inning walk-off single. He was Señor Octubre, Mr. October for the Red Sox in 2004. George Scott also was a possibility here, as was Mo Vaughn, who was as close to a leader as the Red Sox had in the 1990s. He was a black player who also helped to change the racist image of the Red Sox. Vaughn was AL MVP in 1995. He is another in a long line of players whom the Red Sox discarded when they should not have.

Jerry Remy, Second Base – Remy was a speedy player, a good base stealer, and an excellent defensive second baseman. He beats out Marty Barrett for this position in another tough competition.

Rico Petrocelli, Shortstop – Nomar Garciaparra was a possibility here, but Rico had it all. He was great defensively, and one of the best curveball hitters ever. Rico went from being removed for a pinch hitter in game 1 of the 1967 World Series to hitting 2 home runs in game 6. He increased his power, hitting 40 home runs in 1969 and also tied an American League record for fewest errors by a shortstop with only 14 errors in 1969.

Carney Lansford, Third Base – The expected choice at 3B would be Wade Boggs, but this is the best team of the last 43 years, and there was nothing "team" about Boggs, the most selfish player in Red Sox history. Lansford, on the other hand, won an AL batting championship while with Boston with a .336 average in 1981, played an excellent defensive third base, and was also a very good baserunner. After two years in Boston in 1981 and 1982, Lansford was traded to Oakland and went on to be a key player on the Oakland A's team that won three consecutive pennants in 1988-1990. Maybe the Red Sox should have traded Boggs and kept Lansford. They would have been better off if they had.

Carl Yastrzemski, Left Field – Yaz' triple crown season of 1967 (the last triple crown season in baseball history through 2004) was phenomenal. He came through in the clutch time after time. That was not his only good season, though, as he won batting titles in 1963, 1967, and 1968, and narrowly missed winning also in 1965 and 1970. He hit 44 home runs in 1967 and then hit 40 again in 1969. He had 3,000 hits and 400 home runs for his career, all 23 years of which he spent in Boston. He also played a great defensive leftfield, mastering the leftfield wall better than anyone who has ever played there. Yaz also passed on an opportunity to join the Yankees late in his career, which will always endear him to Red Sox fans. Like Fisk, he deserved a championship, and it's a shame that he never got one.

Fred Lynn, Center Field – What a remarkable season Lynn had in 1975, a year in which he won both Rookie of the Year and MVP honors. Lynn was a good hitter and fielder for all of his Red Sox career, hitting a career high of 39 HR in 1979. Lynn was as natural a hitter as the Red Sox have had during this entire 44-year period. It's too bad that contract disputes and free agency reared up during his Red Sox stay as that ultimately caused him to leave, whereas he was a player who should have played his entire career with Boston.

Tony Conigliaro, Right Field – What can you say about a player with so much potential being struck down in his youth? The terrible beaning of August 18, 1967 ultimately ended his career years before it should have. TonyC was a favorite of just about every New England kid who lived in or north of Meriden, Connecticut in the 1960s. He was young, brash, and a powerful righthanded hitter who seemed to be made for Fenway Park. He won the AL HR title in 1965 and was a great clutch hitter throughout his career.

Tommy Harper, Designated Hitter – A case could be made for Jim Rice as DH, but Harper brought speed and hitting to the Red Sox. Harper was unceremoniously dropped after the Red Sox collapse in 1974, making it appear that he was getting more than his share of blame for that collapse. His three-year stay in Boston included 54 stolen bases in 1973, a Red Sox record. Having Harper and Remy at the top of the mythical batting order of this team would be a great way to set the table for Yaz and TonyC.

Tim Wakefield, Long Relief – The numbers indicate that Bob Stanley would be a candidate here, but numbers don't count for everything. Heart and desire do. Wakefield has been with the Red Sox since 1995 and has done absolutely everything asked of him. He has been a starting pitcher in the rotation and he has been a spot starter. He has been a closer and he has pitched in long relief. He volunteered to pitch in relief in a blowout loss to the Yankees in the 2004 ALCS, even though he knew that it would cost him a start in the series. He has been professional in everything that he has done, and has shown class in all of his dealings with the press. He is a real ambassador of the game, and a great representative for the Red Sox. It would have been fitting if the Red Sox had beaten the Yankees in the 2003 ALCS and Wakefield had been named the MVP for his great pitching performances in the first and fourth games.

Best Team Management since 1961

Dick Williams, Manager – Williams was the best manager the team had during this period, and is the man responsible for turning things around in 1967 and making the team a contender. Not only did they win more than they lost, as he predicted that they would, they also became the darling of Red Sox fans everywhere.

Theo Epstein, General Manager – His reign as GM has just begun, but Epstein has certainly done everything that he could to build a strong team. The signings of Kevin Millar, David Ortiz, Bill Mueller and Todd Walker before the 2003 season helped make that team. The additions of Scott Williamson and others during the year were almost enough to push them over the top. The bold acquisition of Curt Schilling for 2004-2007 was a brilliant move that helped end years of frustration for the team at the hands of the Yankees. The trade of Nomar Garciaparra in mid-2004 in which he upgraded the team defense and improved the clubhouse chemistry was a great move that turned a .500 club into a 98-game winner. Epstein has been determined to do everything he can to put his team in position to win. What more can you ask?

John Henry, Tom Werner, Larry Lucchino, Owners – They are willing to spend money to build a team, they hate the Yankees, and attend games sitting in the stands with the fans. All of that is enough to push them ahead of Tom Yawkey who is their only real competition for the ownership spot on this dream team.

Now that we have looked at the best of the last 43 years, let's look at other lists, both of positive and negatives:

Best Trades since 1961

1) Casey Fossum, Brandon Lyon, Jorge De La Rosa, and a player to be named later (presumably Michael Goss) to Arizona for Curt Schilling, 2003.
2) Carl Pavano and Tony Armas, Jr. to Montreal for Pedro Martinez, 1997.
3) Bill Schlesinger to Cubs for Ray Culp, 1967.
4) Nomar Garciaparra to Chicago Cubs in a 4-team trade involving the Cubs, Twins, Expos, and Red Sox, and which resulted in Boston acquiring shortstop Orlando Cabrera and first baseman Doug Mientkiewicz, 2004.
5) Heathcliff Slocumb to Seattle for Derek Lowe and Jason Varitek, 1997.
6) Don Aase to Angels for Jerry Remy, 1978.

7) Mike Easler to New York Yankees for Don Baylor, 1986.
8) Rey Quinones to Seattle for Dave Henderson and Spike Owen, 1986.

Worst Trades since 1961 (with apologies to the selling of Babe Ruth in 1920, which was the worst sports player personnel move in history)

1) Sparky Lyle to NY Yankees for Danny Cater, 1972.
2) Jeff Bagwell to Houston for Larry Anderson, 1990.
3) Earl Wilson to Detroit for Don Demeter, 1966.
4) Dick Stuart to Philadelphia for sore-armed Dennis Bennett, 1964.
5) Bill Lee to Montreal for Stan Papi, 1978.
6) Ferguson Jenkins to Texas for John Poloni, 1977.
7) Pete Runnels to Houston for Roman Mejias, 1962.
8) Ken Harrelson, Dick Ellsworth, Juan Pizzaro to Cleveland for Sonny Siebert, Vicente Romo, and Joe Azcue, 1969.
9) Jim Lonborg, George Scott, Joe Lahoud, Billy Conigliaro, Ken Brett, Don Pavletich to Milwaukee for Marty Pattin, Tommy Harper, Lew Krausse, and Pat Skrable, 1971.
10) Tony Conigliaro, Jerry Moses, Ray Jarvis to California for Doug Griffin, Ken Tatum and Jarvis Tatum (the two players are unrelated), 1970.
11) Dennis Eckersley and Mike Brumley to Chicago Cubs for Bill Buckner, 1984.
12) Carney Lansford, Garry Hancock, and Jerome King to Oakland for Tony Armas and Jeff Newman, 1982.

Red Sox Players who most deserved a championship but didn't get one

1) Carl Yastrzemski
2) Luis Tiant
3) Carlton Fisk
4) Jim Lonborg

Red Sox Players who least deserved a championship but got one with another team

1) Wade Boggs
2) Roger Clemens

Good Free Agent Signings

1) Ken Harrelson (in the era before official free agency)
2) Manny Ramirez
3) David Ortiz

The Possible Dream

4) Jack Clark (didn't work out with the Red Sox but was a very valuable player for the Cardinals and worth a chance with Boston)
5) Jeff Reardon

Worst Free Agent Signings
1) Mike Torrez
2) Bill Campbell

Worst Free Agent Losses (Red Sox player signed by another team)
1) Carlton Fisk
2) Luis Tiant
3) Mo Vaughn
4) Roger Clemens
5) Bruce Hurst
6) Bob Watson

Top Pitchers and Players in Red Sox Post-Season Play, 1967-2004 (* = a World Series year)

Year	Pitcher	Player
1967 *	Jim Lonborg	Carl Yastrzemski
1975 *	Luis Tiant	Carlton Fisk
1986 *	Bruce Hurst	Dwight Evans
1988	Bruce Hurst	Mike Greenwell
1990	Dana Kiecker	Wade Boggs (sigh!)
1995	Mike Maddux	Luis Alicea
1999	Pedro Martinez	Nomar Garciaparra
2003	Tim Wakefield	Trot Nixon
2004 *	Curt Schilling	David Ortiz

What could have been -- a real Boston-NY rivalry if the Red Sox had been smarter with player personnel moves
1920s Boston and Babe Ruth versus Yankees and Lou Gehrig (if Red Sox had kept Ruth)
1940s Boston and Ted Williams versus Yankees and Joe Dimaggio
1950s/1960s Boston and Willie Mays versus Yankees and Mickey Mantle (if Sox had signed Mays when they had an opportunity to do so)
1970s Boston and Carlton Fisk versus Yankees and Thurman Munson
1990s Boston and Nomar Garciaparra versus Yankees and Derek Jeter

Players they could have had but didn't acquire, 1961-2003
1) Alex Rodriguez (but for the greed of Rangers' owner Tom Hicks and the intransigence of Major League Baseball Players Union leader Gene Orza ...)

2) Magglio Ordonez (see comments above for Alex Rodriguez)
3) Tug McGraw (available for Juan Beniquez, 1976)
4) Bartolo Colon (available for Casey Fossum and Shea Hillenbrand, 2003)
5) Joe Rudi (purchased from Oakland in 1976; purchase later overturned by Commissioner)
6) Rollie Fingers (purchased from Oakland in 1976; purchase later overturned by Commissioner)

Games that were most disappointing/disgusting/distasteful
1) October 16, 2003, Game 7, 2003 ALCS, Yankees 6 Boston 5, 11 innings
2) October 2, 1978, AL East Playoff Game, Yankees 5 Boston 4
3) October 25, 1986, Game 6 of 1986 World Series, NY Mets 6 Boston 5, 10 innings
4) September 7, 1978, first game of "Boston Massacre", Yankees 15 Boston 3
5) September 8, 1978, second game of "Boston Massacre", Yankees 13 Boston 2
6) September 9, 1978, third game of "Boston Massacre", Yankees 7 Boston 0
7) September 10, 1978, fourth game of "Boston Massacre", Yankees 7 Boston 4
8) October 16, 2004, Game 3 of ALCS, New York 19 Boston 8

Most memorable games
1) October 20, 2004 – Red Sox complete comeback from being down 3 games to 0 to defeat the New York Yankees in the ALCS, win the series 4 games to 3, and win the American League pennant for the first time in 18 years
2) October 1, 1967 – Red Sox win first pennant in 21 years, on last day of the season behind a great complete-game victory by Jim Lonborg
3) October 17-18, 2004 – Red Sox beat the Yankees in Game 4 of ALCS in 12 innings (on a David Ortiz HR) to begin climb back from 0-3 series deficit
4) October 18, 2004 – Red Sox beat the Yankees in Game 5 of ALCS in 14 innings (on a David Ortiz single) to continue climb back from 0-3 series deficit
5) September 30, 1967 – Red Sox beat Twins to move into a tie for first place on the next-to-last day of season
6) October 27, 2004 – Red Sox sweep St. Louis Cardinals to win first championship in 86 years!

The Possible Dream

7) October 19, 2004 – Red Sox beat the Yankees in Game 6 of ALCS to become the first team to force a seventh game after being down 3 games to 0 in a post-season series
8) Game 5 of 1999 ALCS – Pedro pitches 6 hitless innings in relief to beat Indians 12-8 and complete comeback from 0-2 down to win series 3 games to 2
9) October 21, 1975 – Red Sox win Game 6 of the 1975 World Series as Carlton Fisk hits 12th inning HR to win one of best games in World Series history
10) Game 2 of 1967 World Series – Lonborg nearly pitches perfect game/no-hitter versus Cardinals

Most disliked players (definitely a personal opinion)
1) Wade Boggs
2) Mike Torrez
3) Roger Clemens
4) Rick Burleson
5) Rich Gedman

The Gedman choice is admittedly very personal. In 1982, as the Red Sox were starting batting practice, a group of 5 kids asked Gedman for his autograph. Gedman signed 4 and said that's it, leaving my son as the only child of the 5 without an autograph. Gedman proceeded to go swing a bat even though he was three players away from getting into the cage. He couldn't have signed "Rich Gedman" one more time before doing so? It's not like he had to rush into the cage or risk missing his turn. It's not like he has a long name to sign like Michael Olowakandi or Pembrook Burrows III. This is personal, but hey, if Larry Bird can hold it against Dan Issel for not signing an autograph for him when Bird was a kid, and if Dodger pitching prospect Tommy Lasorda can throw at a player because that player did not sign an autograph for him when he was a kid, then I can put Gedman on this list for not signing an autograph for my son. So there, Gedman.

Appendix C – Red Sox All-Time Record in Post-Season Play

The All-Time Red Sox record in post-season is as follows. The Red Sox starting pitcher for each post-season game played since 1961 is also shown:

1903 Beat Pittsburgh Pirates in World Series 5 games to 3
CHAMPIONS

1904 Won AL pennant but NY Giants refused to participate in World Series, not wanting to recognize the upstart American League

1912 Beat New York Giants in World Series 4 games to 3 (one tie)
CHAMPIONS

1915 Beat Philadelphia Phillies in World Series 4 games to 1
CHAMPIONS

1916 Beat Brooklyn Dodgers in World Series 4 games to 1
CHAMPIONS

1918 Beat Chicago Cubs in World Series 4 games to 2
CHAMPIONS

1946 Lost World Series to Cardinals 3 games to 4

1948 Lost 1 game playoff to Cleveland for AL pennant

1967 Lost World Series to Cardinals 3 games to 4

L	1-2	Jose Santiago
W	5-0	Jim Lonborg
L	2-5	Gary Bell
L	0-6	Jose Santiago
W	3-1	Jim Lonborg
W	8-4	Gary Waslewski
L	2-7	Jim Lonborg

1975 Beat Oakland A's in AL Championship Series, 3 games to 0

W	7-1	Luis Tiant
W	6-3	Reggie Cleveland
W	5-3	Rick Wise

Lost World Series to Cincinnati Reds 3 games to 4

W	6-0	Luis Tiant
L	2-3	Bill Lee
L	5-6	Rick Wise
W	5-4	Luis Tiant
L	2-6	Reggie Cleveland
W	7-6	Luis Tiant
L	3-4	Bill Lee

1978 Lost 1 game playoff to New York Yankees for AL East title

L	4-5	Mike Torrez

1986 Beat California Angels in AL Championship Series, 4 games to 3

L	1-8	Roger Clemens
W	9-2	Bruce Hurst
L	3-5	Dennis Boyd
L	3-4	Roger Clemens
W	7-6	Bruce Hurst
W	10-4	Dennis Boyd
W	8-1	Roger Clemens

Lost World Series to New York Mets 3 games to 4

W	1-0	Bruce Hurst
W	8-3	Roger Clemens
L	1-7	Dennis Boyd
L	2-6	Al Nipper
W	4-2	Bruce Hurst
L	5-6	Roger Clemens
L	5-8	Bruce Hurst

1988 Lost AL Championship Series to Oakland A's 0 games to 4

L	1-2	Bruce Hurst
L	3-4	Roger Clemens
L	6-10	Mike Boddicker
L	1-4	Bruce Hurst

1990 Lost AL Championship Series to Oakland A's 0 games to 4

L	1-9	Roger Clemens
L	1-4	Dana Kiecker
L	1-4	Mike Boddicker
L	1-3	Roger Clemens

The Possible Dream

1995 Lost AL Division Series to Cleveland Indians 0 games to 3

L	4-5	Roger Clemens
L	0-4	Erik Hanson
L	2-8	Tim Wakefield

1998 Lost AL Division Series to Cleveland Indians 1 game to 3

W	11-3	Pedro Martinez
L	5-9	Tim Wakefield
L	3-4	Bret Saberhagen
L	1-2	Pete Schourek

1999 Beat Cleveland Indians in AL Division Series 3 games to 2

L	2-3	Pedro Martinez
L	1-11	Bret Saberhagen
W	9-3	Kent Mercker
W	23-7	Ramon Martinez
W	12-8	Bret Saberhagen

Lost AL Championship Series to New York Yankees 1 game to 4

L	3-4	Kent Mercker
L	2-3	Ramon Martinez
W	13-1	Pedro Martinez
L	2-9	Bret Saberhagen
L	1-6	Kent Mercker

2003 Beat Oakland A's in AL Division Series 3 games to 2

L	4-5	Pedro Martinez
L	1-5	Tim Wakefield
W	3-1	Derek Lowe
W	5-4	John Burkett
W	4-3	Pedro Martinez

Lost AL Championship Series to New York Yankees 3 games to 4

W	5-2	Tim Wakefield
L	2-6	Derek Lowe
L	3-4	Pedro Martinez
W	3-2	Tim Wakefield
L	2-4	Derek Lowe
W	9-6	John Burkett
L	5-6	Pedro Martinez

2004 Beat Anaheim Angels in AL Division Series 3 games to 0

W	9-3	Curt Schilling
W	8-3	Pedro Martinez
W	8-6	Bronson Arroyo

Beat New York Yankees in AL Championship Series 4 games to 3

L	7-10	Curt Schilling
L	1-3	Pedro Martinez
L	8-19	Bronson Arroyo
W	6-4	Derek Lowe
W	5-4	Pedro Martinez
W	4-2	Curt Schilling
W	10-3	Derek Lowe

Beat St. Louis Cardinals in World Series 4 games to 0

W	11-9	Tim Wakefield
W	6-2	Curt Schilling
W	4-1	Pedro Martinez
W	3-0	Derek Lowe

CHAMPIONS

Appendix D – 2004 MLB Team Payrolls

In August 2004 the Associated Press published the following list of the payrolls of the 30 Major League Teams. The summary was listed in the August 17, 2004 Worcester Telegram & Gazette.

Team	Payroll
1. New York Yankees	$ 182,835,513
2. Boston	$ 125,208,542
3. Anaheim	$ 101,084,667
4. New York Mets	$ 100,629,303
5. Philadelphia	$ 93,219,167
6. Chicago Cubs	$ 91,101,667
7. Los Angeles	$ 89,694,342
8. Atlanta	$ 88,507,788
9. San Francisco	$ 82,019,167
10. Seattle	$ 81,543,833
11. St. Louis	$ 75,633,517
12. Houston	$ 74,666,303
13. Arizona	$ 70,204,984
14. Chicago White Sox	$ 65,212,500
15. Colorado	$ 64,590,403
16. Oakland	$ 59,825,167
17. Texas	$ 54,825,973
18. San Diego	$ 54,639,503
19. Minnesota	$ 53,585,000
20. Baltimore	$ 51,212,653
21. Toronto	$ 50,017,000
22. Kansas City	$ 47,609,000
23. Detroit	$ 46,353,554
24. Montreal	$ 43,197,500
25. Cincinnati	$ 43,067,858
26. Florida	$ 42,118,042
27. Cleveland	$ 34,569,300
28. Pittsburgh	$ 32,227,929
29. Tampa Bay	$ 29,506,667
30. Milwaukee	$ 27,518,500

According to the summary in the Worcester Telegram & Gazette, "Figures were obtained by The Associated Press from management and player sources and include salaries and pro-rated salaries of signing bonuses."

Appendix E - Recommended Reading

Bryant, Howard, *Shut Out, A Story of Race and Baseball in Boston*
Publisher: Beacon Press, Copyright 2002.
This book is a chronicle of the history of the Red Sox and the racism that plagued the team through the first 50+ years of this century.

Costas, Bob, *Fair Ball*
Publisher: Broadway Books, Copyright 2000.
Bob Costas is one of our best baseball writers and broadcasters, and has become a real conscience of the game. This book describes a number of things that could be improved in baseball, such as improving the financial aspects of the game, and provides an intriguing alternative to wild-card baseball. It would be very interesting reading for any fan.

Gammons, Peter, *Beyond the Sixth Game, What's happened to Baseball since the Greatest Game in World Series History*
Publisher: Houghton Mifflin Company, Copyright 1985.

Peter Gammons is a well-respected expert on baseball, a former writer for the Boston Globe and current reporter for ESPN. This book describes what happened to change baseball since the positive feelings that came out of Game 6 of the 1975 World Series, a game that many believe to be the best game in baseball history.

Golenbock, Peter, *Fenway, an Unexpurgated History of the Red Sox*
Publisher: G.P. Putnam's Sons, Copyright 1992.

This is a chronological history of the Red Sox with quotes and observations from many players and fans about their experiences with or watching the Red Sox.

Hirschberg, Al, *What's The Matter with the Red Sox?*
    Publisher: Dodd, Mead, Copyright 1973.

    This book was written in the 1970s and describes some of the problems that the Red Sox have had over the years (such as building a team of right-handed sluggers); it is interesting to see that some things have never changed since that time.

Lewis, Michael, *Moneyball – the Art of Winning in an Unfair Game,*
    Publisher: W.W. Norton and Company, Copyright 2003.

    This book describes the inner workings of the Oakland A's, focusing on General Manager Billy Beane and how he has built and continues to build the A's despite a lot of financial constraints. It provides great background on the game, the general manager's role, and how small-market teams can compete in today's game.

Appendix F – Information about the ALS Association

As noted on the cover, portions of the proceeds of sales of this book are being donated to the ALS Association Massachusetts Chapter. I would like to thank Rick Arrowood, President/CEO of the Chapter, and Scott Edelstein, Director of Special Events & Public Relations (who also coordinate the "Curt's Pitch for ALS" program), for all of their help in arranging this.

ALS (Amyotrophic Lateral Sclerosis), or as it is more commonly known, "Lou Gehrig's Disease" is a progressive and ultimately fatal disease of the neurological system. There is no cure. It causes patients to lose all muscular and nerve control, so the muscles weaken and waste away. It ultimately leads to paralysis. ALS manifests itself first in different ways such as falling, losing control of extremities, difficulty in speaking or swallowing, and fatigue. Eventually all bodily control is lost and failure of lungs or heart will lead to death. Having had an uncle die from this disease, I know the effects of the disease and know that it is very debilitating.

On the next page is information provided by the ALS Association Massachusetts Chapter about the services which they provide for people with ALS, including free medical equipment (I've seen some of what they provide and it is really amazing), transportation, Support Groups for patients' families, funding for research, and so on.

Supporting ALS patients and research is a great cause, and the Massachusetts chapter has a lot of dedicated and outstanding people who seem to love being able to help as much as they can. Please take a moment to read the information about the ALS Association and to consider helping out as you are able to do so.

Hope Through Research...
Support Through Patient Services

ASSOCIATION
Massachusetts Chapter

The ALS Association Massachusetts Chapter, Inc. (ALSA-MA Chapter) is a non-profit organization that serves people with Amyotrophic Lateral Sclerosis, more commonly known as Lou Gehrig's disease. We provide free services to over 250 people with ALS, including free durable medical equipment, transportation, respite grants for home health care, financial and legal referrals to patients, and education for their families and caregivers. We also advocate for patient and caregiver rights by hosting our annual ALS Advocacy Day on Beacon Hill at the State level and participating in a nationwide effort at the Federal level. We also pool our research funds with other network chapters, making the ALS Association the largest funding source for ALS research anywhere in the world.

Our mission is fueled by our concern for our patients, but our programs, services, and research efforts are driven by donations from the community. Our ultimate hope is that one day in the near future, there will be a cure, and our services will no longer be needed. However, until that day comes, we will continue to work intensely to improve the lives of patients, and keep up their hopes for a cure.

To become involved with the ALSA-MA Chapter, visit us online at www.als-ma.org, or call 1-888-CURE-ALS. Or, to find out more information about the work that Red Sox Pitcher Curt Schilling, and his wife, Shonda, do with our chapter, visit www.curtspitchforals.org.

ACKNOWLEDGEMENTS

Thanks go to a lot of people for their help with the book and for their encouragement with this writing effort. Specifically, thanks to:

Marjorie Femia, my wife, for listening to me rant and rave about the Red Sox for 31 years of what is an otherwise blissful marriage. Thanks for letting me share the comments, observations, and opinions that you heard so often and know so well, in this book.

Michael Femia, my son, for reading this book and providing feedback, and for providing information about the 1980s and 1990s when I was less interested in the game. Thanks also for all the phone calls after both thrilling victories and heart-breaking defeats.

Steve and Debbie Femia, my son and daughter-in-law, for their willingness to listen to progress reports on the book, for helping with the editing, and for the gifts of the books on what needed to be done to get a book like this published.

Christine Femia, my daughter, for doing a great job of editing the book during Christmas break of her senior year at college and a break from her internship at *Bust* magazine in New York City, and for watching all of the games of the 2004 post-season with us. It was fun.

Tom Mulligan, for all of the e-mail exchanges and phone calls over the years about baseball, the Yankees and Red Sox, Holy Cross, and life in general. Outside of my immediate family there is no one who has heard or read more of my opinions and observations. Some of what is in this book may be familiar to him since I would write it to him and then think 'hmm, maybe I should include that in the book'. Thanks for putting up with those opinions and comments (and for being a very gracious Yankees fan for all of these years). It is always great to see an e-mail from you in my inbox; it helps to make my day.

Dave Meyers, a friend and another big baseball fan with whom I have shared many stories and observations about the game over the years, for reading and editing the book for content and providing some background information and details.

Pat and Fred Link, for their almost weekly encouragement about the book and their continued interest in how it was going. That was, and still is, much appreciated.

Sonia Parikh, Mark Lancisi, Anne Johnson, Jim and Pat Ballard for reading and providing such positive feedback and encouragement about the book.

Dianne Pearson for formatting and pagination assistance.

Nunzy Antonellis for text and cover formatting assistance.

Susan Kaup, for her pictures of the Red Sox victory parade and assistance in contacting a graphics cover designer.

Larry Abramoff, of Chandler House Press and Tatnuck Booksellers in Worcester and Westboro, MA, for all of the help in getting this book printed, and for all of the suggestions and questions about the book. Thanks especially for asking "So what happens if they win it this year?" after discussing the first draft of the book after the 2003 season; that helped result in Section 2 of this book.

Rick Arrowood and Scott Edelstein for agreeing to meet with me, and then agreeing to work with me, so that the ALS Association can benefit from this as well.

Curt Schilling for coming to Boston "to break an 86 year old curse", for being such an inspiration to so many, and for demonstrating that there are still some athletes who are really good human beings.

And thanks to the Boston Red Sox for providing 43 years of material for Section 1 of this book on why they hadn't won, including some very depressing and sad season endings. Thanks also for counter-balancing those 43 years with 2 fabulous and unforgettable years (1967 and 2004) that were exciting from April through October, and for 1 thrilling World Championship. Surprisingly, it balances out. All in all it was well worth the wait.

Index

The Possible Dream

Demeter, Don, 49, 228
Dent, Bucky, 3, 21, 79
Detroit Tigers, 8, 9, 10, 12, 13,
    14, 15, 24, 60, 85
Dominique, Andy, 122, 123
Doyle, Denny, 17, 18, 61, 190
Eckersley, Dennis, 20, 38, 228
Edmonds, Jim, 185, 189, 194
Ellsworth, Dick, 14, 49, 201,
    228
Embree, Alan, 32, 110, 142,
    144, 164, 167, 168, 187
Epstein, Theo, vi, 47, 48, 55,
    78, 95, 99, 118, 202, 227
Evans, Dwight, 17, 22, 91, 200,
    229
Fingers, Rollie, 18, 42, 50, 80,
    89, 230
Finley, Charlie, 51
Fisk, Carlton, 16, 17, 19, 23,
    41, 49, 53, 54, 58, 66, 67,
    69, 73, 91, 92, 223, 224,
    225, 228, 229, 231
Fitzgerald, Ray, 69, 74, 75
Florida Marlins, 83
Fossum, Casey, 47, 78, 227,
    230
Foulke, Keith, 85, 96, 107, 110,
    119, 123, 133, 142, 143,
    161, 162, 163, 167, 170,
    176, 177, 178, 180, 188,
    190, 193, 194, 202, 222
Francona, Terry, 95, 96, 107,
    110, 111, 113, 121, 122,
    127, 129, 131, 132, 135,
    136, 138, 139, 141, 142,
    144, 145, 152, 157, 163,
    164, 167, 168, 169, 170,
    172, 173, 174, 175, 176,
    183, 186, 187, 194, 202, 203
Frazee, Harry, 70
Galehouse, Denny, 28, 31
Gammons, Peter, 24, 37, 74,
    79, 138, 239
Garcia, Karim, 27

Garciaparra, Nomar, 4, 35, 45,
    57, 58, 61, 80, 95, 97, 98,
    101, 102, 103, 104, 106,
    113, 119, 122, 123, 126,
    127, 128, 129, 131, 132,
    134, 135, 136, 138, 139,
    140, 142, 147, 149, 150,
    151, 152, 171, 202, 225,
    227, 229
Gedman, Rich, 23, 24, 58, 61,
    231
Giambi, Jason, 4, 27, 35, 80,
    81, 84, 87, 88, 96
Giambi, Jeremy, 4, 80
Gibson, Bob, 12, 13, 49, 57
Gillis, Don, 20
Gordon, Tom, 96, 177
Gorman, Lou, 51, 52
Gossage, Rich, 22, 37, 60, 79
Gowdy, Curt, 75
Green Bay Packers, 84
Grich, Bobby, 41
Griffey Jr., Ken, 25
Griffin, Doug, 50, 228
Guerrerro, Vladimir, 85, 90, 97,
    170
Guidry, Ron, 20, 21
Hamilton, Jack, 11
Hanson, Erik, 235
Harper, Tommy, 15, 50, 223,
    226, 228
Harrelson, Ken (Hawk), 14, 49,
    228
Harrington, John, 70
Harris, Bucky, 55, 65
Hatteberg, Scott, 45
Henderson, Dave, 22, 23, 51,
    228
Henry, John, v, 70, 95, 99, 104,
    123, 227
Herman, Billy, 40
Hernandez, Orlando (El
    Duque), 103, 159, 160
Hicks, Tom, 98, 99, 106

The Possible Dream

New York Yankees, v, vi, 3, 4,
5, 11, 15, 16, 18, 19, 20, 21,
22, 24, 25, 26, 27, 28, 31,
32, 33, 34, 35, 36, 37, 38,
39, 40, 41, 42, 43, 44, 45,
47, 48, 50, 52, 53, 54, 58,
59, 60, 61, 67, 68, 70, 71,
72, 74, 75, 77, 78, 79, 80,
81, 83, 84, 85, 86, 87, 88,
89, 90, 91, 92, 95, 96, 97,
98, 101, 103, 104, 105, 106,
111, 112, 113, 114, 115,
116, 117, 118, 119, 121,
124, 127, 128, 129, 130,
131, 132, 133, 134, 135,
137, 138, 139, 140, 141,
142, 144, 145, 146, 147,
149, 150, 151, 152, 154,
155, 157, 158, 159, 160,
161, 163, 164, 165, 166,
167, 168, 171, 172, 173,
174, 176, 177, 178, 179,
180, 181, 182, 183, 184,
185, 186, 192, 197, 198,
199, 201, 203, 223, 224,
225, 226, 227, 228, 229,
230, 231, 234, 235, 236
Nipper, Al, 23, 43, 234
Nixon, Trot, 27, 35, 102, 103,
106, 113, 118, 119, 124,
125, 126, 128, 132, 133,
146, 158, 160, 164, 167,
169, 174, 177, 190, 194,
201, 222, 229
O'Connell, Dick, 14, 42, 48, 49,
50, 51, 64, 65, 66, 69
Oakland A's, 8, 16, 18, 19, 24,
26, 36, 42, 44, 47, 50, 52,
58, 72, 78, 80, 89, 113, 225,
234, 235, 236
Oakland A's, 16, 18, 24, 26, 27,
35, 36, 42, 44, 45, 48, 50,
51, 52, 66, 68, 72, 78, 80,
89, 96, 118, 136, 157, 158,
225, 228, 230, 234, 235, 236

Offerman, Jose, 25, 92, 159
Olerud, John, 160, 161, 173,
183
Ordonez, Magglio, 97, 98, 102,
103, 230
Ortiz, David, 26, 27, 28, 33, 34,
35, 47, 48, 101, 102, 109,
116, 118, 121, 123, 124,
125, 126, 127, 128, 131,
132, 133, 134, 139, 140,
142, 150, 153, 157, 161,
167, 168, 169, 171, 173,
175, 176, 177, 178, 181,
186, 187, 188, 190, 222,
224, 227, 228, 229, 230
Orza, Gene, 95, 97, 229
Owen, Spike, 51, 228
Papi, Stan, 37, 228
Pattin, Marty, 50, 228
Pavano, Carl, 51, 83, 227
Paxton, Mike, 19
Pennant Fever Grips Hub, 72
Pesky. Johnny, 40, 54, 64
Petrocelli, Rico, 8, 10, 11, 12,
14, 40, 222, 223, 225
Pettitte, Andy, 27, 34, 35, 97,
98
Philadelphia Phillies, 7, 42, 77,
88, 95, 126, 137, 198, 233
Piazza, Mike, 59, 98
Pittsburgh Pirates, 54, 84, 85,
233
Posada, Jorge, 4, 28, 32, 33,
80, 106, 133, 134
Puckett, Kirby, 69
Pujols, Albert, 185, 189, 194
Radatz, Dick, 7, 40, 223, 224
Raines, Tim, 73
Ramirez, Manny, 27, 34, 61,
62, 71, 72, 85, 97, 98, 102,
104, 106, 109, 111, 112,
113, 115, 116, 118, 121,
123, 124, 126, 128, 133,
134, 135, 137, 138, 139,
141, 142, 144, 150, 153,

154, 157, 158, 159, 160,
163, 167, 168, 169, 171,
172, 173, 175, 176, 178,
181, 186, 187, 188, 189,
190, 222, 228
Reese, Pee Wee, 64
Reese, Pokey, 64, 103, 109,
110, 113, 117, 122, 124,
126, 127, 129, 137, 152,
153, 167, 183, 222
Remy, Jerry, 21, 22, 25, 60, 75,
109, 162, 223, 225, 226, 227
Renteria, Edgar, 187, 190, 193,
194
Revenue sharing, 86, 88
Rice, Jim, 16, 19, 21, 22, 42,
60, 67, 226
Rivera, Mariano, 34, 129, 133,
146, 160, 161, 173, 175, 177
Roberts, Dave, 147, 160, 161,
162, 167, 175, 176, 177, 202
Robinson, Frank, 16, 50, 58,
95, 203
Robinson, Jackie, 53, 54, 61,
62, 63, 64
Rodriguez, Alex (A-Rod), 85,
95, 97, 98, 99, 101, 102,
104, 106, 112, 115, 123,
126, 127, 132, 134, 145,
146, 147, 150, 152, 160,
164, 172, 173, 174, 176,
180, 182, 183, 229, 230
Rodriguez, Alez (A-Rod), 128
Rohr, Billy, 11, 14
Rolen, Scott, 185, 189, 194
Romo, Vicente, 14, 49, 228
Rose, Pete, 58
Rudi, Joe, 18, 19, 41, 42, 50,
80, 89, 230
Russell, Bill, 54
Ruth, Babe, 53, 54, 67, 70, 79,
89, 228, 229
Ruth, George Herman (Babe),
183, 194
Saberhagen, Bret, 235

San Diego Padres, 7, 36, 89,
122
San Francisco Giants, 78, 81,
104, 121, 137
Sanders, Tom, 54
Santiago, Jose, 8, 11, 13, 14,
65, 233
Satriano, Tom, 14, 49
Sauerbeck, Scott, 34, 47
Schilling, Curt, 51, 77, 78, 81,
85, 88, 90, 95, 96, 101, 102,
103, 105, 107, 110, 111,
114, 115, 116, 117, 118,
119, 121, 123, 125, 126,
127, 135, 136, 138, 139,
140, 141, 142, 143, 144,
145, 151, 152, 153, 154,
157, 158, 159, 162, 164,
165, 166, 167, 168, 171,
172, 176, 178, 179, 180,
181, 186, 188, 189, 191,
192, 193, 199, 200, 202,
222, 223, 224, 227, 229, 236
Schourek, Pete, 45, 235
Scott, George (Boomer), 8, 9,
11, 12, 13, 14, 19, 22, 24,
35, 50, 51, 64, 65, 224, 228
Seattle Mariners, 22, 25, 141,
142, 143, 158
Seaver, Tom, 19, 51, 89
Selig, Bud, 105
Shea Stadium, 22, 23, 59
Sheffield, Gary, 85, 88, 96, 97,
103, 104, 111, 113, 127,
129, 133, 134, 145, 161,
164, 172, 173, 174, 176,
180, 182, 183
Siebert, Sonny, 14, 49, 228
Sierra, Ruben, 134, 163, 164,
168, 177, 178, 180, 183
Smith, Reggie, 11, 12, 14, 49,
51, 64
Soriano, Alfonso, 77, 104, 139
Springsteen, Bruce, 26, 74

The Possible Dream